# The World News Prism

WITHDRAWN

*To the many journalists around the world who have been killed,*
*kidnapped, or jailed for reporting the news.*

# The World News Prism

## *Challenges of Digital Communication*

### Eighth Edition

### William A. Hachten
### and James F. Scotton

A John Wiley & Sons, Ltd., Publication

This eighth edition first published 2012
© 2012 John Wiley & Sons, Ltd

Edition history: Iowa State University Press (1e, 1981; 2e, 1987; 3e, 1992; 4e, 1996; 5e, 1999; 6e, 2002); Blackwell Publishing Ltd (7e, 2007)

Wiley-Blackwell is an imprint of John Wiley & Sons, formed by the merger of Wiley's global Scientific, Technical and Medical business with Blackwell Publishing.

*Registered Office*
John Wiley & Sons Ltd, The Atrium, Southern Gate, Chichester, West Sussex, PO19 8SQ, UK

*Editorial Offices*
350 Main Street, Malden, MA 02148-5020, USA
9600 Garsington Road, Oxford, OX4 2DQ, UK
The Atrium, Southern Gate, Chichester, West Sussex, PO19 8SQ, UK

For details of our global editorial offices, for customer services, and for information about how to apply for permission to reuse the copyright material in this book please see our website at www.wiley.com/wiley-blackwell.

The right of William A. Hachten and James F. Scotton to be identified as the authors of this work has been asserted in accordance with the UK Copyright, Designs and Patents Act 1988.

*Library of Congress Cataloging-in-Publication Data*

Hachten, William A.
   The world news prism : challenges of digital communication / William A. Hachten, James F. Scotton. – 8th ed.
      p. cm.
   Includes bibliographical references and index.
   ISBN 978-1-4443-3858-4 (pbk.)
1. Foreign news. 2. Communication, International. 3. Journalism–Political aspects. 4. Digital media. 5. Mass media and globalization. I. Scotton, James Francis, 1932- II. Title.
√ PN4784.F6H3 2012
   070.4′332–dc23

2011018167

A catalogue record for this book is available from the British Library.

This book is published in the following electronic formats: ePDFs (9781118114179); ePub (9781118114186); Kindle (9781118114193).

Set in 10.5/13pt Minion by Thomson Digital, Noida, India
Printed in Malaysia by Ho Printing (M) Sdn Bhd

1   2012

# Contents

# Preface to the Eighth Edition

No matter where people live in the world, most "news" or public information is local. People care about what happens in their community, their country, their region. Yet in today's interconnected and globalized world, people everywhere easily learn about and are affected by important international news – terrorist attacks, wars, civil strife, economic upheavals, and great catastrophes such as earthquakes and tsunamis, that occur in distant lands. More than ever before in history, more people are both informed and almost everywhere now have opinions – whether about globalization, the United Nations, nuclear proliferation, or about who should lead their nation. The on-rush of digital communication – the Internet, social media, cell phones – is helping make this possible.

In early 2011, international news made a dramatic comeback fueled by a series of unexpected political revolutions first in Tunisia and then Egypt where President Hosni Mubarak was ousted and then throughout the Arab world in rapid succession to Bahrain, Libya, Yemen, Jordan, Syria, and elsewhere. The streets of long-standing authoritarian Arab states were suddenly filled with angry, mostly young, protestors demanding freedom, democracy, human rights and jobs. Communication media had clearly facilitated the uprisings. Protestors were mobilized and informed by cell phones, the social media of Facebook and Twitter and news of these startling events were transmitted to Arab publics by the Internet and Al Jazeera and other Arabic broadcasters as well to the rest of the world.

Unrest, protests, and brutal repressions continued on including warfare with Libya against NATO forces and rebels.

In March 2011, Japan took over page one when the island nation was struck by a magnitude 9 earthquake followed by a massive tsunami that devastated large areas taking a toll estimated at 30,000 dead and missing victims. Severe damage to several nuclear power plants prolonged the calamity to the world's third largest economy. With prolonged revolution in the Arab world and quake/tsunami turmoil in Japan, television coverage of foreign news in 2011 was at its highest levels since the 9/11 attacks ten years earlier. News, it has been said is a process and it may be years before the full implications of the "Arab spring" and Japan's recovery will be known.

The terrorist attacks on New York's World Trade Center and the Pentagon in Washington, DC abruptly altered the lives of Americans and sharply impacted on international news communication. With the collapse of those two skyscrapers and about 3,000 lives lost, Americans (and many others) no longer felt secure and personally safe from the perils of a dangerous world. Terrorist hijackings and bombings were not new – from 1983 to 2001, ten attacks had claimed the lives of 100 or more Americans. But the 9/11 attacks were the largest violent taking of life on US soil since the Civil War. Most of us agreed that the nation was at war with terrorism – the first war of the twenty-first century.

So, as in early 2011, on 9/11 the news media responded quickly, professionally, and at times magnificently. Global television – up-to-the-minute and non-stop, with vivid color video and without commercial interruptions – reported the horrifying details of the tragedy to every corner of the world. The horrific but awesome video of the two airliners crashing into the twin towers of the World Trade Center was etched into the minds of millions. Supplemented by radio, the Internet, and print, much of the world saw the same video and reports as Americans and Britons. This elicited unprecedented responses of sympathy and empathetic support from many other nations. Yet in some places of the Muslim world, there was elation and celebration. Yet in 2011, Arabs generally supported the anti-authoritarian uprisings in their societies.

The evolving events – war against the Taliban in Afghanistan, and the quick military defeat of Saddam Hussein's army followed by the long insurgent conflict in Iraq – were followed with great interest. The _reporting_ of the horrific events and the world's _response_ were reminders of how much we have become a global society. Not just in trade and economic affairs but in social and political ways, we are increasingly coming together. But continuing acts of terrorism also were grim reminders that deep divisions between rich and poor countries remain. Democratic societies, with their open borders and individual freedoms, were vulnerable to stealth attacks. Radical terrorism was termed the dark underside of globalization.

As the first decade of the twenty-first century ended and 2011 political eruptions began, the world was still an unstable and dangerous place as war ground on in Afghanistan and terrorism threats emerged in the failing states of Somalia and Yemen. As nations slowly emerged from a global recession, people everywhere sought news to plot their futures and to comprehend the import of the multiple Arab uprisings.

Yet another less apparent series of technological changes in news communication has both facilitated and disrupted the traditional news media and the many publics or audiences for serious news and commentary throughout the world. The digital media – the Internet, personal computer, email, cell phones, bloggers and social web sites, Twitter, Facebook, and so on – have encroached on and reduced the journalism practiced by the great newspapers and journals, news services, and television and radio services that have historically reported the world to itself. News printed on paper or broadcast on television screens and radio receivers has been sharply diminished. The audiences have been diminished as well.

In this revised edition, we will show how the news media have responded to great crises as well as to technological changes. Journalists from everywhere flocked to the Middle East even as armed forces mobilized. But within months, media coverage and public interest in Iraq had diminished.

Only subsequent events and history will determine how significant the events will become in modern history. But there is no doubt that the year 1989 was historic. Then, the world watched on television in dazzled amazement as communist regimes were toppled in Poland, East Germany, Hungary, Czechoslovakia, Bulgaria, and Romania. Two years later, the Soviet Union itself, after a right-wing coup failed, went through a convulsive revolution of its own, outlawing the Communist Party and its media as well as dismantling the Soviet Union itself. These historic events also heralded the end of the Cold War, and the demise of the propaganda or "information wars" that had enlivened international communication for forty-five years. However, new propaganda wars, now focused on terrorism and the relations of Muslim nations with the West, have gained momentum in recent years.

The post Cold War world of the 1990s proved to be a harsh and forbidding place. The forces of intense nationalism and unleashed ethnic animosities have led to civil wars, genocide, terrorism, political instability, and economic and social chaos starkly evident in the prolonged and agonizing strife engaging the Bosnian and Kosovo Muslims, Croatians, and Serbs of the former Yugoslavia. Elsewhere, various experiments in democracy and market economies sputtered and foundered.

The decade of the 1990s was also one of great global economic expansion. In China and throughout East and South Asia, economies grew at spectacular rates and world trade expanded as a new phenomenon, *globalization*, was recognized and elaborated. Globalization is an inexact expression for a wide array of worldwide changes in politics, communications, business and trade, life styles, and culture. Even before the quake Japan's economy has had severe problems. In our new post-Cold War world with its increasingly globalized economy, economic concerns have sometimes taken precedence over political concerns.

Elsewhere, over 120,000 innocent civilians died in an irrational six-year civil war in Algeria, a half dozen nations have fought a nasty and prolonged regional war over the Congo, genocide flared up again in Rwanda and Burundi, and in Israel bitter violence continued with the Palestinians; and North Korea's erratic and starving Communist regime, with its potential nuclear threat, has worried the West. Other global concerns: India and Pakistan have both tested nuclear devices but may have moved somewhat toward reconciliation. In the horrendous earthquake in Pakistan in October 2005, Indian soldiers joined Pakistani troops in relief efforts after 86,000 died. Peace and stability were tantalizingly near, but not fully realized, in Northern Ireland. The recent disastrous earthquakes in Haiti and Chile brought forth an unprecedented surge of relief funds and manpower to alleviate the great suffering that still continues.

Recently, as the world has worried over potential nuclear bomb threats in Iran and North Korea at the same time genocide has appeared in Sudan and has challenged the United Nations to intervene in the Darfur conflict, which has claimed over 180,000 lives and made 2 million people homeless refugees.

International communication in general has been affected by world events as it has continued to expand its reach. International broadcasting has become less propagandistic and more informative and entertainment-minded. In most countries, journalists have enjoyed greater access to news. New independent and outspoken publications and broadcast outlets have sprouted like mushrooms in spring. Communication satellites transmitting news and pop culture have proliferated, and media audiences have greatly expanded, especially in China and India.

Personalized digital media have proved to be a many headed hydra that has greatly increased the ability of people everywhere (and we mean everywhere) to receive news and comment AND to communicate it onward. But the old model of global communication based on a few great news organizations has been undermined and diminished. The downsizing of print and broadcast media have significance for global news communication. But the future of media is unclear – just as it was when Gutenberg's printing press shook up the middle ages.

Further, personalized media – videos, VCRs and DVDs, audiocassettes, personal computers, cell phones, and fax machines – have continued their rapid global penetration, as did cablevision and the Internet. Western Europe has been going through its own regional communication revolution, with transnational competition between commercial cable and satellite systems, as it moves haltingly toward economic integration.

The ongoing rush of technological innovations in foreign reporting has accelerated. Direct broadcasting from portable transmitters to satellites and then back to dish antennas – bypassing complicated, expensive ground installations – has become commonplace. Small portable earth terminals, for example, have enabled broadcast journalists reporting remote news events to send their video reports directly to satellites and thus to the whole world. The cell phone and the videophone have played unexpected roles in news dissemination. A news report in Afghanistan or, for that matter, in almost any faraway troubled area, can instantly become a global news event. In just a few years, the Internet has become a player of great and ominous potential in international communication for both journalism and as a device that lets people share ideas freely on a global network. Bloggers and even hackers have joined the fray as controversial conveyors of news and comment that critique and challenge traditional news media.

In this age of information, communications systems are at the leading edge of social, economic, and political change. With the unprecedented growth in global telecommunications, an informed global community has developed a more immediate concern with both world news and the symbiotic relationship between events and those who report them. For this eighth edition, the text has been thoroughly revised, with new material added to every chapter. More attention has been given to significant media developments in developing nations, particularly those in the Arab world – some of which have been producing many more media users who respond in different ways to the world news prism. The chapters on China and the Middle East provide in-depth analyses in the ways that digital media are changing traditional societies.

– W.A.H. and J.F.S.

# Introduction

*After years of global fretfulness about the brute effectiveness of modern armaments, it turned out during one of the most pervasively revolutionary years of the twentieth century, if not of all recorded history, that the most potent single weapon in nearly every conflict was the video camera. In nation after nation, vastly superior military forces were stood off and frequently compelled to retreat before the symbolic and testimonial power of televised images.*

*– William A. Henry III*

As the tragic and war-stained twentieth century (and the old millennium) came to an end, we were reminded both of the changes as well as continuities that have marked journalism and international communications in our times. In 1900, all the elements were in place in Western nations – great metropolitan newspapers, rotary presses and linotypes, the typewriter, the telegraph and the undersea cable, the Associated Press, Reuters, and other cooperative news gatherers – as building blocks for the changes to come. News was recognized as a valued and useful commodity in itself and as an essential means of comprehending and coping with a strange and distant world. At the same time, sensationalism and trivia had long been standard fare in the press and entertainment media.

But no one could have foreseen the political and social changes to come in our tumultuous times as a result, in part, of the greatly enhanced speed, volume, and reach of international news and public knowledge. Journalists and broadcasters jetting about the globe with videocameras, Comsat phones, and laptop computers reported great events instantly via satellite

*The World News Prism: Challenges of Digital Communication*, Eighth Edition.
William A. Hachten and James F. Scotton.
© 2012 John Wiley & Sons, Ltd. Published 2012 by John Wiley & Sons, Ltd.

and Internet networks and, in so doing, often became participants and catalysts in global news stories. Sometimes they became celebrities themselves.

For over a century, the press has reported news from abroad, but it has been only in the past three decades that we have seen how great events abroad vividly illustrate the technotronic age, the melding of technology and electronics, that planet Earth has entered. It is a new era of information whose potential we but dimly perceive; whose complicated gadgetry only few of us totally grasp; whose social, political, and economic consequences are accelerating change and cleavages among the nations of the world.

For the world we live in today is changing rapidly, in no small part because worldwide television, communication satellites, high-speed transmission of news and data, and other computer and electronic hardware and software (including the Internet) have transformed the ways that nations and peoples communicate with one another. The fact that a news event can be transmitted almost instantaneously to newsrooms and onto television and computer screens (and into cell phones) around the world can be as important as the event itself. Long-distance mass communication has become a rudimentary central nervous system for our fragile, shrinking, and increasingly interdependent, yet fractious, world.

Journalism has been undergoing rapid changes. In what journalist and biographer Walter Isaacson has called a "glorious disruption" the traditional journalism of print on paper is rapidly giving way to journalism by digital technology. As a result, newspapers, news services, broadcast stations and networks, and news and commentary magazines have been sustaining great losses in circulations, audiences, and advertising revenues. These financial setbacks make it difficult to fully report global news and commentary. Basically, there is more information and news than ever before circulating the globe but there are fewer serious professional journalists reporting and verifying it. The Internet with its proliferating blogs, emails, web sites, and so on, spew out vast amounts of information and data but much of it is unverified, inaccurate, biased, propagandistic, opinionated or just downright wrong.

People everywhere have more access to much more information than ever and also have an enhanced ability to communicate themselves through the Internet, cell phones, and others devices like Twitter, Flickr, YouTube, and so on. But what the public is not getting is sufficient hard news that is verified, confirmed, and reliable.

The Western press, found mainly in North America and Europe, is struggling to find a new business model that will enable the "old media" to survive economically. The future of global news depends on it. And there are other disconcerting side effects.

The accelerating speed and efficiency of news media transmission has often created severe strains on the standards and ethics of responsible journalism. The same system can and does report much trivia, sensation, and misinformation. The news eruptions that followed the death of Michael Jackson and the travails of golfer Tiger Woods illustrated how news now breaks twenty-four hours a day, around the clock, instead of at the more leisurely pace that prevailed before the rise of twenty-four-hour cable television news and interactive news on the Internet. As fierce competitors such as MSNBC, the Fox Channel, and CNN with their talk and opinion - shows have proliferated on cable as well as blogs online, some news organizations have relaxed their rules on checking and verifying sources. There is a growing sense that getting it first is more important than getting it right. One result is journalism that is sometimes shaky, inaccurate, or worse, and with it has come a serious loss of public trust in news media. The rapid reporting of all aspects of the already mentioned Tiger Woods scandal in 2009 illustrated how the Internet enflamed and accelerated widespread coverage of salacious news of little serious importance and soon the story had spread to all news media.

High among the various factors contributing to the collapse of communist regimes (and their press) was certainly the global impact of Western communications in all their diversity and seductive appeal. For throughout the 1980s, two great groundswells rolled through the seas of international communication. On an incoming tide, the methods of organizing and distributing news and mass culture developed in Western democracies had washed inexorably over the globe, driven by innovations in media technology and expanding audiences, along with a resurgence of market economies on a global scale.

Some have suggested that increasingly the US-Anglo model of journalistic values and news-making practices have, for better or worse, become a universal standard for the rest of the world. (More will be said about this later.)

On an outgoing tide, the theory and practices of communist or Marxist/ Leninist public communication have become widely discredited by the many millions living under communist regimes, as well as their own journalists and rulers. The resounding rejection was directly related, of course, to the worldwide failures of socialist political economies and, particularly, the rejection of communist political rule in Eastern Europe. The crowds that protested communist regimes in Warsaw, Beijing, East Berlin, Prague, Budapest, Sofia, and Moscow in 1989 were also calling for more open and free media systems – the kind they knew about from images and sounds from the West. Expanding waves from these astonishing events radiated to the former Third World. Even African countries felt pressures for multiparty democracy.

Chronic crises and instability in Afghanistan, Pakistan, Iran, and Iraq have unsettled the strategic Middle East and Western media coverage is often slipshod and inadequate to inform the outside world.

Africa – beset by economic stagnation; drought and famine; political unrest and corruption; and brutal civil wars in Sudan, Somalia, Congo, and Rwanda – has in fact retrogressed. Hopes for meaningful democracy in Kenya, Zimbabwe, Ivory Coast, and Congo have all been dashed recently. It is no coincidence that, with the exception of South Africa, these troubled nations have inadequate media systems and cannot participate fully in a globalized world.

Today's uni-polar world, with the United States as its uncertain and often unpopular leader, is challenged not only by terrorism but other related problems, such as resurgent nationalism, poverty, racism, and religious fundamentalism. To these can be added the ups and downs of a sometimes faltering global economy.

This book analyzes the changing role of transnational news media in our evolving globalization and its impact on rapidly changing news events. In the ongoing concern about terrorism, global news media have played a major role both in informing the world and in organizing and facilitating responses to terrorism. (The media are also an unwilling accomplice of terrorism by publicizing the atrocities and carrying the email messages of terrorists.) Throughout this book, the emphasis is often on the role of US news organizations, yet we acknowledge that news media of many other nations – East and West – contribute to this cooperative activity of reporting the world to itself. And as the world modernizes, journalists of more and more nations are contributing to the flow of international news and popular culture.

News has increasingly become a powerful political and diplomatic force. For example, when US television shows stark pictures of starving Somali mothers and children, American public opinion becomes concerned, and the White House watches, hesitates, and then sends in the military to help feed the starving and keep the peace. A few months later, a dozen American soldiers are killed in an ambush in Somalia, and the US public is outraged at seeing on television the body of an American soldier dragged through the streets of Mogadishu. Soon, the White House announces that troops will be withdrawn.

News, instantaneous and vivid, speeds up history as it directly influences diplomacy and government policies. At the same time, in this age of satellites, the Internet, and shortwave radio, tyrants find it impossible to keep unflattering news about their regimes from reaching their own people. (Yet terrorists use the Internet to inform their followers and coordinate acts of terror.) On the one hand are the technological and operational changes taking place in the international news media, with their enhanced capability for global communication that is reshaping "spaceship Earth." Wider communication often seems to exacerbate political and cultural conflicts between the West and Islam, between rich and poor nations. Also, there are the frictions and the problems these changes have wrought, including conflicts over transnational news gathering and the impact of television programming, motion pictures, videos, radio broadcasting, and other aspects of mass culture, most of it coming out of the United States and Europe.

Another area of concern is that, when no crisis intrudes, serious international news seems often to be shunted aside for more profitable content. "Infotainment" – scandal, sensation, celebrities – has become more and more the staple of news media in many countries.

Before 9/11, network television news programs, from which most people get their news, had sharply cut back on the amount of foreign news on the major networks. Similar trends were seen among the news magazines. This reflects (or explains) why Americans and others have been showing a declining interest in news from abroad. The terrorism crisis of 2001 reversed this trend, but only for a few months.

This book deals with various facets of the changing media and their impact on transnational journalism and mass communication. It is intended to provide some insights into how and why international news communication is evolving. Few of us can appreciate, much less fully understand, the meaning of the global information revolution we are living through. The major components of this quiet revolution are the computer, the Internet and telecommunications, principally the communication satellite plus other sophisticated electronic devices that have become as much a part of our lives as the electric light.

We may not be aware of how our perceptions of the world are being changed by the transformed news system, but we quickly learn to take that system for granted. If there is another terror attack on a major city or another major earthquake in Haiti or Chile, we expect to see live television reports the same day or on a twenty-four-hour news channel, such as BBC World or CNN, within the hour via satellite. We are fascinated but not surprised to see detailed, computer-refined pictures of the exploration of planet Mars or the dramatic saga of the space shuttle as well as the grim daily war stories from the Middle East.

In a broader context, the fact that information of all kinds, including urgent news, can now be communicated almost instantly to almost anywhere has profound implications for international organization and interaction. News of Iraq's invasion of Kuwait, for example, had an almost immediate impact on the price of gas at the pump and initiated an international diplomatic reaction resulting in mass deployment of US military forces. And the world's subsequent perceptions of the crisis and war were certainly shaped and, at times, distorted by the flickering images on television screens. Instant information is often not the whole truth or a complete picture and, on occasion, does sharply distort images that people receive.

Still, global news has many uses. The global financial media's day-to-day reporting of financial crises in Asian stock markets and currencies, and their effects on the financial markets and economies of Asia. Europe, and America, illustrates how many millions around the world, including small stockholders, rely on fast, accurate information in their daily lives. The global economy simply could not function without the flow of fast and reliable information provided by the growing global business media – both print and electronic.

A new global society of sorts is emerging rapidly and inexorably, though experts disagree about its extent and nature. (Many nations, especially in the Middle East and Africa, do not feel a part of it.) The media of mass communication, along with global telecommunications, air transportation, and growing interdependence of national economies, are providing the essential linkages that make interaction and cooperation – and stealth terrorist attacks – possible.

Full understanding of the nature of this new society requires that today's students of international communication be conversant with world politics and economics, including recent history, and be quick to recognize significant trends as they occur. Further, they must understand national and cultural differences and keep up with technological innovations in communication media, such as the Internet and social media, and with changing journalistic practices.

Communication satellites are just one example of the truly revolutionary impact that communication technology has had on the modern world. The earlier role of transistor radios in the Third World was another; today the small hand-held video camcorder is having news effects undreamed of. As we will see, the Internet is beginning to be perceived as yet another technological marvel that may dramatically alter international communication. FM radio, cell phones, and cable television are each having unexpected impacts in developing nations.

The interplay of these elements makes the study of international communication fascinating and important. The major emphasis throughout this book is on the journalistic aspects of international communication – the new challenges and perils of reporting the news, the important but imperfect and controversial ways that journalists and mass communicators keep the world informed. Further, the cultural and entertainment facets of media are often significant as well.

Several chapters concern the changing media – the ways that international journalism is adapting to altered global conditions, changing concepts of news, and utilizing the new hardware of our information age.

Currently, for the first time in history, all nations, however remote, have stepped onto the stage of the modern world. What happens in Rwanda or Indonesia, or Afghanistan, can have global significance and often sends repercussions around the world, in part because events happening there are reported. More importantly, a much greater degree of interdependence among all peoples and nations has developed.

The world has been evolving an international news system that moves information and mass culture ever faster and in greater volume to any place on Earth where an antenna can be put on a shortwave radio receiver, where dish antennas can receive television programs from a communication satellite, or, increasingly, where there is a personal computer with a modem hooked onto the Internet. The cell phone with connections to the Internet is becoming a potent player in global communication. Although politics, economic disparities, cultural and linguistic differences, and ideology keep us apart on many issues, the international news system has on occasion made us one community, if only briefly – as when Neil Armstrong took that "one giant leap for mankind" in 1969. An estimated 600 million people throughout the world watched that first walk on the moon, and they sat before their television sets not as Chinese, French, Africans, or Japanese, but as earthlings watching in awe as one of their kind first stepped onto another planet.

Actually, the reporting of Armstrong's moon walk has further relevance for this book because the new information age is partly an outgrowth of the exploration of space. The communication satellite, high-speed data transmission, and miniaturized computer technology are by-products of space technology, and all are playing integral roles in the transformation of international communication and transnational journalism.

The modern practices of globally collecting and distributing news are only about 100 years old and were initiated by the news agencies of Britain, the United States, and France. Today, the world agencies – the Associated Press (United States), Reuters (Britain), and Agence France-Presse (France) – are still an important but far from only, conduit of transnational news, although they and other media have been transformed by digital technology. Change has been coming so quickly that it is often difficult to stay up-to-date with the ways in which news is being moved. And to understand the future potential of say, the Internet, is like trying to perceive in 1905 what the absurd horseless carriage or the telephone would do in time to the cities and life styles of the twentieth century.

Furthermore, technology and global reach are modifying some of the institutions of transnational communication. Subtly and almost imperceptibly, various media, including the news agencies, are evolving from national to increasingly international, or better, to supranational institutions of mass communication. Concomitantly, English is clearly the world's leading media language.

The international news media, furthermore, are unevenly distributed among nations, creating serious frictions between the haves and have-nots in mass communication. The explosion of communication technology has coincided with the post World War II decolonization of the Third World, and the penetration of Western news and mass culture into the newly independent nations, as well as into the former communist bloc. This has been perceived by some as a new attempt to reassert the domination of the former colonial powers. Certainly, the Western media – and the nations behind them – are much resented in many of what are now referred to as "failed nations."

Part of this book focuses on the differences that frustrate and at times inhibit the flow of international news and divide journalists and mass communicators: political and ideological differences, economic disparities, geographic and ethnic divisions. The media of all nations, it can be argued, reveal biases imposed by the constraints of nationalism and parochialism. When US soldiers are engaged in a military clash in Afghanistan, the subsequent news report on NBC television will differ from that carried on Al Jazeera, the Arabic broadcaster. There is no "true" news report of any event, only a variety of conflicting views out of which hopefully a consensus of sorts can be reached about what exactly happened.

The conflicts and frictions in international communication arise in part from divergent concepts of mass communication. In the concept of the press that has evolved in Western democratic nations, journalists are relatively independent of government, free to report directly to the public that uses the information to understand the world and to assess its governors. This view is unacceptable to authoritarian nations, which control and manipulate their media to serve better the goals of the state and their often unelected leaders. In numerous, mostly impoverished nations, a similar theory – the developmental concept – has emerged, which holds that mass media must be mobilized to serve the goals of nation building and economic development.

The deep differences between the media-rich and media-poor nations reflect closely other differences between rich and poor nations. Despite the impressive gains in the technical ability to communicate more widely and quickly, the disturbing evidence is that in some ways the world may be growing further apart rather than closer together. Most of the benefits of the communication and information revolution have accrued to the industrialized nations of the West, and to Japan and the Pacific Rim nations. For an individual to benefit fully from the news media, he or she ideally should be literate, educated, and affluent enough to have access to a variety of news sources. Unfortunately, in our unfair world, the largest share of such individuals are found, for now, in the few industrialized democracies. Yet the world's two most populous nations, China and India, have greatly increased the audiences and readership of their media.

The world's system of distributing news can be likened to a crystal prism. What in one place is considered the straight white light of truth travels through the prism and is refracted and bent into a variety of colors and shades. One person's truth becomes, to another, biased reporting or propaganda – depending on where the light strikes the prism and where it emerges. As we understand the optics of a prism for measuring the spectrum of light, so must we understand and accept the transecting planes of different cultural and political traditions that refract divergent

perceptions of our world. Obviously, Islamic terrorists have a radically different view of the world than most Europeans have.

We must acknowledge how the light refracts for us. In considering the problems of international communication, we have tried to be sympathetic to the views and frustrations of people in non-Western nations and the enormous difficulties they face. Journalism is a highly subjective pursuit, tempered and shaped by the political conditions and cultural traditions of the particular society where it is practiced; the news and the world do look different from Shanghai, Lagos, or Baghdad than they do from Chicago.

As products of the Western press tradition, we believe journalists in their pursuit of the news should be suspicious of, and disagree at times with, other political leaders and other journalists as well as the owners of the media. For the essence of journalism is diversity of ideas and the freedom to express them. We agree with Albert Camus, who wrote:

> A free press can of course be good or bad, but certainly without freedom, it will never be anything but bad. . ... Freedom is nothing else but a chance to be better, whereas enslavement is a certainty of the worst.

And in the dangerous, strife-ridden world of the twenty-first century, we believe that the billions of people inhabiting this planet deserve to know more about the events and trends that affect their lives and well-being. Only journalists who are free and independent of authoritarian controls and other constraints can begin the difficult task of gathering and reporting the news and information we all have a right and need to know.

# 1

# News Communication for a Global System

*Globalization is not simply a trend or a fad but is, rather, an international system. It is the system that has now replaced the old Cold War system, and like that Cold War system, globalization has its own rules and logic that today directly or indirectly influence the politics, environment, geopolitics and economics of virtually every country in the world.*

— Thomas L. Friedman, *The Lexus and the Olive Tree*

The rapid integration of the world's economy, loosely called globalization, has been facilitated by an information revolution driven by communication technologies that provide a nervous system for our world today. Globalization is a broad and inexact term for a wide array of worldwide changes in politics, economics, trade, finance, life styles, and cultures. To its critics, globalization is trendy and controversial; they see the world becoming a consumer colony of the United States, led by Coke, McDonald's, Nike, and the vast pop-culture output of Hollywood. How people feel about globalization often depends a lot on where they live and what they do.

With just a visit to a mall, one is struck by the plethora of products and services from many distant lands. In the past thirty years, much of the world's economy has become increasingly integrated; direct foreign investment has grown three times as fast as total domestic investment. But globalization is more than buying and selling; some see it as a

*The World News Prism: Challenges of Digital Communication*, Eighth Edition.
William A. Hachten and James F. Scotton.
© 2012 John Wiley & Sons, Ltd. Published 2012 by John Wiley & Sons, Ltd.

profound interchange of cultures – a communication revolution that is dissolving our sense of boundaries, our national identities, and how we perceive the world.

Deregulation of telecommunications systems and computerization have been called the parents of globalization. Three technologies in particular – computers, satellites, and digitalization – have converged to produce a global communications network that covers the Earth as completely as the atmosphere. Today's era of globalization is characterized by falling telecommunications costs, thanks to microchips, satellites, fiber optics, and the Internet.

For example, some 400 million viewers world wide watched together on television as Spain defeated Holland in the 2010 World Cup in South Africa.

The popular culture of the West – movies, television shows, music CDs, video- and audiocassettes, books, magazines, newspapers – has been flowing increasingly about the world. It can be argued that the world is beginning to share a popular culture, based only in part on that of the West. Critics differ about what happens when cultures meet.

Rather than fight, cultures often blend. Frederick Tipson noted, "More like a thin but sticky coating than a powerful acid, this cosmopolitan culture of communication networks and the information media seems to overlay rather than supplant the cultures it interacts with."[1] When cultures receive outside influences, it is said, they ignore some and adopt others, and soon begin to transform them. An example can be something called *bhangra pop* in India – music that sounds like Jamaican reggae but is played on Indian instruments and then amplified.

Critics of this global media market castigate globalization for several reasons: the centralization of media power; and heavy commercialism, which is linked to declines in public broadcasting and public service standards for media performance. Media are seen as a threat to democracy because of lessened public participation and concern with public affairs. Press critics have other concerns about these corporate giants. The news media, they argue, risk becoming submerged and neglected inside vast entertainment conglomerates that are primarily concerned with entertainment profits.

Most of these criticisms are leveled at Western media, and these critics neglect to consider how globalization has spurred the growth of media and their audiences in the developing non-Western nations.

Others see globalization in more positive terms. It is argued that many millions more people than ever before now have access to news and information, especially in such countries as China and India and much of Southeast Asia. Globalization means that multitudes now have many newfound choices: how they will spend their leisure time; what they will watch or read; what to buy with newly acquired personal income from rapidly rising standards of living. Anthropologist James Watson wrote, "The lives of Chinese villagers I know are infinitely better off now than they were 30 years ago. China has become more open because of the demands of ordinary people. They *want* to become part of the world – I would say that globalism is the major force for democracy in China. People want refrigerators, stereos, CD players."[2]

Journalist Thomas Friedman wrote that globalization is essentially about change, which is a reality and not a choice: "Thanks to the combination of computers and cheap telecommunications, people can now offer and trade services globally – from medical advice to software writing to data processing – services that could never be traded before. And why not? A three-minute call (in 1996 dollars) between New York and London cost $300 in 1930. Today it is almost free through the Internet."[3]

The primacy of the issue of globalization reminds us of the extent to which most of us now think and act globally – as a matter of course. In his book, *The World is Flat: A Brief History of the 21st Century*, Friedman expands his earlier views and sees dramatic changes in the forces for global leveling from the fall of the Berlin Wall, which eliminated the ideological divide in the world, to the rise of the Internet and technological changes that have led to new economic models of production and collaboration, including outsourcing and offshore manufacturing. Now nations such as China and India, as well as others in South Asia, have prospered in dramatic ways. The integration of some 3 billion people into the global economy is of major importance. Just one facet of this global flattening is that the media of communications have become increasingly pervasive in these rapidly modernizing places. Literally many millions are now, through the Internet, cell phones, satellite television, and publications, are "in touch" with the greater world. But while the new technologies are closing gaps between parts of India and China and the advanced industrial nations, the gaps between those countries and Africa have been widened. The world's nations may not have a level playing field, but the world is changing in critical ways. And for many millions in those nations considered to be "developing," their standards of living have improved rapidly.

## A Big, Cloudy, Blue, Agate Marble

Perhaps one of the most significant photographs of modern times was taken during the Apollo 11 mission to the moon. The astronauts photographed the earthrise as seen from the moon, and there was our planet, like a big, cloudy, blue, agate marble. The widely reprinted picture illuminated the fragility and cosmic insignificance of our spaceship Earth.

That stunning image coincided with the worldwide concern about ecology and global pollution; even more, it made it easy to grasp why many scientists already treated that cloudy, blue marble as a complete biological system, in which change in one part will inevitably affect other parts.

Certainly in the years since, concerned persons around the world have become more aware of our global interdependence. Although some experts disagree, an important trend of our times is that the world is becoming a single, rudimentary community. Today's world must grapple with an agenda of urgent and complex problems, most of them interrelated: overpopulation; poverty; famine; depletion of natural resources (especially energy); pollution of the biosphere; regional political disputes; continuing arms buildup, including the nuclear threat; global warming, and the widening gap between rich and poor nations, which seems exacerbated by economic integration. Recent events have pushed terrorism high on the agenda. Terrorist acts are somber reminders of how much hate and anger divide our diverse societies.

These and other global crises ebb and flow on the world's news agendas, but they are truly international in scope; the amelioration – much less solution – of any of them requires cooperation and goodwill among nations. To achieve that, there first must be information and understanding of these challenges, for these are crises of interdependence. No one nation or even combination of nations can deal effectively with such global concerns as international monetary crises, pollution of the air and oceans, population control, terrorism, regional warfare, and widespread famine and food shortages, yet the blinders of nationalism and modern tribalism continue to influence political leaders everywhere to react to international problems with narrow and parochial responses. The news media in all nations will reflect the national views and prejudices of their own societies on these pressing global concerns. It's not necessary that all nations agree on how to respond – and here is where the news media come in – but there should be general agreement about what the problems are.

Lester Brown, an authority on global needs, described the problems of our times as "unique in their scale." Previous catastrophes – famines, floods, earthquakes, volcanic eruptions – were local and temporary. But now, the world's more pressing concerns can be solved only through multinational or global cooperation, yet the institutions to cope with them are largely national. And because each technological innovation seems to create new problems but not the political will capable of resolving them, Brown sees global conditions worsening in the years immediately ahead. Brown's view of world problems, although shared by many, is still not truly understood by great numbers of people. Americans, for example, periodically turn inward and become self-absorbed, failing to comprehend how domestic problems have roots in events that may occur thousands of miles away.[4]

Westerners and some leaders of developing countries are becoming aware that population growth is putting intolerable pressures on the Earth's land, water, and energy resources as well as its economies.

The world's population in 2008 was 6.8 billion with 37% of its population living in China and India. The US Census Bureau projected that in 2025 India will surpass China. The other most populous countries are, in order, the United States, Indonesia, Brazil, Pakistan, Bangladesh, Nigeria, Russia, and Japan.[5]

Africa is currently gripped by one of the greatest population explosions ever recorded. Over the past 60 years Africa's population has quadrupled to 1 billion people, an epic baby boom that threatens to trap a generation of children in poverty and strangle economic progress on the world's poorest continent. With low rates of contraception and high social pressures to have large families, African women bear 5.3 children each on average, compared with 2.1 in the United States. By 2050, Africa's population will reach 2 billion.[6]

Scientists and development experts have been racing to increase food production by 50% in the next two decades to feed this growing population. The global number of hungry people increased to 1.02 billion in 2009 or nearly one in seven, according to the UN Food and Agriculture Organization. A central problem is whether food can be grown in the developing world where the hungry can actually get it at prices they can afford to pay. Poverty and difficult growing conditions plague the places that need new food production most – in sub-Saharan Africa and South Asia.[7]

The world's political structures, many believe, must be reshaped to enable us to cope with these global challenges: hence the great importance, despite their shortcomings, of international organizations such as the United Nations and its attendant agencies. Recently, there have been frequent calls for reform of the United Nations.

Public opinion polls have long shown that many people are uninformed about international affairs. For example, one Gallup Poll found that half of all Americans did not know that the United States had to import petroleum to meet its needs.

As important as formal education is, its influence sometimes does not change attitudes or improve understanding until a generation or two later. In immediate terms, the media flow of information and news throughout the globe can have a greater impact than education on the world's ability to understand its problems and dangers. Since World War II, an intricate and worldwide network of international news media has evolved, providing an expanded capability for information flows. This relationship between the capacity and the need to communicate rapidly has resulted from the interaction of two long-term historical processes: the evolution toward a single global society and the movement of civilization beyond four great benchmarks of human communication – speech, writing, printing, and electronic communications (telephone and radio) – into a fifth era of long-distance instant communication based on telecommunications and digital computer technology. The latter are key components of globalization.

Harold Lasswell believed that the mass-media revolution has accelerated the tempo and direction of world history. What would have happened later has happened sooner, and changes in timing may have modified substantive developments.[8]

Paradoxically, even with this greatly enhanced capability of involvement in world affairs, comparatively few people are well informed or even care much about what happens beyond their borders. Many who follow the news on television have only a superficial knowledge of events such as the cancelation of an election in Nigeria or a stock-market crash in Indonesia. But for those comparative few who do follow public affairs closely (and they are found in every nation), perceptions of the world are being formed and reshaped by this revolution in long-distance instant communications.

Our ability, or lack of it, to use the fruits of this technological revolution is directly related to our success or failure to act decisively and in concert as a world community. International experts worry whether the world can organize itself and deal effectively with what have been called the seven major interrelated world problems: mass poverty, population, food, pollution, energy, military expenditure, and the world monetary system. To organize, though, we must communicate, since communication is the neural system of any organization. The extent of its ability to communicate determines the boundaries of any community – be it a primitive tribe in Papua New Guinea or a global society – and only expanded and more effective communication can make possible a viable global community.

The technology to circulate that information exists, but the barriers of illiteracy, parochialism and nationalism, poverty, and political constraints keep too many people in the world from receiving it.

The illiteracy situation is particularly vexing. Here are some facts and figures:

- There are about 1 billion non-literate adults (persons fifteen years and above).
- 98% of all non-literate adults are in developing nations.
- Two-thirds of all non-literates are women.
- One half of all non-literates are in China and India.
- It has been estimated that 30 to 50 million people are added each year to the numbers of non-literates due to population increases.
- So, worldwide the percentage of adult illiteracy is declining, but the absolute number of non-literates is increasing.

Over the long run, worldwide illiteracy dropped from 38.5% in 1970 to about 18% in 2005. Yet there is much room for improvement: currently about 670 million school-age children are not in school.

Literacy is the key skill for modernization, education, and use of mass media and computers. Illiteracy is widespread in Africa, so it is no wonder that there are only about 125 daily newspapers in all of Africa, compared with more than 1,770 dailies in the United States. In any country, therefore, the proportion of people able to receive news and information will vary greatly according to the availability of news media and the ability of people to use them. Those living in such "information societies" as Japan, Western Europe, or the United States are overwhelmed with information and news, whereas throughout the many poor nations only a tiny fraction of persons is able to participate in the international news flow. Regardless of where they live, however, too few people take advantage of opportunities to acquire and use information about the solution of urgent transnational problems.

## The Importance of Foreign News

Much of the essential information we need for our personal lives comes from the news media. Our economy, our society, and our government would have difficulty functioning without the flow of reliable news and information. An open, democratic society without independent news media is impossible to imagine.

Foreign news is a special genre of news. It is not just from afar but also news of widespread significance. The earthquake/tsunami of late 2004 in South Asia was major news everywhere. Even more thoroughly reported were the devastating earthquakes in Haiti and Chile in January 2010 and Japan in 2011. Serious journalists and editors have long held that important information from overseas should be reported capably and thoroughly, even though most people are primarily concerned about what happens in their own communities or to themselves personally. Yet foreign news is perceived through the distorting prisms of culture and personal predilection.

Throughout our turbulent times, events beyond our borders have directly affected, and disrupted, many lives: two world wars, a worldwide depression, the rise of Hitler and Stalin, decolonization of great empires, the Cold War, and, more recently, the rise of an interdependent global economy. In an open, democratic society, the public must know what is happening in the outside world in order to judge how well their government and leaders respond to challenges from abroad. The history of independent journalism clearly shows that the best and most responsible news media have always given high priority to foreign news. This is still true today, especially for a handful of great daily newspapers.

Yet for many in recent years, foreign news did not seem as important and relevant as it was before the Cold War ended. Who is to blame: the press, our political leaders, or the public? Perhaps all three. Without a crisis demanding our attention – a famine and civil war in Sudan, genocide in Rwanda, civil war and aerial bombing in Bosnia and Kosovo – the average daily paper carries usually only about six short items from abroad – unless American soldiers are involved, as in Somalia, Afghanistan, or Iraq.

Most people rely on television for their news, yet anyone regularly watching network news is aware that foreign news has been typically reduced to several short items ("And now the news from abroad...") unless some video with violent footage is available (50% of television's foreign coverage does portray violence). Critics say that serious foreign news on television has been pushed aside in favor of scandal, celebrity, or the so-called "you news" – self-help and advice stories.

The public apparently does not mind. A recent survey of the US public by the Pew Research Center found that among regular users of the news media, the topics of most interest were, in this order, crime, local news about people and events, and health news. International news ranked ninth, well behind sports, local government, science, religion, and political news. Another 2001 poll (before 9/11), by Andrew Kohut, found that fewer than one in five Americans was strongly interested in serious news programs and publications – international, financial, government, and politics. Gender, generation, and education are keys: college-educated men over forty years of age and older have the most interest; lesser-educated, younger women have decidedly the least.[9]

Other surveys conducted by the Pew Research Center in 1997 found that the percentage of people following foreign news dropped from 80% in the 1980s to 20% in 1990. The decline was most precipitous among young people, who were turned off by such traditional categories as international politics, security, war, and peace. The relatively few serious news stories that attract the attention of adult Americans are those that deal with national calamities or the use of American military force. The obverse is that readers in the affluent West show little interest in tragic and harsh news stories coming out of developing nations. The admirable group, Doctors Without Borders, who aid destitute people abroad, annually lists what it considers the "Most Under-Reported Humanitarian Stories." Their twelfth annual list, for 2009, was expressed in vivid headlines:

1   "Unrelenting violence in eastern Democratic Republic of Congo."
2   "Somalis endure violence and lack access to health care."
3   "Precarious situation for people in South Sudan and Darfur."
4   "Thousands injured in final stages of Sri Lanka's decades-long war."
5   "Civilians suffer from violence and neglect in Pakistan."
6   "Politics of aid leaves many Afghans cut off from humanitarian assistance."
7   "Civilians trapped in violent war in northern Yemen."
8   "Woefully inadequate funding undermines gains in treatment of childhood malnutrition."
9   "Funding for Aids treatment lags despite millions in need."
10  "Lack of research and development of treatment plagues patients with neglected diseases."

These "top ten" lists not only point out the world's acute health need but also highlight some shortcomings in global reporting.

We agree with Stephen Hess of the Brookings Institution, who argued that we have become a nation with a two-media system, especially in regard to foreign news. Hess wrote, "Our society is awash in specialized information (including foreign news) available to those who have the time, interest, money, and education to take advantage of it. The other society encompasses the vast majority of Americans, who devote limited attention to subjects far removed from their necessary concerns (again, foreign news). They are content to turn to the top stories of television networks' evening news programs and their community's daily newspapers for the information."[10] We would argue that this happens in other affluent nations as well.

Yet perhaps this diminished interest in international events is not as significant as it would seem. Recent polls show that although the public is turned off by some foreign news, it does crave engagement in the world's crises, but not in ways defined by government, academics, and the media. For example, a University of Maryland poll found that 74% of people wanted a sharing of power internationally, whereas only 13% wanted the United States to assert itself as the only superpower. Also, although Congress held up $1.5 billion in overdue assessments for the United Nations, a Pew Center survey found that Americans hold the organization in high regard. The Pew survey found broad support for cooperative action to halt global warming, even if it meant applying fuel consumption standards leading to higher US gasoline prices.

In short, publics everywhere seem highly concerned about issues they see as directly affecting their own lives. The British clearly felt their lives threatened by the July 7, 2005 terrorist attacks. They are also concerned about immigration and trade negotiations that could have an impact on their jobs and taxes, as well as environmental issues such as global warming, resource depletion, health threats, drug trafficking, and other cross-border crime.[11]

## Moving Together or Apart?

Whether the problem is pollution of the seas or proliferation of nuclear weapons, the fact remains that international society is marked by the absence of effective collective procedures, by competition rather than cooperation, and by the lack of a commitment to a common goal. The world is ruled by nation-states, not by an effective international organization, and each state will usually act according to its own interests and needs. In several African nations, such as Somalia, Liberia, and Congo, an even more discouraging trend has emerged: the complete breakdown of a nation into warring camps without a coherent central government. Some academics argue that the apparent thrust toward global unity and globalization is actually misleading. Political scientist Steven Krasner of Stanford believes that the idea that the world has fundamentally changed lacks historical perspective. The international transfer of ideas, trade, and capital has been going on for four or five centuries, he says. Others agree that the idea of global integration has been overblown and that we are not yet up to the late nineteenth-century standard of integration. They argue that the current globalization is a return to a process interrupted by two world wars.[12] From the mid-1880s to the Great Depression, the world experienced a similar age of globalization. The volumes of trade and capital flows across borders and the flow of labor across borders, relative to populations, in the pre-World War I era of globalization was similar to what we are living through today. But today, powerful communications, including the media, drive our current globalization.

Others feel that the world is both converging and diverging at the same time. In 1993, *The New York Times* listed forty-eight nations where long-suppressed ethnic, religious, and sectional conflicts had surfaced. Policy makers say the ethnic conflicts are actually the third wave of this century, with the first having taken place after World War I and the second with the explosion of anti-colonial movements in Africa and Asia after World War II. Most of these nations' ancient rivalries and bigotry have remained largely unaffected by communication technology. The rise of international terrorism to the top of the world's agenda is further strong evidence of global divisiveness. Also, the sharp opposition of many Western nations to the US invasion of Iraq certainly indicated a shattering of political consensus. It is too early to assess the importance of the Arab revolutions of 2011.

On the other hand, powerful technetronic forces are binding the world together – circulating news, ideas, and information faster and in greater volume than ever before. These technologies are transforming many economic enterprises into truly global businesses. Further, countless more individuals are, through education and media participation, joining the modern world. So, although global integration may seem both real and illusory, there may be encouragement in the futuristic views that science fiction writer Arthur C. Clarke expressed more than twenty-five years ago regarding the communication satellite:

> What we are now doing – whether we like it or not – indeed, whether we wish it or not – is laying the foundation of the first global society. Whether the final planetary authority will be an analogue of the federal systems now existing in the United States or the USSR I do not know. I suspect that, without any deliberate planning, such organizations as the world meteorological and earth resources satellite system and the world communications satellite system (of which INTELSAT is the precursor) will eventually transcend their individual components. At some time during the next century they will discover, to their great surprise, that they are really running the world.
>
> There are many who will regard these possibilities with alarm or distaste and may even attempt to prevent their fulfillment. I would remind them of the story of the wise English king, Canute, who had his throne set upon the seashore so he could demonstrate to his foolish courtiers that even the king could not command the incoming tide.
>
> The wave of the future is now rising before us. Gentlemen, do not attempt to hold it back. Wisdom lies in recognizing the inevitable – and cooperating with it. In the world that is coming, the great powers are not great enough.[13]

Some signs of this trend are visible; a slow but perceptible movement toward internationalization of the world's news media is taking place. The world's news agencies, a few newspapers and magazines, and both radio and television broadcasting (CNN and BBC World in particular) are transcending the national states from which they arose and are serving international audiences. With this has come, from the West, a pervasive popular culture. Such a transition will be welcomed by some as a contribution to better world understanding or resented by others as efforts by some nations to impose their models of mass communication and pop culture on everyone.

The technological capability for worldwide communication has never been greater, but then never have truly global problems and challenges seemed more urgent. Not enough people anywhere understand these problems or are in a position to cooperate with others in resolving them. Serious questions can be posed about the quality and adequacy of today's system of global news communication, but little doubt exists about the importance to the world of the newspapers, news agencies, and broadcasters that report the world's news to itself.

# Notes

1. Erla Zwingle, *National Geographic*, August 1999, 12.
2. Zwingle, "Goods Move. People Move. Ideas Move. And Cultures Change," 13.
3. Thomas Friedman, *The Lexus and the Olive Tree* (New York: Anchor Books, 2000), xviii.
4. Lester R. Brown, *World Without Borders* (New York: Vintage Books, 1973), 10–12.
5. Sam Roberts, "In 2025 India to Pass China in Population Estimates," *New York Times*, December 16, 2009, A16.
6. Shasshank/Bengali, "Population Boom in Land of Bust," *Wisconsin State Journal*, December 14, 2009, 1.
7. Neil MacFarquhar, "Experts Worry About Feeding the World as its Population Grows," *New York Times*, October 22, 2009, A5.
8. Harold Lasswell, "The Future of World Communication; Quality and Style of Life," Papers of the East-West Communication Institute, Honolulu, no. 4 (September 1972), 3.
9. Andrew Kohut, "Balancing News Interests," *Columbia Journalism Review*, July/August 2001, 58.
10. Stephen Hess, *International News and Foreign Correspondents* (Washington, DC: Brookings Institution, 1996), 8.
11. Barbara Crossette, "US Likes Its Foreign Affairs in Non-Traditional Terms, Polls Say," *The New York Times*, December 28, 1997, 8.
12. Susan Wels, "Global Integration: The Apparent and the Real," *Stanford Magazine*, September 1990, 46.
13. Arthur C. Clarke, "Beyond Babel: The Century of the Communication Satellite," in *Process and Effects of Mass Communication*, W. Schramm and D. Roberts, eds. (Urbana: University of Illinois Press, 1971), 963.

# 2

# Changing Ideologies of Press Control

*Hypocrisy is the homage that vice plays to virtue.*
— Duc de La Rochefoucauld

*Abuses of the freedom of speech ought to be repressed, but to whom dare we commit the power of doing it?*
— Benjamin Franklin

The impressive technological improvements in international news exchanges cannot give editors and broadcasters any real control over how news will be perceived as it emerges from the global news prism, whose planes and surfaces have been cut and polished by diverse and frequently antagonistic political and social systems. As the news passes through the prism, what one journalist considers to be truthful, objective reporting can bend into what another journalist elsewhere in the world considers to be distortion or propaganda.

Despite our impressive technological expertise, political and regional differences and cultural conflicts prevent the international news process from working smoothly and harmoniously. More and faster news communication across national borders does not automatically lead to better understanding; often, it results in enmity and distrust, because the cultural and social differences that characterize the world community preclude even agreement on what is legitimate news. As mentioned, one person's truth is another person's propaganda, and vice versa.

As a result, international journalism has often been the subject of rancor and mutual suspicion. Mass communication's powerful ability to publicize, to expose, to glorify, to criticize, to sensationalize, to denigrate, and to

*The World News Prism: Challenges of Digital Communication*, Eighth Edition.
William A. Hachten and James F. Scotton.
© 2012 John Wiley & Sons, Ltd. Published 2012 by John Wiley & Sons, Ltd.

mislead or propagandize is universally recognized and often feared. At one time or another, government leaders in every land become unhappy or dismayed with the press. In the West, a president or prime minister may complain bitterly that his or her programs are unfairly reported by press opponents and try to bring pressure to bear on the offending publication.

In an African country, an offending foreign correspondent may be thrown into jail or expelled from the country. In Iraq under Saddam Hussein, Farzad Bazoft, an Iranian-born journalist with a British newspaper and carrying a British passport, was executed after he investigated an explosion at a secret chemical plant. Under duress and perhaps torture, Bazoft confessed to spying for Israel. The incident illustrated the often narrow line between espionage and journalism in Iraq, as elsewhere. Throughout the world today, journalists have become the victims of violence from those who do not want some particular information reported.

The differing perceptions about the nature and role of journalism and mass communication are rooted in divergent political systems and historical and cultural traditions, and are broadly reflected in five political concepts of the press found in the world today: (i) Authoritarian, (ii) Western, (iii) Communist, (iv) Revolutionary, and (v) Developmental.[1] These are normative concepts that reflect how the media ideally should perform under certain political conditions and social values. We believe that an understanding of these contrasting approaches to the role and function of transnational journalism can help to clarify some of the issues that divide the world's press.

Authoritarianism is the oldest and most pervasive concept and has spawned two twentieth-century modifications: the Communist and Developmental concepts. The Western concept, under which the press in Western democracies with market economies generally functions, represents a fundamental alternative to the Authoritarian concept and contains elements of both eighteenth-century political liberalism and twentieth-century views of Social Responsibility. The Revolutionary concept has one trait in common with the Western: they both try to operate outside governmental controls. The Developmental concept is a declining pattern associated with the developing nations, most of which still lack adequate media resources, as well as effective political and economic institutions. As the twenty-first century rolls along, political ideology is becoming less important as a raison d'être for press concepts or theories. The collapse of communism and one-party states in the third world has effectively headed many undemocratic governments and their media into the broad corral of authoritarianism. A concurrent trend has been the widespread US-UK. or Western model as the predominant press concept. Just as many autocratic regimes call themselves "the Democratic Republic of. . .." or the "People's Kingdom of . . ." they also proclaim their media free of government restraint and "servants of the people" thus reminding us of what a great Frenchman said about hypocrisy as the homage that vice plays to virtue.

Newspapers, television, and other media, always and everywhere, function within some kinds of governmental, societal, and economic constraints. Even the "freest" or most independent press system must deal with varying degrees of regulation by political authority. In the relationship between government and mass communication, the basic question is not whether government controls the press but the nature and extent of those controls. All press systems exist somewhere along a continuum, from complete controls (absolute authoritarianism) at one end to no controls (pure libertarianism) at the other. Absolute freedom of expression is a myth. Beyond that, controls on the press are so varied and complex that it is difficult, if not impossible, to compare press freedom in one nation with that in another. In one country, newspapers may be under harsh, arbitrary political restraints; in another, they may be under more subtle, yet real, economic and corporate restrictions. As Hallin pointed out, "news media around the world vary in their styles, structures, and social and political roles. The differences are less dramatic in 2004 than they were a generation ago. 'Globalization' resulted in a considerable degree of homogenization of media systems, as a similar, mainly commercial structure and a common culture of journalism have increasingly spread around the world. However, the differences among the media systems continue to be striking."[2]

A basic tenet of the following analysis is that all press systems reflect the values of the political and economic systems of the nations within which they operate. The trend toward globalization notwithstanding, print and broadcast systems as well as digital media are still controlled and regulated by their own national governments. And in this era of increasing transnational communication, journalists from an open society must work often and collect news abroad in a closed or autocratic society, thereby increasing opportunities for friction between divergent concepts. The long struggle of journalists to freely report and publish news from abroad without hindrance from government has now become expanded to include the Internet, emails, and cell phones. As will be seen efforts to censor the Internet and its many services such as the Google and Yahoo search engines, and so on, are becoming the new frontier of the struggle for international free expression.

## Authoritarian Concept

Authoritarian political systems were the norm at the time the printing press was invented by Gutenberg in the mid-fifteenth century and, in the years since, more people have lived under an authoritarian press concept than under any other. The basic principle of authoritarianism is simple: the press is always subject to direct or implied control by the state or sovereign. A printing press (or, later, a broadcasting facility or a search engine) cannot be used to challenge, criticize, or in any way undermine the sovereign. The press functions from the top down. The king, or ruler, or the party decides what will be published because truth (and information) is essentially a monopoly of those in authority. Reality is what the government says it is.

To the authoritarian, diversity of views is wasteful and irresponsible, dissent an annoying nuisance and often subversive, and consensus and standardization are logical and sensible goals for mass communication. There is a certain compelling logic behind this.

Under traditional authoritarianism, the press operates outside government and is permitted to gather and publish news, but it must function for the "good of the state." The government usually leaves the press alone as long as it does not criticize authority or challenge the leadership in any way. If the press does attack authority, then the political authority intervenes, imposing censorship or even closing down publications and jailing editors. Under the Authoritarian concept, the constraint of potential censorship, if not actual prior restraint itself, always exists. Editors and reporters exercise a good deal of self-censorship, but never know for sure just how far they can go without triggering official disfavor and intervention. They must support the status quo and neither advocate change, or criticize the nation's leadership, nor give offense to the dominant moral or political values.

The Authoritarian concept is alive and well today in other South Asian nations, especially Singapore and Malaysia. Singapore, despite its prosperity and economic ties to the West, has been unusually hostile to foreign publications, having restricted or banned distribution of *The Asian Wall Street Journal*, *Time*, *Asia week*, and *Far Eastern Economic Review* at various times.

Authoritarianism is widespread today, especially if, as some scholars aver, the Communist and Developmental concepts are understood to be variations of traditional authoritarianism. According to Freedom House, the global declines in press freedom continued in 2009 – the seven straight years of deterioration in the former Soviet Union, the Middle East, and Africa. "Not free" or authoritarian nations included some of the largest – China, Russia and its former republics, most of Africa, and all of the Middle East except for "partly free" Egypt. Libya, Iran, Tunisia, Syria, and Saudi Arabia were nations where journalists and bloggers faced harsh repercussions for expressing independent views.

Authoritarian media systems of all Arab nations are now in a state of flux and uncertainty. Many apparently democratic nations with political parties and elected presidents are not in fact very democratic because rulers often act arbitrarily, dissidents and minorities lack legal rights, and local journalists operate under strict controls, including harassment, torture, and imprisonment.

In many nations, especially in Latin America, the media have moved back and forth between freedom and controls as the governments have changed from military to democratic regimes and back again. During 2009, South American nations were all "partly free" except for "free" Chile and Uruguay and "not free" Venezuela controlled by dictator President Hugo Chávez. However, Freedom House noted that Mexico, Bolivia, Ecuador, Guatemala and Nicaragua all registered declines in press freedom during 2009.

Foreign correspondents pose a special challenge to authoritarian regimes, and Western journalists often encounter a variety of difficulties: entry visas are denied; stories are censored; telephone and Comsat facilities are refused; and sometimes reporters are harassed, mistreated, jailed, or expelled.

## The Western Concept

The Western concept represents a distinct deviation from the traditional authoritarian controls and evolved during the rise of democracies in Europe and North America. During the long constitutional struggle in England between the Crown, the courts, and the Commons and, later, in the United States, a press relatively free of arbitrary government controls slowly evolved. In fact, one definition of freedom of the press is the right of the press to report on, comment on, and criticize its own government without retaliation or threat of retaliation from the government. This has been called "the right to talk politics." Historically, seditious libel meant criticism of government, laws, or officials. The absence of seditious libel as a crime has been considered the true pragmatic test of a country's freedom of expression, because politically relevant speech is what press freedom is mostly about. By this demanding test the Western concept – the right to talk politics – is comparatively rare.

Although many authoritarian governments give it lip service, a free or independent press is usually found in only a dozen or more Western nations that share these characteristics: (i) a system of laws that provides meaningful protection to individual civil liberties and property rights (here, common-law nations, such as the United States and Britain, seem to do better than nations, such as France or Italy, with codified legal traditions); (ii) high average levels of per capita income, education, and literacy; (iii) governance by constitutional parliamentary democracy, or at least with legitimate political oppositions; (iv) sufficient capital or private enterprise to support media of news communication – that is, market economies; and (v) an established tradition of independent journalism.

Among Western media, Hallin and Mancini identify three models: the liberal model found in the United States, Britain, Canada, Ireland, Australia, and New Zealand; the "polarized model" found in Italy, Spain, and France, to an extent; and the "democratic corporatist" model found in Scandinavia and Central European states.[3] Any list of other nations meeting these criteria for a Western press today would certainly include the Netherlands, Belgium, Austria, Iceland, Israel, and Switzerland. In addition to these Western nations, highly developed and westernized Japan surely should be added. And India, the world's largest democracy, has enjoyed a remarkably free press despite its diverse problems.

Journalists in many other nations support and practice the Western concept but, because of political instability, their media over the years have swung back and forth between freedom and control.

By and large, the Western nations that meet the criteria include those that do most of the world's news gathering from other nations and whose correspondents most often come into conflict with authoritarian regimes. This is because the Western concept holds strongly that a government – any government, here or abroad – should not interfere in the process of collecting and disseminating news. The press, in theory, must be independent of authority and, of course, exist outside government and be well protected by law and custom from arbitrary government interference. And so an independent press usually means one situated in a democratic, market economy and enjoying the same autonomy as other private business enterprises. As globalization spreads, more and more nations are evolving in this direction.

The ideals of Western libertarian journalism are, to a large extent, a by-product of the Enlightenment and the liberal political tradition reflected in the writings of John Milton, John Locke, Thomas Jefferson, and John Stuart Mill. Primarily, there must be a diversity of views and news sources available, a "marketplace of ideas" from which the public can choose what it wishes to read and believe, for no one person or no authority, spiritual or temporal, has a monopoly on truth. United States Judge Learned Hand expressed it well:

> That [newspaper] industry serves one of the most vital of all general interests: the dissemination of news from as many different sources, and with as many different facets as is possible. . . . It presupposes that right conclusions are more likely to be gathered out of a multitude of tongues than through any kind of authoritarian selection. To many this is, and always will be, folly; but we have staked upon it our all.[4]

Underlying this diversity of views is the faith that citizens will somehow make the right choices about what to believe if enough voices are heard and government keeps its hands off. In American Constitutional theory, this libertarian view is based upon certain values deemed inherent in a free press: (i) by gathering public information and scrutinizing government, the press makes self-government and democracy possible; (ii) an unfettered press ensures that a diversity of views and news will be read and heard; (iii) a system of free expression provides autonomy for individuals to lead free and productive lives; and (iv) it enables an independent press to serve as a check on abuses of power by government.[5]

Carried over to the international context, the Western concept argues that there must be a free flow of information, unimpeded by any inter-vention by any nation. ("Free flow," it is argued, does not necessarily mean a balanced or two-way flow of news, as desirable as that may be.) No government anywhere should obstruct the gathering and dissemination of legitimate news. Only news media free of official restraints will be credible to readers and viewers here and abroad. Advocates say that the Western concept serves the cause of global news flow in several important ways. It makes possible the gathering and dissemination of reliable and accurate news. In a global economy, the business press plays an essential role of providing fast and reliable news of global business and finance.

A free press, operating on a global scale, provides news and important information to peoples living in authoritarian regimes that censor their own media. International shortwave radio broadcasters – the BBC, VOA, and others – relay news and information from Western news gatherers, as do the interactive news media on the Internet.

Western news media, of course, are not without their shortcomings. Critics claim that too many news media have become submerged into giant, entertainment-oriented conglomerates, all primarily concerned with making a profit. In so doing, Western media are accused of slighting serious news in favor of sensation, scandal, and celebrity. Furthermore, Western media certainly are not immune to pressures from their own governments. Political freedom does not preclude economic and corporate interference with journalistic practices. A privately owned media system will, in varying degrees, reflect the interests and concerns of its owners. Yet to stay independent of external controls, including government, the publishers and broadcasters must be financially strong and profitable. Journalistic excellence and profitability are not identical goals, although some of the best news media are also very profitable; for some owners, however, making money is the primary purpose of journalism, and independence and public service mean little. Then, too, diversity at both national and international levels appears to be in decline, and the marked increase of media conglomerates and ownership concentration has reduced the number of independent voices heard in the marketplace. Further, Western news media have suffered loss of both credibility and audiences due in part to the rising and increasingly harsh political rhetoric within democratic societies.

The significance and effectiveness of the Western concept depends on the "basics" of serious, professional journalism. These basics have been laid out most clearly by Bill Kovach and Tom Rosenstiel in their fine book *Elements of Journalism*. They are: (i) journalism's first obligation is to the truth; (ii) its first loyalty is to its citizens; (iii) its essence is a discipline of verification; (iv) its practitioners must maintain an independence from those they cover; (v) it must serve as an independent monitor of power; (vi) it must provide a forum for public criticism and compromise; (vii) its practitioners have an obligation to exercise their personal conscience; (viii) it must keep the news comprehensive and in proportion; (ix) citizens, too, have rights and responsibilities when it comes to the news (FN Kovach and Rosenstiel, *The Elements of Style*, New York: Three Rivers Press, 2007, 1).

Viewed from a slightly different perspective, a free press provides three kinds of news: (i) accountability news; (ii) explanatory news, and (iii) investigative news. All are essential to the proper functioning of a free press in its relationships to government and society – whether foreign or domestic (FN Alex S. Jones, "Losing the News: The Future of the News in that Feeds Democracy," New York: Oxford University Press, 2009).

But as this book argues in several places, the traditional Western concept is in dire economic straits. Declines in circulation and broadcasting audiences, steady losses in advertising revenues, and aging publics, have all contributed to the "glorious disruption" of the "old media" by digital and electronic media. In this time of confusion and uncertainty about the future, the traditional media – printed newspapers and magazines, books, and cable outlets are all trying to find a "new business model" that will enable them to survive in this period of rapid change. No one is predicting the future with any real confidence – just as no one in the fifteenth century could foresee the future impact of Gutenberg's moveable type on paper. But without doubt, innovations in media technology are moving at a far faster pace then ever before.

In some democracies, such as Norway and Sweden, the government maintains diversity of political views by providing subsidies to the newspapers of various political parties, a practice not without potential danger to press independence.

Some modifications of the Western concept fall under the rubric of Social Responsibility. This view holds that the media have clear obligations of public service that transcend moneymaking. Public service implies professional standards for journalists as well as reliable and objective reporting. The media are obligated, in addition, to ensure that all voices and views in the community are heard. Further, government is granted a limited role in intervening in media operations and in regulating conditions if public interests are not being adequately served. Government regulation of broadcasting in its earliest years in the United States, for example, represented an example of the Social Responsibility position.

Two other related modifications are the Democratic Socialist concept and the Democratic Participant concept, suggested by Robert Picard. Expressing fears concerning the abuses of private ownership, the Democratic Socialist theory says that state action is needed to institute new forms of ownership and management and to intervene in the economics of the media.[6] Similarly, Democratic Participant theory reflects a reaction against commercialization and monopolization of the privately owned media, as well as against the centralism and bureaucratization of public broadcasting. Denis McQuail summarized several of its principles: (i) media should exist primarily for their audiences, and not for media organizations, professionals, or clients of media; (ii) individual citizens and minority groups have rights of access to media (rights to communicate) and rights to be served by media according to the peoples' own determination of need; (iii) the organization and content of the media should not be subject to centralized political or state bureaucratic control; and, finally, (iv) small-scale, interactive, and participative media forms are better than large-scale, professionalized media.[7]

These evolving views, which represent some disillusionment with mass-media performance, are found throughout Western democracies, but especially in Northern Europe. Their major disadvantage is that such decentralized, small-scale media are less able to check the abuses of government and corporate power, whether at home or abroad. Yet this debate illustrates a built-in advantage of the Western concept: it enjoys the freedom to criticize and reform its own media system through democratic processes, something that is lacking in the other concepts.

Finally, the Western press concept, with its emphasis on the individual's rights to send and receive information, is well suited as a conceptual framework for the new "personalized media" – computers with modems, faxes, interactive television, and bloggers on the Internet – that are now playing a growing role in international communication (see Chapter 4, "The Internet, Comsats, and Bloggers"). But as yet the Western nations have not yet acquired all the necessary legal and regulatory framework needed for the new electronic media. Issues of communications freedom and privacy are examples. Yet it is evident that the new media are more accepted and are more free in a libertarian framework than in any variation of the authoritarian concept of the media.

## The Rise and Fall of the Communist Concept

For more than seventy years, the Western concept of the press had been under direct challenge by advocates of the communist press theory, just as capitalism itself was under assault by Marxist/Leninist economic doctrines. Lenin had written that "'freedom of the press' of a bourgeois society consists in freedom of the rich systematically, unceasingly, and daily in the millions of copies to deceive, corrupt, and fool the exploited and oppressed mass of the people, the poor."[8]

Many intellectuals and writers were convinced that the Western liberal democracies and their press were outdated and doomed and that the USSR's communism and its party-controlled media were the wave of the future. Even among its critics, the Leninist theory was seen as something new and different – certainly more positive and meaningful than the traditional Authoritarian concept.

Mass media controlled and directed by the Communist Party, Lenin argued, can concentrate on the serious task of nation-building by publishing news relating to the entire society's policies and goals as determined by the top party leadership. To Lenin, the press was an integral part of the Communist Party, which was itself seen as a teacher to instruct the masses and lead the proletariat. The basic postulates of the theory deriving from Marx and Engels with rules of application of Lenin were summarized by McQuail:

> Media should serve the interests of, and be in control of, the working class and should not be privately owned. Media should serve positive functions for society by socialization to desired norms, education, information, motivation, and mobilization. Within their overall task for society, the media should respond to wishes and needs of their audiences. Society has a right to use censorship and other legal measures to prevent, or punish after the event, anti-societal publication. Media should provide a complete and objective view of society and the world according to Marxist-Leninist principles. Media should support progressive movements at home and abroad.[9]

Aside from normative theory, the characteristics of the Soviet press concept that set it apart from Western journalism were these: it was, first, a planned and completely government- and party-controlled system that permitted no competing private media. As Lenin said, there is no freedom for the enemies of socialism; his concept would avoid the abuses of the capitalist press. Second, this one-party press enjoyed a monopoly on news, both coming in and going out. Information was controlled by the state; the Party version of events was all that mattered. This condition lasted through the Stalin years, when foreign broadcasts were jammed and foreign publication barred at the borders. Third, news itself was defined as "positive" information that furthered the goals of the Party, not information of direct interest or relevance to the lives of the Soviet people themselves. A plane crash or a nuclear accident was not news; a government farm report or a new tractor factory was. Finally, the press, in concert with the Communist Party and secret police, was used to control the people as well as to promote government policies and prepare the public for future policy changes.

The communist media faithfully served the Party's ruling elite, but their fatal flaw was that they did not serve the interests of the people themselves. As the peoples under communist regimes in Central and Eastern Europe, deprived of political freedoms, saw their economies crumble and fall behind those of the West, they became increasingly disillusioned with their own mass media, which spoke only for authority and failed to criticize or report weaknesses in the ruling communist elites. In the USSR, much of the same disillusionment existed, but it can be argued that some impetus for reform came from above as Mikhail Gorbachev's *glasnost* policies led to media changes beginning in 1985, well before the upheaval of 1991.

The communist press theory unraveled over a number of years. First came loss of faith in Leninist ideology: the slogans and buzzwords became increasingly empty. From the 1970s onward, Marxist press advocates no longer extolled the superiority of communist theory and focused instead on criticizing Western media. The practices of communist mass communication, especially as a means of controlling and leading public opinion, continued with some modifications into the 1980s, but without the old ideological fervor. In the Soviet Union's final stages, the communist media were reduced to playing a role similar to that of the secret police: another means of controlling the people.

Concurrently, Western mass communication kept intruding on the closed societies of Eastern Europe and appears to have facilitated the demise of communist regimes. The Soviet media's monopoly on news began to crack early in the Cold War. The BBC World Service, the Voice of America, Radio Free Europe, and other Western broadcasters were widely heard. East Germans watched Western television beamed from West Berlin and the Federal Republic of Germany. Alternative and unofficial forms of publication flourished in the USSR, and the West learned a new word, *samizdat* ("self-publishing" in Russian).

Despite efforts to keep them out, Western rock music and videocassettes found their way into communist cultures and became hugely popular.

The nuclear accident at Chernobyl in April 1986 signaled a change in the Soviet media's handling of a major "bad news" story. At first, the Soviet government made an extraordinary effort to deny that any catastrophe had occurred, and restricted information even while airborne radiation was detected in Scandinavia and Poland. This reflexive retreat into secrecy illustrated the Kremlin's traditional unwillingness to concede any failings before its people and the world. But abroad, the Kremlin was harshly criticized for failing to provide prompt information about the radioactivity spreading across Europe and for neglecting to warn its own citizens. Gradually, Soviet media were forced, by Western media coverage, to report details even though they were released weeks after the event.

The news void on Chernobyl was filled in part by Radio Free Europe and Radio Liberty, which provided breaking news to communist bloc listeners. In such emergencies, Eastern Europeans were likely to turn to Western radio for information unavailable elsewhere. To obtain information by radio, Voice of America officials reported, people traveled out of the cities to rural areas where jamming was ineffective. Finally, four years later, in April 1990, the Soviet Union finally acknowledged that the medical, environmental, and political consequences of the Chernobyl disaster had been much greater than the Kremlin had ever frankly discussed.

As the Chernobyl disaster showed, the communist media could not deal with foreign competition, something unforeseen in Lenin's closed-system press theory. With Mikhail Gorbachev's proclamation of *glasnost* and *perestroika* in the mid-1980s, changes in media theory and practice accelerated. A Soviet weekly, *Argumenti i Fakti*, with a circulation of more than 20 million, published in 1989 the most detailed account of Stalin's victims yet presented to a Soviet mass audience, indicating that about 20 million Soviet citizens died in labor camps, forced collectivization, famine, and executions. The same year in Warsaw, the first independently published daily newspaper in the Eastern bloc appeared: *Gazeta* supported the newly legalized Solidarity trade union. And, in East Germany, the communist media turned on their former masters and behaved like Western investigative reporters. *Neues Deutschland*, the main communist paper, *Berliner Zeitung*, and *Junge Welt* all published accusations of corruption and profiteering by high Communist Party officials under Erich Honecker. East German television, a week earlier a subservient tool of the Honecker regime, ran a series of sixteen reports depicting the high living of top Party members. These revelations scandalized the public and reinforced the outcry that forced the Honecker regime from power. From East Berlin to Warsaw to Prague to Budapest to Moscow, the communist theory of the press has been left in shambles – in effect, tossed into the much-utilized dustbin of history.

Russia's media have increasingly been endangered since Vladimir Putin became president and began presiding over an alarming assault on press freedom. The Kremlin imposed censorship on news about the lingering civil war in Chechnya, orchestrated legal harassment against private media outlets, and granted sweeping powers of surveillance to security forces. During 2000–2001, numerous violent attacks on journalists were carried out with impunity across Russia. In April 2001, the Kremlin-controlled Gazprom corporation took over NTV, the country's only independent national television network. Within days, the Gazprom coup had shut down a prominent Moscow daily and ousted leading journalists from the country's most prestigious newsweekly. Despite Gazprom's insistence that these changes were strictly business, the Committee to Protect Journalists reported that the main beneficiary was Putin himself, whose primary critics have now been silenced. Many of NTV's best journalists joined TV-6, which was Moscow's only independent television outlet and had a smaller, but still loyal audience. But then, in December 2001, a Russian court also shut down TV-6. The station's managers and most outside analysts called it a Kremlin plot to force it off the air. Authoritarian may be the best adjective to describe Russia's news media today. By 2004, press freedom and free speech had become so restricted in Russia that Freedom House downgraded the country to "Not Free" – the only country to be so downgraded that year. Russia had become a nation where, it was said, you could kill a journalist and get away with it. Putin's government had failed to solve the murders of eleven important journalists. The national television media were working almost completely under the Kremlin's fist. Newspaper and magazine journalists now show independence at their own peril. Russia extended its press hostility to ABC Television News when it barred all journalists working for the US network on August 30, 2005. The crackdown came in retaliation for ABC's *Nightline* broadcast interview with a Chechen rebel leader who had carried out terrorist attacks in Russia.

By 2009, Russia became the third deadliest country for journalists after Algeria and Iraq, according to the Committee to Protect Journalists (CPJ). Since 2000, when Putin was elected, at least seventeen journalists had been killed because of what they reported. None of these murders has been solved. As Nina Ognianova of CPJ put it: "the process of squeezing critical journalism out of the public space is now complete" (FN "Killing the Russian Media" + (editorial) *New York Times*, May 24, 1907, 22).

The CPJ said journalists became targets because they were scrutinizing powerful people by reporting on corruption or other misconduct (FN Clifford Levy, "Press Group Seeks Inquiry into Killings in Russia," *New York Times*, September 10, 2009, A5). Fear of violence, it was said, has led to a growing climate of self-censorship with many journalists reluctant to carry out investigative reporting. Under Putin and his stand-in, Dmitry Medvedlov the Russian media system is essentially authoritarian.

Russia provided a harsh example for its fifteen former republics, all of which but the three Baltic states have seen a decline of press freedom. In Turkmenistan, Belarus, and Ukraine (under its former leader Kuchma) ways were found to thwart, control, or even kill journalists.

## Revolutionary Concept

Lenin provided both some of the ideology and rationale for another and more ephemeral view: the Revolutionary. Simply stated, this is a concept of illegal and subversive communication, using the press and other media to overthrow a government or wrest control from alien or otherwise rejected rulers.

Lenin in his famous work *What Is to be Done?* (written in exile before the 1917 Revolution) proposed that the revolutionaries establish a nationwide, legal newspaper inside czarist Russia. Such a paper could obviously not advocate revolutionary goals, but its distribution system could be an excellent mechanism for a political machine. The newspaper, Lenin postulated, would be a cover for a far-flung revolutionary organization. The early *Pravda*, although it was not a legal newspaper (and was edited by Stalin at one time), was published outside czarist Russia, and smuggled copies were widely distributed – a fine example of the Revolutionary concept.

The revolutionary press is a press of people who believe strongly that the government they live under does not serve their interests and should be overthrown. They believe they owe such a government no loyalty whatsoever. Pure examples are difficult to find, but one surely was the underground press in Nazi-occupied France during World War II. The editors and journalists of the clandestine press literally risked their lives to put out their papers and pamphlets. Other examples of the Revolutionary concept were the *samizdat*, the secretly typed and mimeographed copies of books, political tracts, and the like that were passed at great risk from hand to hand among dissidents inside the Soviet Union.

The history of anticolonialist movements in the former third world is replete with examples. Throughout the British Empire, especially in West Africa, political dissidents published small newspapers, often handwritten, that first expressed grievances against the British rulers, then encouraged nationalism, and finally advocated political independence. Aspiring political leaders such as Azikiwe, Awolowo, Nkrumah, Kaunda, and Kenyatta were all editors of these small political newspapers that informed and helped organize the budding political parties and nationalist movements. The British authorities were surprisingly tolerant, even though they disapproved of and sometimes acted against the publications and their editors.

Much in the Anglo-American political tradition supported these newspapers, and the editors claimed the rights of British journalists. Had not Thomas Paine used political pamphlets to help expel the British from the American Colonies? Had not Thomas Jefferson said that the people have a right to revolution, including the right to subsequent revolutions if that proved necessary?

In the post-independence years, radio broadcasting has become a valuable tool of revolutionary groups seeking to overthrow the fragile governments of developing nations. Black Africa has been plagued with numerous coups d'état, and during times of acute political crisis, radio broadcasting has often played a significant role as the primary medium of communication in most nations. So rebels have recognized the importance of controlling information at the political center of power. Hence, insurgents have often seized the radio station before heading for the presidential palace. Military struggles during a coup attempt frequently occur outside the broadcast station, because if rebels can announce over the nation's only radio station that a coup has been accomplished (even while the issue is still in doubt), it helps achieve the desired end.

In Iran, two other communication devices – the photocopying machine and the audiocassette – have proved useful in revolutionary efforts. The revolution of the Ayatollah Khomeini has been called the first cassette revolution. Thousands of cassette recordings of the Ayatollah's speeches propagating his revolutionary ideas were played in the mosques, which were not kept under surveillance by the Shah's secret police. These small, portable instruments were able to reach millions while circumventing the government-controlled press, radio, and television. At the same time, when revolutionary "night letters" and pamphlets arrived mysteriously at offices in Tehran, sympathetic secretaries made many photocopies, quickly and more secretly than possible with a printing press.

Anthony Sampson said that "the period of television and radio monopolies may prove a passing phase, as we find ourselves in a much more open

40 *Changing Ideologies of Press Control*

field of communications, with cassettes and copied documents taking the place of the books and pamphlets that undermined eighteenth-century governments." He suggested an epitaph for the Shah's regime: "He forgot the cassette."[10]

Personalized media, with their interactive capabilities, all present challenges to centralized autocracies trying to control news and information. The continuing struggle of Chinese dissidents for civil rights is an example of the Revolutionary concept. That struggle goes on with dissidents now using the Internet and cell phones to advocate democratic change in China. Twitter and cell phones played a crucial role in the violent political protests in late 2009 over Iran's challenged election (see Chapter 5) and in the Arab revolutions in 2011.

## Developmental Concept

By its very nature, the Revolutionary concept is a short-term affair: the successful subversive use of communication to topple a despised regime is self-limiting. After goals are achieved, the gains must be consolidated and then another concept takes over. In recent decades, a variation on the Authoritarian concept – the Developmental concept – has emerged in the wake of political independence in impoverished nations throughout the developing world.

The Developmental concept is an amorphous and curious mixture of ideas, rhetoric, influences, and grievances. As yet, the concept is not clearly defined. Some aspects are taken straight from Lenin and the communist concept of the press. Perhaps of greater importance are the influences of Western social scientists who have posited a major role for mass communication in the process of nation-building in newly independent countries. American academics such as Wilbur Schramm, Daniel Lerner, and others, all democrats at heart, have argued that the communication process is central to the achievement of national integration and economic development. In so doing, they may have unintentionally provided a rationale for autocratic press controls.

Other more radical academics, mostly Europeans, have echoed Marxist views and added a touch of anti-Americanism to the concept, for the concept is to some extent a critique of and reaction against the West and its transnational media. It also reflects the frustrations and anger of poor and media-deficient nations.

The Developmental concept is an approach to mass communication in nations that are clearly lacking in newspapers, broadcasting, and other media – the world's "have-nots" in media resources.

In general, the concept holds that:

- All the instruments of mass communication – newspapers, radio, television, motion pictures, national news services – must be mobilized by the central government to aid in the great tasks of nation building: fighting illiteracy and poverty, building a political consciousness, assisting in economic development. Implicit here is the Social Responsibility view that the government must step in and provide adequate media service when the private sector is unable to do so, as is the case in many poor nations.
- The media therefore should support authority, not challenge it. Dissent or criticism has no place, in part because the alternative to the ruling government would be chaos, it is argued. Freedom of the press, then, can be restricted according to the development needs of the society.
- Information (or truth) thus becomes the property of the state: the flow of power (and truth) between the governors and the governed works from the top down, as in traditional authoritarianism. Information or news is a scarce national resource; it must be utilized to further the national goals.
- Implied, but not often articulated, is the view that individual rights of expression and other civil liberties are somewhat irrelevant in the face of the overwhelming problems of poverty, disease, illiteracy, and ethnicity that face a majority of these nations. (Critics argue that the concept provides a palatable rationale for old-fashioned authoritarianism.)
- This concept of a guided press further implies that in international news each nation has a sovereign right to control both foreign journalists and the flow of news back and forth across its borders. Good examples of this concept were Ghana under Kwame Nkrumah, Tanzania under Julius Nyerere, and Zimbabwe under Robert Mugabe.

Some critics argue that central to the Developmental concept is a rejection of the Western view. As British journalist Rosemary Righter has written, there is a growing feeling that the Western model of the press is undesirable in itself. Instead of backing diversity and free flow, the mass media must adopt a didactic, even ideological, role of explaining to the people their part in forging a new social order.[11]

Western news media are attacked on several scores. To begin with, some critics say that the Western international media are too monopolistic and powerful; they penetrate too widely and effectively. The world news organizations – the AP (the Associated Press), CNN, Reuters, the BBC, and AFP (Agence France-Presse) – are particular targets, charged with creating a clear imbalance, a one-way flow, and a near monopoly of news that favors the affluent North. Furthermore, Western media represent an alien viewpoint, which they impose on nations trying to build independent modern identities. Traditional cultures, it is charged, have been threatened by the inundation of news and mass culture – television programs, pop music, movies, videocassettes, and audiocassettes – principally from the United States and Britain. Such domination, it is argued, amounts to cultural aggression. But nonetheless, in recent years, the Western approach has been gaining wider acceptance.

Finally, a few proponents of the Developmental concept have long charged that the Western media are part of an international conspiracy by which the economic and political interests of the capitalist nations are using global mass communication to dominate, even subjugate, the developing nations. Some advocates of this concept argue that the world needs a "new international information order" to redress these imbalances.

The Developmental concept is a view of mass communication from the many nations of the former third world, where most citizens are people of color, poor, ill-nourished, and illiterate, and it reflects resentments against the West, where people are mainly Caucasian, affluent, and literate. The concept is related as well to what some feel is the major problem facing the world today: the widening gap between the rich and the poor, debt-ridden, "failed" nations. The same nations that decry the trade and GNP (gross national product) imbalances between North and South also excoriate the Western news media. Echoes of the Developmental concept are being heard in current protests and demonstrations against globalization.

By the mid-1990s, the Developmental concept appeared to be losing momentum among developing nations. The current global trends toward more democracy and market economies appear to have boosted the Western press concept, but the odds that many of the new democracies will succeed are not good. At the same time, the communist press concept appears to have disappeared as a viable press theory. Communist regimes persist in North Korea, Cuba, and the People's Republic of China, but the ideological fervor and justification seems to have waned – only authoritarianism remains.

China has jettisoned Marxist economic theory while holding onto centralized, totalitarian controls over its people. The resulting mix has been called "market socialism," and has produced a rapidly growing economy that seems to have something in common with the corporate capitalism or neo-authoritarianism of its Asian neighbors, South Korea, Singapore, and Malaysia. The Chinese people have been prospering economically, but enjoy little freedom of expression as China has emerged as a major economic force in the world (for more on China, see Chapter 7).

The controversies engendered by these conflicting concepts of mass communication have long been marked by rancor, but this, too, has shown some signs of abating. Currently, ideological conflict between press systems seems to have clearly subsided, if only temporarily. Some would argue that in today's world only two concepts of the press are viable: the Authoritarian approach, which insists on its right to control news and information and restrict its circulation; and the Western concept with its variations, which argues that news and information, like knowledge itself, belong to all people and that journalists have the right to pursue and report news wherever it can be found.

Yet there remain valid arguments on all sides of these political and cultural confrontations, each reflecting differing social and political traditions that are difficult to reconcile. But as the international news system becomes more integrated and interdependent, the conflicts over how news and information are to be controlled may diminish. Although few if any nations fit neatly into any of these five normative concepts of the press, the concepts are still useful in illustrating some of the divergent perceptions of the nature of news and how it should be disseminated.

Despite the variety of news and views refracted through the world news prism, the great bulk of foreign news is still gathered and disseminated by Western news media. In recent years, two clear trends have emerged: the triumph of the Western or liberal concept of the press and the reality that many more millions of people, mostly in the Eurasian landmass, have joined the vast world audience of international communication. Both trends are integral aspects of the globalization of the media.

# Notes

1. For this analysis, the authors owe a debt to the classic book by Fred Siebert, Theodore Peterson, and Wilbur Schramm, *Four Theories of the Press* (Urbana:

University of Illinois Press, 1956). In 2004, another important book, *Comparing Media Systems: Three Models of Media and Politics*, by Daniel Hallin and Paolo Mancini (Cambridge University Press, 2004) has added new insights to the interaction between media and political structures.

2. Daniel Hallin and Robert Giles, "Presses and Democracy," in *The Press*, G. Overholzer and K. H. Jamieson, eds. (New York: Oxford University Press, 2005), 4.
3. Hallin and Giles, "Presses and Democracy," 5.
4. *Associated Press v. United States*, 52 F.Supp.362, 372 (1943).
5. See Vincent Blasi, "The Checking Value in First Amendment Theory," *ABA Research Journal*, no. 3, Summer 1977, 521–649.
6. Robert Picard, "Revisions of Four Theories of the Press," *Mass Comm Review*, Winter/Spring 1982–1983, 27.
7. Denis McQuail, *Mass Communication Theory: An Introduction* (Beverly Hills, CA: Sage, 1983), 96–97.
8. Mark Hopkins, *Mass Media in the Soviet Union* (New York: Pegasus, 1970), 55.
9. McQuail, *Mass Communication Theory*, 93–94.
10. Anthony Sampson, "Rebel Poli-Techs," *The New York Times*, May 5, 1970, 15.
11. Rosemary Righter, *Whose News: Politics, The Press, and the Third World* (New York: Times Books, 1978), 14–15.

# 3

# Global News Under Stress

*What we are building now is the nervous system of mankind, which will link together the whole human race, for better or worse, in a unity which no earlier age could have imagined.*

— Arthur C. Clarke

When an unexpected global calamity occurs, such as the recent earthquakes in Japan, Haiti, Chile, or China, news media immediately begin gathering all available details about the horrendous events (for unusual aspects of reporting the stories, see Chapter 5).

The earthquake and tsunami stories, like most major news stories, were essentially reported by journalists working for news organizations of Western nations. To their clients, news has – like electricity, water, and gas – become an essential service that is taken for granted. By merely turning on a radio or television set or picking up a newspaper at the door, or logging on to the Internet, people expect to find the latest news, whether it is from the Middle East, Europe, Africa, or wherever. (This is not the case, however, among the rural poor of developing nations.)

Indeed, most people in the industrialized world cannot remember when important breaking news was not available immediately (like any other public utility) at the flick of a switch; the technicalities of news delivery are of little public concern and only dimly understood at best. The fact is, however, that global news communication is of fairly recent origin. The far-flung apparatus or "system" through which news flows around the world has evolved and expanded greatly since World War II, along with

*The World News Prism: Challenges of Digital Communication*, Eighth Edition.
William A. Hachten and James F. Scotton.
© 2012 John Wiley & Sons, Ltd. Published 2012 by John Wiley & Sons, Ltd.

our modern information society. We learned, for example, about the important battles of World War II many hours or often several days after they began – and then only through radio or newspapers. About thirty years later, the daily clashes in Vietnam were delivered in full color on our home television screens at dinner time, sometimes on the same day they occurred.

Naturally, the public's perceptions of warfare have always been colored by the way journalists have reported them, but color television pictures of modern wars, including US dead and wounded, had an unusually strong impact on public attitudes. And today, with the ongoing war in Afghanistan, the public follows many dramatic news events in real time. Hence, the impact is greatly enhanced.

In our time, and particularly since 1945, an intricate web of international communications has been spun about the planet, greatly expanding the capability for news and political interaction at a time when the need for information has become so much more urgent. This rapid growth of what Colin Cherry termed an "explosion" in mass communication around the world has had widespread significance: for international relations and world politics; for the flow of news and information; for the cultural impact abroad of motion pictures, television, and video from the West; and for the institutions of international communication, including news agencies, broadcast networks, international newspapers, magazines, and the now ubiquitous Internet and its digital progeny. Today, the world reacts politically and socially much more quickly, and perhaps emotionally, to events than ever before.

As we become, in various ways, a more interdependent world community with common problems and dangers, if not common values and goals, the world's ability to communicate effectively with all its parts has been greatly expanded. We now have an expanding global economy, and we are trying to develop institutions to deal with it. Reliable news and adequate communications are of prime importance in today's world.

This communication explosion has three broad dimensions: geographically, vast areas of Africa, South and East Asia, and Latin America have been drawn into the global communication network for the first time; the amount of traffic and the number of messages carried in the system have multiplied geometrically; and the technical complexity of both the new hardware and the skills and specialized knowledge needed to maintain and run the network has become increasingly sophisticated.

"For two thousand years and more the means of distant communications were various postal services, derived from the Roman cursus publicus, working at the speed of the horse (up to and including the Pony Express); and then the explosion hit us, not immediately upon the invention of the telegraph, but nearly a century later," Cherry wrote. "It is the sheer suddenness of the explosion which is of such profound social importance, principally following the Second World War."[1]

Advancing from crystal sets in 1920 to a television service in 1937 took, as Cherry pointed out, only seventeen years. The first transistor appeared in 1948, and electronic memory chips, the silicon brains of microcomputers, came soon after that. The first Sputnik went up in 1957, and only eight years later Early Bird, the first generation of the global INTELSAT system of communication satellites, went into operation in 1965 and brought television pictures from Europe. Just twenty-five years later, INTELSAT VI was in the heavens and, compared with Early Bird, had fifty-five times more power and a total communications capacity that had increased 170 times. Comparing the communications capacity of Early Bird INTELSAT I to INTELSAT VI, a major carrier of international news, is like comparing the height of a toolshed with a skyscraper in New York City.[2] Today, the Internet with its rambunctious progeny – interactive newspapers, online broadcast media, email and many bloggers – has added additional dimensions to international news, including gossip, advocacy, and misinformation.

## The International News Tradition

The expanded international news system is largely an outgrowth of Western news media, especially those of Britain, the United States, and, to a lesser degree, France and Germany. A world news system exists today because the peoples of Western democracies wanted world news, and the great independent newspapers, news magazines, news agencies, and, later, broadcast organizations have cooperated and competed to satisfy those wants and needs. Editors and correspondents, working for independent (that is to say, non-governmental) and profit-making news organizations, have developed the traditions and patterns of providing the almost instantaneous world news upon which people everywhere have come to rely. The credibility and legitimacy that such news generally enjoys rests on its usually unofficial and independently gathered nature as well as its informational or generally objective content. The enduring ethic of Western journalism was summed up more than 100 years ago by an editor of *The Times* of London:

> The first duty of the press is to obtain the earliest and most correct intelligence of the events of the time, and instantly, by disclosing them, to make them the common property of the nation. The duty of the journalist is to present to his readers not such things as statecraft would wish them to know but the truth as near as he can attain it.

That nineteenth-century statement represents a journalistic ideal; actual practice is often much different. Some transnational media have close, compromising ties to their governments, and all independent media are subject to varying kinds of controls and influences from the corporate interests that own them. Nonetheless, the news media of Western nations have more freedom and independence to report world news, and hence more credibility, than media of other nations. And because of greater financial resources and technology, Western media have a greater capability to report world news. Although the press in different nations will differ sharply about the facts and importance of particular news stories, the process is essentially one of international cooperation.

Cooperation is still an integral part of global news flow but digital disruption is rapidly changing how foreign news is gathered and distributed. The names of the leading media are still familiar, – *New York Times*, Associated Press (AP), British Broadcasting Corporation (BBC), *The Wall Street Journal*, *Washington Post*, *Financial Times*, *Daily Telegraph* (of London), *The Economist*, *Time*, National Broadcasting Corporation (NBC), National Public Radio (NPR), and more recently Al Jazeera (in English and Arabic) very important for the Arab World. But today much of the world news collected by these media appears as well on the Internet or web sites, Google, Yahoo, and other "search" sites and on thousands of online editions of newspapers, magazines, and radio and television broadcasters. Further, the well known "old media" have gone digital in various ways. The *New York Times* and *Washington Post* have online editions that reach more people than their print edition. *The Wall Street Journal* charges a fee for online readers who do no take the paper versions. The great BBC, long the leader in short wave and AM radio world news and a leader in television news, has been a major presence on the global Internet.

These media are still reporting world news but as emphasized elsewhere, their financial wherewithal to do it has been sharply restricted by falling circulations, declining audiences, and advertising losses to the "free" online media like Google, Yahoo, and other "new media." The dozen or more "old media," though weakened financially at home, still have the authority and stature to authenticate the serious news for the world and create a consensus for what is considered to be the major news from abroad.

Serious regional publications and other media, such as, (to name a few), the *Guardian* of London, *Le Monde* of Paris, *Frankfurter Allgemeine* and *Der Spiegel* of Germany, the *Times of India*, and numerous other media around the world still contribute to world news flow. So in 2011, global journalism faced this anomalous situation: the traditional providers of world news were financially weakened and less capable of covering the news but at the same time, due to the abrupt digital explosion, vastly more information and news went out to even the most remote corners of the world. Currently, however, comparatively little revenue ever finds its way back to the journalists and news organizations, who dug out the original facts and pulled the big story together. This has caused such important news organizations as the ABC News and the Associated Press to restructure and downscale their news operations. For example, in early 2010, ABC News announced sharp layoffs of news gathering staff that effected 300 to 400 people or roughly 25% of the news division of 1,500 staffers. ABC News called it a "fundamental transformation." The network, as well as NBC and CBS have lost audiences, the result of competition from cable, the Internet and changing consumer habits. CBS News, a chief competitor, said that month it was laying off dozens of employees. ABC said it would reduce its news bureaus structure by replacing some bureaus with more flexible so-called digital journalists who work on their own in foreign capitals.[3]

Some press and broadcasting organizations use their own correspondents to report foreign news, but the global workhorses and the linchpins of the world news system have long been the so-called world news services: the AP, AFP, and DPA, which are in effect "newspapers for newspapers." It is no coincidence that they come from the United States, Britain, France, and the former Soviet Union. (With the breakup of the USSR, TASS, now Information Telegraph Agency of Russia, or ITAR-TASS, has slipped considerably in importance.) In a general sense, great powers have been great news powers. Today, however, the continued importance of France and Britain in world news may owe more to relationships developed during their imperial pasts than their geopolitical importance today.

In 2005, the Associated Press, with 242 bureaus, a total staff of 3,700, and more than 6,000 subscribers, processed 20 million words and 1,000 photos daily and had an annual revenue of about $630 million. Yet, as a cooperative mainly owned by US newspapers, the AP is an important cog in the world news system but not as central as in previous times. After a decade of watching the newspapers and rival news services shrink, the 161- year-old AP said in 2007 that it was refitting itself to deal with the twenty-four-hour news cycle it helped create. The AP will change the way it files, edits, and distributes news, opening four new regional editing hubs and expanding its multimedia packages for entertainment, business, and sports reports. And the company is moving toward an all digital platform it calls the "Digital Cooperative."

Some of the great newspapers of the world – *The Times, The Daily Telegraph*, the *Financial Times, The Independent*, and the *Guardian* (UK); *Le Monde* of France; *Frankfurter Allgemeine* of Germany; *Neue Zürcher Zeitung* of Switzerland; *Asahi* of Japan; *New York Times, Washington Post*, the *Los Angeles Times, The Wall Street Journal*, and others in the United States – maintain their own correspondents abroad. The same is true of the extensive broadcasting systems BBC, CBS, NBC, ABC, CNN, and others, as well as the leading news magazines such as *Time, The Economist, L'Express*, and *Der Spiegel*. Other important regional dailies are the *The Hindu* and *The Times of India, Al Ahram* of Egypt, and the *New Straits Times* of Singapore.

Several newspapers, such as *New York Times, Washington Post*, and the *Los Angeles Times*, as well as the *Guardian*, syndicate their news and sell it to other newspapers at home and abroad. As a result, their news stories and features supplement as well as compete with the world news agencies. It is well to remember that once a news event is reported – the death of a king or a major earthquake – this information becomes the common property of journalism and can be repeated anywhere; only the precise wording of a news story can be copyrighted, and this rarely becomes a factor in news flow.

A survey in 2002 reported on the foreign bureaus of major US papers. The *New York Times* had forty reporters in twenty-six bureaus; *Washington Post* had twenty reporters in twenty-six bureaus; and the *Los Angeles Times* had twenty-one reporters in twenty-six bureaus. Maintaining reporters abroad is very expensive for newspapers, especially for regional papers like *Knight-Ridder* which had fourteen reporters in fourteen bureaus. *USA Today* had four reporters in four bureaus. Other regional papers with five or more bureaus included the *Chicago Tribune* (ten), *Newsday* (five), *The Dallas Morning News* (five), *The Baltimore Sun* (five), and *The Boston Globe* (five). These numbers have been dropping as papers find other ways to get foreign stories.

There has been some expansion in overseas coverage because of the expanded interest in overseas business and financial news, a key aspect of the global economy. This interest explains the 119 reporters in forty bureaus of *The Wall Street Journal*, with its business focus and overseas editions. Reuters and Bridge News (formerly Knight-Ridder financial news) have hundreds of overseas staffers to report specialized business news. Bloomberg News, another financial news service, has had reporters in sixty-two countries.

People receive more and more of their news from electronic sources, especially television. As a result, two television news services, Reuters TV (formerly Visnews) and Associated Press Television News (APTN), as well as the great Western networks, have been playing an increasingly important role in the international news system. Live feeds from another continent are usually identifiable as the work of the network involved, but the source of the news on tape or film is not as evident. Most viewers are unaware that much of the foreign news viewed on television is supplied by two television news agencies, dominated by American and British interests.

Reuters TV, the biggest and best known, is the world's leading supplier of international news video and film for television, servicing more than 409 customers in eighty-three countries, and is distributed by both satellites and air-mailed videocassettes. Reuters TV says it reaches 1.5 billion people daily. In 1992, Reuters bought out its co-owners, NBC and BBC, and changed its name from Visnews. Reuters TV staffs thirty-eight bureaus and works with contract crews in about seventy countries.

The pivot of these services is APTN, also located in London, which remains a center and clearinghouse for international news exchanges. APTN was founded in 1994 as Associated Press Television, and in 1998 it merged with Worldwide TV News (WTN) to form APTN. Both services have exchange agreements with the US networks, ABC, CBS, NBC, and CNN, all of which maintain several bureaus overseas. The US networks sell some of their news products abroad and thus contribute to the interchange that makes the international news system work. Video news agencies like these do not produce programs that television viewers can use. Rather, they provide footage of an event with only natural sound and very little editing. This is sent out via an encrypted video stream that is distributed on three satellites for global coverage.

Eurovision, the regional television exchange system in Western Europe, gets about 40 to 50% of its material from Reuters Television and APTN. The majority of television systems around the world depend on these two services for all of their world news on television. In numerous small African nations, often a lone television service depends on a five-minute package of world news from Reuters TV for its entire foreign coverage.

It can be said with some, but not much, exaggeration that a Westerner's right to know is the world's right to know. For any news story that gets into the European or US news media can, and often does, flow rapidly around the world and can appear in local media anywhere if it gets by the various gatekeepers that select and reject the news of the day. Stories about unrest in Chechnya, the war in Afghanistan or terrorist bombings in Pakistan can and often will be read or viewed or listened to in Africa, Asia, and Latin America.

There is some basis to complaints about this Western-dominated system. But the West does not enjoy a closed monopoly of world news; any news organization is free to report world news, but few as yet have the capability and credibility for so doing. Moreover, far ranging and technically sophisticated as it is, the world's present news system is not as pervasive and efficient as it might be, considering the world's diversity and its need for information. Yet the new digital media have been providing more and more news and information to the global flow.

## Global Television News

The successful establishment of the twenty-four-hour Cable News Network (CNN), with its global reach, has been a major innovation in international news as well as in the competitive US cable television news. Ted Turner, the Atlanta, Georgia, broadcaster, launched the around-the-clock news service to attract viewers to cable television and to compete in news with the three major US networks. Started in 1980, its growth and success have been impressive – and imitated. From a single network available to 1.7 million US households to its current 23 networks reaching some 260 million households worldwide, CNN is seen in more than 200 countries. So when a world crisis such as the Arab nations uprisings occur, CNN plays a major role in informing the world quickly.

During an international crisis, CNN plays a special global role. Whereas ABC, CBS, and NBC will issue news bulletins and then go back to scheduled programming and perhaps do a late-evening wrap-up, CNN stays on the air for long stretches of time, continually updating the story. The three major networks' version of the story will be seen in the United States; CNN's version will be seen all over the world. Overseas, travelers often can watch CNN in their hotel rooms, foreign television services pick up the whole service or some news programs from CNN, and individual television viewers can get it from their satellite dishes or subscribe to the service locally.

During prolonged crises, such as the first Gulf War, CNN can play a key role with its extensive coverage of all facets of a story. Indeed, CNN's international position often makes it a player in diplomacy as well as a reporter of major events. With its reports available in all world capitals, political leaders and diplomats watch closely and are willingly interviewed on CNN in order to get their views widely known. (CNN recognizes its near-diplomatic status, and reporters are aware of the danger of being manipulated by their interviewees, whether they are George W. Bush or a spokesman for Osama bin Laden.)

Recently, CNN has not been without its problems and its critics. When there is not an international crisis or a celebrity scandal or trial, viewership of CNN drops off sharply, and revenues from advertising have declined as well. During the O.J. Simpson trial, audiences soared when CNN provided gavel-to-gavel coverage, often to the neglect of foreign news coverage. As of 2010, CNN has been lagging in its cable ratings in the US with Fox, Msnbc, and CNBC.

It can be argued that CNN is primarily a technological innovation in international news by reason of its ability to interconnect so many video sources, newsrooms, and foreign ministries to so many television sets in so many remote places in the world. In this regard, CNN has undoubtedly had a major impact on diplomacy as well as global news. Nonetheless, a television news channel of true global reach was an innovation whose time had come and, as proof of that, CNN now has serious competition at home and abroad.

In 1991, the BBC began its own World Service Television (WST), now called BBC World, and has been expanding it rapidly. Since 1997, BBC World has been challenging the dominance of CNN International. BBC World has a twenty-four-hour international current affairs television channel with BBC news, documentaries, interviews, and so on. Unlike the radio service, it is commercially funded and is widely carried on satellite and cable.

In what has been called the newest public utility, the 24/7 cable-news-television industry, CNN has been bucking stiff competition from MSNBC and Fox News Channel (FNC). MSNBC is owned jointly by NBC and Microsoft, and has averaged a higher daily audience than CNN. Fox News Channel, which appeals to a more conservative audience than the other two cable channels, has been making large gains. Since 9/11, the cable channels have been competing fiercely. During the first week of coverage, CNN pulled in a near-record number of viewers. CNN was first among all cable networks for the week of September 10–16, pulling in 3.07 million cable and satellite households. That was 1 million more households than second-place FNC. However, in early 2002, FNC pulled ahead of CNN and has stayed there ever since. During the Arab uprisings, CNN has bounced back.

Both Rupert Murdoch, owner of FNC, and NBC have had their sights on global networks similar to CNN International and BBC World. Some experts argue that in normal times the overwhelming interests of audiences everywhere are not about global news per se but, in a more focused way, about their own region and locality. Yet as the most recent global crisis shows, global television news takes center stage once again by reporting, explaining, and influencing the world's response to great events.

The success of CNN and BBC World illustrates the ways that media technology can shape the contours and impact of international news – and will continue to do so. International radio broadcasts, both shortwave and medium wave, are also major purveyors of global news. But because of their roles in public diplomacy, the BBC World Service and the Voice of America are discussed in Chapter 12.

With the greatly enhanced technological reach of international communication, the location of a sender or receiver is no longer as important as it once was. The key gatekeepers of the world news system are still concentrated in New York City, London, Paris, and similar metropolitan centers, but it is not necessary to be in those cities to follow the news of the world. A shortwave radio or a satellite dish, and now a computer with an Internet connection, or a cell phone can keep a person almost anywhere in touch with the day's principal events. Furthermore, distance has become increasingly less a factor in the cost of long-distance news communication, whether it takes place through a private telephone, computer or fax messages, television reception, or news reports bounced off satellites or now even Twitter. Essentially the same technological process (and at the same cost) is required to send a news flash via satellite from London to Paris as from London to Tokyo. And the greater the traffic on the system, the lower the unit cost of the messages sent. International communication is tied to computer technology, and in that explosive field the costs of computers are dropping as rapidly as their efficiency is increasing. In addition, the capacity of communication satellites to carry information is expanding. Much of the content of the international news system concerns popular culture – video, movies, music in its many forms, youth life styles and attire – all of which appeal to a global youth culture found literally everywhere. Besides traditional news, the system carries news about the widely known and admired icons of pop culture, the singers, musicians, dancers, rappers, and movie stars. The commonalities of this youth culture were well shown on July 2005, by the Live 8 concerts in eight major industrial nations plus South Africa, in an effort to pressure leaders at the Group of 8, then meeting on aid, to mitigate poverty in Africa. Over 1 million young people attended, while another 5 million watched AOL's live video streams on their computers. The music, performers, and their message resonated around the world.

Media habits of foreign students at the University of Wisconsin illustrate how global communication has changed. For many years, if a foreign student wanted news from home, he might go to the university library and consult a newspaper from his home land, if he was lucky enough to find one. Today, he turns on his computer and consults the university's DATN (digital academic television network) service to find a television channel from his native country. DATN has thirteen channels from overseas including China, France, Germany, Italy, Japan, Korea, Qatar, Russia, and Saudi Arabia. According to the linguistic choices, foreign students (and their families) have their choice of such channels as NTV America Russia, TV5 États-Unis France, DW-TV Germany, Al Jazeera English Qatar, tvK Korea, CCTV4 China, TV Asia, RAI International Italy, or TV Japan.

## Cracks in the Conduits

If technology is the good news, then performance in recent years is the bad news. In earlier years, the American "national media" – particularly the *New York Times*, the *Washington Post*, the *Los Angeles Times*, *The Wall Street Journal*, CBS, NBC, ABC, *Time*, and *Newsweek* – which set the news agenda for other media, did much of the gathering of news from abroad with the help of news agencies.

But that situation changed around 1989 when the Cold War ended. The television networks and the news magazines gave much less attention to serious foreign news. One indicator: In its heyday, CBS maintained twenty-four foreign bureaus; by 2002, it had nine reporters in only four capitals:

London, Moscow, Tel Aviv, and Tokyo. Dan Rather admitted to Harvard students, "Don't kid yourself, the trend line in American journalism is away from, not toward, increased foreign coverage."[4]

Max Frankel, former editor of the *New York Times*, wrote, "A great shroud has been drawn across the mind of America to make it forget that there is a world beyond its borders. The three main television networks obsessively focus their cameras on domestic tales and dramas as if the end of the Cold War rendered the rest of the planet irrelevant. Their news staffs occasionally visit some massacre, famine, or shipwreck and their anchors may parachute into Haiti or Kuwait for a photo op, but these spasms of interest only emphasize the networks' apparent belief that on most evenings the five billion folks out there don't matter one whit."[5]

Foreign news is expensive to gather and often not of interest unless American lives – as soldiers or terrorism victims – are at stake. Instead, network television and the news magazines shifted their resources and considerable talents into high-profile stories of scandal, celebrity, and sensation.

However, a few major US daily papers still report the world. The best and most comprehensive foreign reporting, some of very high quality, comes from just four daily newspaper groups, those owning the *New York Times*, the *Washington Post*, and *The Wall Street Journal*, and the *Los Angeles Times*. This small group plus the AP and Reuters are the prime sources for foreign news. It should be noted that a good deal of serious foreign news is available to radio listeners of National Public Radio's two daily programs, *All Things Considered* and *Morning Edition*. Major British and European newspapers and broadcasters still cover world news in large part because their readers demand it.

Another deep concern for the US news media is that the public's assessment of the accuracy of news stories was, as of November 2009, at its lowest level in more than two decades of Pew Research surveys. Americans' views of media bias and independence now match previous lows. Just 29% of Americans said that news organizations generally get their facts straight, while 63% said that they are often inaccurate. In the initial survey of this series in 1985, 55% said news stories were accurate while 34% they were not. That percentage has fallen sharply by the late 1990s and has remained low over the last decade. Similarly, only about a quarter (26%) now say that news organizations are careful that their reporting is not politically biased, compared with 60% who say that news organizations are politically biased. And the percentages saying that news media are independent of powerful people and organizations (20%) or are willing to admit their mistakes (21%) now also match all-time lows.

In America, political attitudes appear related to media views. Democrats hold considerably more positive views than Republicans of CNN, MSNBC, the *New York Times* network news, and views of National Public Radio. By contrast views of Fox News and to a lesser extent, *The Wall Street Journal*, are more positive among the Republicans than Democrats.[6]

But in their handling of foreign crises or calamities, Americans can rally behind their media. The events of September 11, 2001, demonstrated that the news media of America and other Western nations responded, and responded magnificently, to the challenges of the new war on terrorism. Several months later, after the crisis had eased somewhat, the media, particularly television, went back to their old habits of not much news from abroad. But in 2011 when the Arab nations erupted, interest in foreign news returned.

## Notes

1. Colin Cherry, *World Communication: Threat or Promise?* (New York: Wiley Interscience, 1971), 57–58.
2. Joseph Pelton, "Heading for Information Overload," *Inter-Media*, Autumn 1988, 19.
3. Brian Stelter and Bill Carter, "ABC News Plans to Trim 300 to 400 from Staff," New York Times, February 24, 2010, B5.
4. Stephen Hess, *International News and Foreign Correspondents* (Washington, DC: Brookings Institution, 1996), 61.
5. Max Frankel, "The Shroud," *New York Times Magazine*, November 27, 1994, 42.
6. Pew Research Center, "Press Accuracy Rating Hits Two Decades Low, 1985–209" people-press.org/report, November 18, 2009.

# 4

# Digital Media:
# Global, Interactive, and Free

*We are laying the foundations for an international information highway system. In telecommunications we are moving to a single worldwide information network, just as economically we are becoming one global marketplace. We are moving toward the capability to communicate anything to anyone, anywhere, by any form – voice, data, text, or image – at the speed of light.*

– John Naisbitt

*If it's digital, it's eventually going to be free.*

– Chris Anderson

*The Internet has made information available. Google has made information accessible.*

– Hal Varian

The so-called new media (some not so new) – camcorders, cell phones, satellite phones, bloggers on the Internet, Twitter, Facebook, Flickr, My Space, YouTube, Google – have been transforming the traditional ways that news has been gathered and reported. When the tsunami roared through Indian Ocean beaches, drowning thousands, in late 2004, the first video and photos the world received came from camcorders held by tourists caught in the deluge. Long before press photographers could reach the disaster areas, the vivid video was being viewed by millions around the world.

Similarly, when London subways were attacked by terrorists on July 7, 2005 (7/7), the first dramatic photos came from Londoners trapped

*The World News Prism: Challenges of Digital Communication*, Eighth Edition.
William A. Hachten and James F. Scotton.
© 2012 John Wiley & Sons, Ltd. Published 2012 by John Wiley & Sons, Ltd.

underground, who recorded the scenes on their cell phones. Many of these dramatic pictures were quickly available to the world, not on television screens or in newspapers but on bloggers' web sites.

In both cases, the news media's role of providing the "first draft of history" was being challenged by ordinary citizens with a gadget in their hands. The effect is to accelerate the speed with which news and pictures of great events travels about the globe. Compare these recent news stories with the US presidential election of 1920 – the first reported by radio. Station KDKA in Pittsburgh kept a few people informed about election tabulations and newspapers carried the final results the next day. But it was two weeks before many people in scattered rural areas learned the news that Warren Harding had defeated James Cox for the presidency.

The drastic differences between then and now dramatize the reality that the mechanics of delivering the news to an interested public is a significant factor in the communication process. New technologies have been shaping and changing editorial content in diverse ways. News, particularly international news, has over the years been directly affected by each new invention. The postal service, telegraph, cable, telephone, and radio in turn have each greatly extended the reach of foreign correspondents and world news agencies and the speed with which they can deliver news, each innovation supplementing rather than replacing earlier methods of communication.

Like other institutions and organizations, the news media – newspapers, news services, radio stations, television, cable channels and networks, and news magazines – are being strikingly altered by the information revolution. News communication is being dramatically affected by ongoing revolutionary changes in communication satellites, computers, digitalization, miniaturization, and the Internet.

To these "old" media must now be added the Internet, which has been playing a facilitating and supplementary role in the rapid dissemination of a fast-breaking story – either a trivial Hollywood scandal or the ominous events of the latest terrorist attacks. Online news junkies have quick access not only to more news but also to a heady mix of unconfirmed rumor, conjecture, commentary, discussion, and conspiracy theories. Sometimes, rumor and conjecture find their way into the legitimate news media. Further, the Internet and the twenty-four-hour cable news cycle can greatly accelerate a story, often to the detriment of traditional journalistic practices such as verifying sources and creating context. More and more people are getting their news from cable and the Internet.

The "glorious disruption' of international journalism is being deeply influenced by two basic trends: first, how the news is received and to whom it goes (the audience and readers of news) and second, the changing ways that news and commentary are gathered and communicated. Most of the traditional journalism practices persist but much is changing as well.

These days more and more people are getting their news from web sites. The busiest US web sites during May 2008 were:

Yahoo News with 35.8 million unique visitors;
MSNBC sites with 35.2 million unique visitors;
AOL News with 22.5 million unique visitors;
New York Times.com with 21.3 million unique visitors;
Tribune Newspapers with 16.2 million unique visitors;
Gannett Newspapers with 14.6 million unique visitors;
Google news with 11.4 million unique visitors;
ABC News sites 11.1 million unique visitors;
USA Today.com with 10.8 million unique visitors;
Fox News sites with 10.1 million unique visitors;
CBS News sites with 9.2 million unique visitors;
Washington Post.com with 9.2 million unique visitors;
McClatchy Newspaper Network with 9.1 million unique visitors;
Hearst Newspapers Digital with 8. million unique visitors.[1]

The audience for online news tends not to stick with a single site and further, research has shown that with a vast array of digital sources, "promiscuous" news consumption goes only so far. Only 35% of people who go online for news have a favorite site and just 21% are more or less "monogamous" relying primarily on a single Internet source, according to the Pew Research Center. But 57% of that audience relies on just two to five sites.[2]

With Internet news appearing in digital words, pictures, and videos, the concept of who is a "journalist" has been changing. A journalist is no longer primarily a trained professional in a bona fide news organization. Any of the untold millions carrying a small camera, phone camera, or video recorder, tape recorder, and so on. Can witness an event of importance or news interest, and then record it and send it on to a news channel. For example, an open cell phone call from North Korea being dialed and connected to a phone in Seoul, South Korea, sent out news from the most closed and controlled society on earth.

Iraqi authorities who executed Saddam Hussein learned that the prying eyes of television can belong to anyone with a small cell phone in their pocket. Police angrily searched for those who recorded and distributed a secret video of the execution, after the grainy footage appeared on the Internet and later on Iraqi television giving a much different view of the execution than the Iraqi government presented to the public.

But in a world so awash with information, the selection and editing of news becomes ever more important. An estimated 70% of Americans carry cell phones and nearly one quarter of all phone users – an estimated 55.6 million Americans have phones with video capability. Hence, the possibility of fraud and distortion becomes apparent with the arrival of what has been called "maybe journalism" – a best guess at the news it might well have been and built on a bed of pure surmise. In Hong Kong, a computerized "news event" of the Tiger Woods SUV crash – with a robotic-looking blonde simulation of Woods' wife chasing him with a golf club – became a top global online video of the moment. The brief digitally animated piece was created by Next Media, a Hong Kong firm serving gossipy newspapers in Hong Kong and Taiwan. It turns out about 20 such stories daily. Despite the flawed Chinese-only soundtrack, the video achieved global fame in the week after it went on. There were 1.7 million viewers on YouTube alone.[3]

Scandals about prominent celebrities such as Tiger Woods or Michael Jackson spread at lightning speed through the Internet and cable television and then are usually picked up by more serious media. Such stories get worldwide distribution in a matter of seconds and as with Woods, the "news" just keeps on flowing as more details surface and the various outlets such as TMZ.com, Twitter, Facebook, and so on. And other digital media interact by adding more details and thus embellishing the story and giving it a longer life.

## Google vs. Old Media

Digital news has been infiltrating and changing the news media for many years but many recent changes seem associated with the spectacular success of Google, the leading Internet search company. Directly competing with print news media, Google has in 12 years utterly transformed the media landscape. Google directly challenges news media because it provides so much "free news," has usurped a large share of print advertising revenue; and has beguiled or bewitched many young people who no longer read newspapers. As a result news media based on print and paper are experiencing several severe financial difficulties and finding it difficult to gather news, especially news from distant places.

By April 2009, an estimated 1.6 billion people worldwide were connected to the Internet – with less than 25% of them in America. While digital firms like Yahoo and Google have boomed between 2000 and 2009, numerous printed papers have faced huge financial losses and some have shut down. During that period, 167,000 US newspaper jobs were lost. Potential buyers are wary of buying properties with doubtful profitable futures.

The print media were hardest hit; less so radio and television; book publishing's fate is being currently decided and the music business has been turned upside down.

For newspapers, the trends were clear: circulation and advertising have been falling; newspaper readers are aging; debt service and production costs are rising and stock prices are way down. Giving away online newspapers did not help print editions. More and more newspapers closed including the *Rocky Mountain News* and the print edition of the *Seattle Post Intelligencer* plus threatened closing of numerous others. Newspaper advertising dollars fell by nearly one third 2005 and 2008 – a reflection of new competition.

Amazingly the traditional media did not see this upheaval coming. For example, they did not recognize that Craigslist which carries free local classified advertising in many cities on the Internet as a serious threat to newspapers' classified ads, a major source of revenue for daily newspapers. The same news available on so-called "dead tree" papers was available free on digital news sites. Google has eliminated barriers to finding information and knowledge – and news. The Internet, it has been said, makes information available. Google has made news accessible. Newspapers and other print publications are scrambling to find a new business model that will make ink journalism profitable again.

President John Hennessy of Stanford, where Google was born, said "We made one really big mistake in the Internet which is hard to reverse now. We should have made a micropayment system work. Viewers would pay a small fee for news or information on the Web."[4] Auletta's book traces the rise of Google and its impact on news media.

But by now, the vast global audience on the Internet is well accustomed to NOT paying for information on the net. And Google, the biggest and fastest of information providers, has been called "the biggest company in the world based on giving things away."[5] Other Silicon Valley companies modeled themselves on Google have not been charging fees. These include Twitter, Facebook, MySpace, Flickr, some email services, Wikipedia, and Craigslist.

Driving this trend are the steeply declining prices of three essential technologies: computing power, digital storage, and transmission capacity. Digital content (including news) has become, as was once predicted about electricity, too cheap to meter. Whatever it costs to deliver a video today will cost half as much a year from now, say experts.

Google has been called the poster child of "free" – for its millions of users no charges turn up on credit cards.

The specter of digital free seems to stymie efforts by ink on paper media to come up with a viable (i.e. profitable) business model. But *The Wall Street Journal*, the *New York Times* and the *Washington Post*, among other media firms, have been considering ways to extract fees for online news. Some readers of online news in the United States and several other Western countries are willing to pay to read online news including mobile devices. In a 2009 survey, 48% of American interviewees said they would pay to read news online. That result tied with Britain and these totals were among the lowest nations in some of which 60% of readers would pay to read. Asked how much they were willing to pay Americans averaged $3 a month, tied with Australia for the lowest figure and less than the $7 average for Italians. Other nations included France, Spain, Norway, and Finland. Consumer willingness and intent to pay is related to the availability of a rich amount of free content and there is more, better, richer "free" content in the United States than elsewhere. In every nation, the people who were willing to pay the most were the people who already pay the most for news: avid newspaper readers.[6]

A conspicuous exception to the trend is Japan where no online journalism of any kind has yet posed a significant threat to Japan's monolithic but sclerotic news media. For years, the online newspaper *Jan Jan News* competed against Japan's blandly conformist press offering articles on taboo subjects like whaling. But these digital efforts could attract neither readers nor revenue and closed in early 2010. *Jan Jan News* was the last of four online papers offering reader-generated stories. The Japanese media landscape is dominated after several decades by the same few large papers like Yomiuri Shim bun, the world's largest newspaper with a 10 million daily circulation.[7]

## The Key Role of Satellites

In our concern with how international news moves about the globe, the significant changes initiated by communication satellites, a major by-product of the space age, must be recognized. Recently, there has been a quantum jump in the ability of people to talk to and see one another. Marshall McLuhan once wrote that we were experiencing a "global electronic village" being created by television. John Naisbitt countered that it is in fact the communication satellite that is "creating a super tribal community unlike any environment previously known to mankind since the Tower of Babel."[8]

In the past thirty-five years, global telecommunications by satellite have achieved remarkable results. Joseph Pelton pointed out that "trillions of dollars of electronic funds transfers and hundreds of millions of dollars of airline reservations flow through global networks each year. Billions of conversations carry on international business, diplomacy, finance, culture, and recreation as a matter of routine."[9] Included in these vast communication flows are, of course, the world's news in pictures, sounds, data, and words.

Our interest is with the impact of telecommunications on international news flow. And the most immediate short-term effect of Comsats (that is, communication satellites) is a reduction in the cost of long-distance communications and a corresponding increase in the amount of words, data, and images exchanged. In other words, more news is flowing at less expense. We have seen dramatic changes in long-distance telephone calls, which form the bulk of traffic on the INTELSAT system; that system is operated by a multinational consortium controlling long-distance point-to-point Comsat communications.

Arthur C. Clarke dismissed the notion that Comsats are merely an extension of existing communication devices and do not engender much change. He placed Comsats in the same class as the atomic bomb and automobile, "which represent a kind of quantum jump which causes a major restructuring of society." Clarke recalled a parliamentary commission in England over 100 years ago when the chief engineer of the post office was asked to comment on the need for the latest American invention, the telephone. The engineer made this remarkable reply: "No Sir. The Americans may have need of the telephone – but we do not. We have plenty of messenger boys."[10]

That telephone, in time, came to have its own revolutionary impact on modern life, and now the personal letter has been replaced by the long-distance call as well as by fax and email. And telephone services, as has been noted, constitute the primary activity today of communication satellites and are the major source of revenue for INTELSAT. (The telephone and its wireless version, it should be noted, are major tools as well in news gathering – formerly local tools but now used globally.)

At the end of the 1970s, the traffic of INTELSAT still consisted mostly of people talking to people, but since the mid-1980s, at least half the information volume has consisted of machines communicating with other machines. The mind-boggling information-carrying capacity of INTELSAT VI is driving this trend, and INTELSAT VII, launched in 1993, followed by INTELSAT VII-A, in 1995, have continued it. Pelton developed a term, TIUPIL, to show the relationship between human capabilities of processing information and the speed of the information machines – present and future. A "TIUPIL" represents the "Typical Information Use Per Individual Lifetime" and was defined as twenty billion bits of information: the total information received by a person who lives seventy years and processes some 27,000 written or spoken words a day. A TIUPIL can be transmitted on INTELSAT VII in a matter of just seven seconds, or about nine times a minute. "Soon we will have networks of satellites capable of sending up to 100 billion bits of information in a second. This means we will have machines capable of processing information thousands or even millions of times faster than the human brain," Pelton wrote. "If one asks why we need such high-speed machines, the answer is clearly for machine-to-machine communication. Once we have communication satellites and fiber optic cables capable of handling super high-definition, 3-D television, the meeting of telephone or human data requirements will be small potatoes indeed."[11]

Although they have been called microwave relay towers in the sky, Comsats do have broader, unique properties. They do not link just two points, but many. They can simultaneously receive and transmit to many places, sending a panoply of message forms – television, telephone, telex, photo facsimile, fax, and high-speed computer data. For example, an increased mobility of money is a result of the computer revolution.

Today, satellite systems are operational at the international (intercontinental) level, the regional (continental) level, and the domestic (national) level. Satellites extend the range of over-the-air broadcasting systems, but they have a much greater impact on satellite-cable networks. CNN and various other cable services extend their reach dramatically by being tied in with cable services. In addition, numerous specialized satellite systems are functioning, such as those designed for military, data relay, and maritime and aeronautical purposes.

INTELSAT is the largest and oldest system, with fifteen satellites (plus backups) over the Pacific, Atlantic, and Indian Oceans. Some 120 nations, each with its own earth segment, belong to the consortium, and any two member countries can communicate directly without going through former colonial capitals. User countries, territories, and possessions total about 170, operating internationally on almost 1,500 pre-assigned pathways. INTELSAT also functions as the carrier for national domestic services in about thirty countries.

Comsats have greatly expanded the capacity of news media to move international news around the globe, but the ability of the satellites to relay color television signals, giving that medium a global impact, is what has made Comsat technology such a significant mass communication development. This is true even though television use accounts for a comparatively small proportion of the monthly revenue of INTELSAT.

When Early Bird, the first commercial Comsat, was launched in 1965, the principal television use was expected to be for occasional live events such as sports, state funerals, space missions, and the coverage of disasters and wars. Although reportage of such major events still accounts for much television traffic on INTELSAT, the most extensive and consistent use of the global system is for daily television news "packages" sent from one country to another. The US networks – NBC, CBS, and ABC – plus CNN daily incorporate satellite news feeds from their correspondents in various parts of the world or, for special coverage, sporadically purchased from foreign broadcast news services, such as Reuters Television or APTN.

Innovations in communication technology are changing both the ways that global news is gathered and disseminated and the ways that individuals receive the news. The speed and scope of foreign news reporting is constantly expanding as the use of laptop computers is increasing. Foreign correspondents have long said that their worst problems are not censorship or other authoritarian restraints, but logistics – getting to the remote news scene, such as an earthquake in Chile or a civil war in Congo, and then getting the story out. The technology to solve part of that problem has been developed and increasingly utilized: especially small portable computers that can transmit stories over phone lines (or by wireless) directly to newsroom systems. Initially, these portables were used to cover golf matches, auto races, football and basketball games, and court trials, but now journalists covering the whole range of news carry them.

A major technological advance for television reporting was the development of new, highly portable "satellite uplinks," which can be disassembled, checked as baggage, and flown to the site of a breaking story in order to feed back live reports. A "flyaway" dish can become a temporary CNN or ABC bureau in just the time it takes to get one on the scene. Other innovations useful to reporters in the field (as well as to individual citizens) are the portable wireless telephone and the video telephone.

This advance means that an editor can telephone a foreign correspondent, whether he or she is covering a conference in Geneva or a war in Central Asia. And that correspondent can, if necessary, send in the story by his or her cordless telephone or by videophone to a television station.

Another significant aid for reporters today is databases, which are collections of text or numbers that are stored in computers. Online databases, of which there are now thousands, are mainly for the retrieval of information by researchers who can tap into a data bank through telephone lines attached to a computer terminal. Increasingly, newspapers and broadcasters have used such sources for investigative and general reporting. Distance is not a factor, for in a matter of minutes a US reporter can gain access to anything printed in a British newspaper or a journal in Japan. Closer to home, the reporter can call up and scan the full text of about seventy dailies offered by various newspaper databases; such as the Nexis database, which carries more than 140 international newspapers, magazines, news services, and newsletters.

A further utilization of Comsats that is changing the structure of daily journalism is facsimile production and distribution of national and international newspapers, pioneered by *The Wall Street Journal*. Each day, a fax of every page of the paper is sent from its production plant in Chicopee, Massachusetts, to twelve or thirteen various printing plants around the country. The page-size fax pages are processed onto offset pages. *The Wall Street Journal* has extended this expertise to Asia for its subsidiary, *The Asian Wall Street Journal*. This kind of technological innovation, plus an informative, well-written news product, has moved *The Wall Street Journal* to 2,011,999 in circulation in 2008.

Another national daily newspaper, the Gannett Company's *USA Today*, has employed the same facsimile production methods, circulating 2,293,310 copies in 2008 from thirty US printing sites. In 1985, *USA Today* began beaming facsimile pages of its international edition to Singapore for printing and distribution in the Far East. Other publications routinely utilize facsimile transmission technology, including the *International Herald Tribune* of Paris, *Die Zeit* of Hamburg, *China Daily*, *The Economist*, *Time*, and *Newsweek*. The national edition of the *New York Times* is printed in several regions of the United States to facilitate its same-day delivery across the nation.

## Personalized Media

Innovations in information media – personal computers with Internet connections, photocopiers, printers, fax capabilities, modems, videocassettes, cordless and mobile telephones, interactive television, databases, cable, and satellite connections – all often considered "personalized media," are having profound effects on the audience or recipients of international news. In fact, the term *audience* is itself becoming a bit obsolete, because it implies a mass of passive receivers of communication. Increasingly, personalized media are supplementing traditional media in the affluent West, but less so in developing countries.

In today's information societies, an individual is no longer a passive recipient of news or entertainment, but now is an "information seeker" who can select or choose his or her news or information from a widening variety of sources, many of which governments are unable or unwilling to control. Further, individuals themselves, such as those involved in computer networking, become sources of information; that is, communicators. Autocratic governments find it difficult to control personalized communications.

With a personal computer and a modem connected to a telephone or wireless, a person can tap into the fast-growing Internet system, providing access to many thousands of web site databases, including news publications and other current information from home and abroad. Further, that receiver can become a sender by freely communicating with other computers through the web sites or Internet, email, and various networks and bulletin boards.

The printed word has changed as well. Fax, the same technology that sends the *International Herald Tribune* from Paris to Hong Kong, sends millions of documents, letters, and messages across continents and oceans. Facsimile transmissions have played a role in challenging or even toppling unpopular regimes, from Iran to Panama to China to the collapsing Soviet Union. Not only does fax foster immediate human interaction across great distances, it also facilitates the vital flow of information into and out of repressive regimes.

Digital recorders, both video and audio, have greatly enhanced the ability of individuals to choose what they will hear or see and, as a result, have expanded rapidly in recent years even to remote corners of the Southern Hemisphere.

Much of the talk of an "information superhighway" involves the idea of a merging of computers, telephones, and televisions (video, text, and sound) to provide new delivery systems and content options. Two models for the so-called "infobahn" are offered: broadcast and the Internet. In the broadcast model, entertainment would be the driving force, leading to the 500-channel future, with features such as video on demand, interactive home shopping, entertainment, and advertising. The latter model is on the lines of the Internet, the vast computer/communications network begun in 1969 that now connects many millions worldwide. The two models still exist and compete side by side.

## The Internet and International News Flow

The potential of the Internet for international news communication is being realized, but is still a work in progress. Daily, the Internet carries more news than 1,600 daily newspapers that can supply a worldwide audience of 1.6 billion Internet users as of 2009. More and more Internet users are getting their news online and from media in far-off places.

An Internet user in Pakistan, Paris, or Pretoria can read the online edition of the *New York Times*, *The Times* of London, or *Die Zeit* of Hamburg. Major newspapers and other news media, such as magazines, radio and television broadcasters, and cablecasters, from a variety of mostly Western nations – what was formerly called the "foreign press" – are available in ways never before possible for those with the means and inclination to log on. The impact on journalism education is obvious: Instead of going to a university library to peruse back copies of several dozen foreign newspapers, a journalism student today using his or her computer can read, study, and compare hundreds of publications and broadcasting outlets of many countries. Many other related sources are available as well. For example, by calling up www.memri.org, the web site of the Mideast Media and Research Institute, a student can read translations from Arabic of what the Arab press and broadcasters are reporting and proclaiming about the war on terrorism and revolution among Arab nations.

The BBC's impressive utilization of the Internet has placed the broadcast giant in direct competition with British newspapers. Starting its online operations in 1998, the BBC now has 525 sites. It spends $27 million on its news web site and this is backed by the BBC's vast news gathering resources, including 5,000 reporters scattered around the world, which is funded by its annual £2.8 million subsidy from the British government. The success of the BBC's news web site clearly troubles British newspapers. Its audience has increased from 1.6 million unique weekly users in 2000 to 7.8 million in 2005. The news web site has a breadth and depth that newspapers have difficulty keeping up with.[12]

The Associated Press has adopted the Internet to distribute its articles and photographs over the global Internet. In so doing, it has followed other mainline news organizations into uncharted journalistic territory. The AP's great rival, Reuters, announced similar plans to reposition itself as a high-flying Internet player. Reuters plans to spend $802 million to shift its delivery systems to the Internet.

The Internet incorporates many elements of various print and electronic media that have preceded it. Computers can be used to send and receive text, sound, still images, and video clips. Yet for all its versatility, the Internet is not expected to replace its predecessors, but to take its place alongside them as a social, cultural, and economic force in its own right. No longer a curiosity, the Internet has become another way for to people find out what is happening in the world.

Much news or information on the Internet is of dubious value and may be deliberately wrong or misleading. During the weeks after the September 11 attacks, the Internet was overwhelmed with wild rumors, deliberate misinformation, and conspiracy theories. But the discriminating and critical viewer could still find solid, reliable information because the world's best news organizations – newspapers, news magazines, television, and radio services – were reporting the real news daily. (An important role for professional online news media is to act as a check on unreliable and unsubstantiated reports.)

Cyber news so far is complementing the traditional news media, but may soon become a new kind of journalism. John V. Pavlik wrote, "Since networked news can be interactive, on-demand, and customizable; since it can incorporate new combinations of text, images, moving images, and sound; since it can build new communities based on shared interests and concerns; since it has the almost unlimited space to offer levels of reportorial depth, texture, and context that are impossible in any other medium – new media can transform journalism."[13]

Perhaps the single most significant characteristic of the Internet is that it is a communication device that lets people share ideas (including news) on a global network. This feature suggests that international news communication has made tremendous strides in the past twenty-five or so years, which is the age of the personal computer. A PC with a modem, either hooked up to a telephone line or wireless, means that the world – literally the world – is more available than ever before. Not only individuals but professional news media now can reach and hold not just audiences or readers, but also communities of people with shared concerns literally anywhere in the world.

## Bloggers Join the Fray

Internet journalism and international news have been influenced by the rapidly growing army of bloggers. A "blog" (web and log) is technically someone's record of the web sites he or she visits. Bloggers have been called one-person Internet blabbermouths, who pop off to anyone who will listen. They criticize each other but, more importantly, they take on the mainline media. Sometimes right and often wrong, they provide a kind of instant feedback loop for media corrections. They often write personal diaries and commentaries, with the best of them weighing on the pressing issues of the world. They report news items that the traditional media ignore or suppress, and they provide links to other bloggers with something to say. Anyone can be a blogger and no one is in charge.

Their sheer numbers are mind boggling: in mid-2005, a web site, Technorati, reported an astonishing growth: nearly 80,000 new blogs are created every day and there are some 14.2 million in existence, and of these 55 per cent remain active. In December 2009, one online source, Netcraft Net Services, reported a total of 233,848,493 web sites on the World Wide Web. There was an increase of 47 million last names and 7 million active web sites over the previous seven months. News related web sites were a tiny fraction of this vast total. The influence of blogs on news flow is increasing. Some are quoted on regular media and some media have their own blogs – and being on the Internet, their reach and influence can and does become global.

In Madrid, David and Alfonso Rojo publish the Periodista Digital, a widely read blog with 115,000 registered subscribers. Daily, about 4,000 people log on to headlines about the highs and lows of public life in Spain. Doreen Carvajal reported that "The Web is a sprawling space that has spawned new breeds of digital gadflies like the Rojos and an assortment of self-appointed cybermonitors of the conventional news media of Europe. Across the world, their sharp comments can evoke an array of reactions: amusement, insults, public outrage, blunt legal threats. Yet these web sites and blogs are scoured by the policy makers and the political elite."[14]

A popular German blog, Bildblog, attracts 300,000 readers a month, mainly because of its fact-checking of Germany's largest daily, the tabloid *Bild*, with a 3.8 million circulation. Four journalists with other day jobs scrutinize *Bild* for errors and miscues. The site attracts about 10,000 visitors a day.

Richard Posner wrote that "in effect, the blogosphere is a collective enterprise – not 12 million separate enterprises but one enterprise with 12 million reporters, feature writers, and editorialists with very little costs. It's as if Reuters or the AP had millions of reporters, many of them experts, all working for no salary for free newspapers that carried no advertising." If Posner is correct, the influence of the bloggers on international news media may be considerable, even if far flung and almost impossible to measure.[15]

Communications over the Internet have greatly multiplied and amplified the voices, information, exhortations, and diatribes passing through the world news prism. More people than ever before are getting information, tuning in, tuning out, and forming opinions. This is what freedom of expression is all about.

Thoughtful persons in mainstream journalism – the "news business" – are well aware of the importance as well as the many pitfalls for journalism on the Internet. Publishers, broadcasters, and journalists believe that the news media must be involved with the Internet, but neither they nor anyone else seems to know where this brave new world of communication is headed.

Journalism by bloggers stressed the importance and primacy of "citizen journalists" but print journalists say news bloggers lack the professional reporters who ask powerful people, here and abroad, blunt and impertinent questions, report back reliably and in plain language to a general audience. Moreover, bloggers lack the resources of a professional newsroom which can edit, critique; supplement a story with further verified information. Global news is a process – not a single report. Such journalism, the old pros say, is better able to serve as a watchdog overseer on powerful authority whether local, national or global. Media coverage of the extensive oil disaster in the Gulf of Mexico is a good example. These are part of the basics of the US/UK model of serious journalism which is spreading around the world and needs to be more widely emulated in online journalism.

Internet journalism is still in its infancy and is continuing to expand as readers, especially younger ones, turn to the Internet for a fast take on the news. The beneficiaries of this continued audience growth continue to be the largest and best-known national news organizations – those that stress national and international news.

The Internet is still an ancillary news source for most people, after broadcasting and newspapers, yet the audience for news and information sites is growing. Some of the most frequently used US news web sites are www.msnbc.msn.com, www.cnn.com, www.nytimes.com, www.abcnews.go.com, www.usatoday.com, www.washingtonpost.com, www.time.com, www.latimes.com, www.foxnews.com, and www.wsj.com.

## International Concerns about Cyber News

The rapid spread of interactive journalism has raised some nagging issues. For example, who will benefit and who will not? Globally, the information revolution has been flourishing mainly in America, Western Europe, and other industrialized countries. The poor nations want the new media, but lack the economic and social infrastructure to utilize and sustain them. Not many of Africa's fifty-four countries are linked to the Internet, and experts warn that unless Africa gets online quickly, what is already the world's poorest continent risks ever-greater marginalization. Without network connectivity, large areas of Africa will be prevented from participating in many evolving aspects of life on this planet. As in all nations, the younger, better educated, and more affluent are using the Internet; the poor, the undereducated, and the elderly have no way to access the information highway. But some major gains have been made in India and China.

Among Western democracies, there are unresolved questions about how much freedom of expression (including press freedom) can be legally permitted on what is being recognized as the most participatory market-place of ideas the world has yet seen. The Internet faces more draconian censorship from authoritarian regimes or despotic rulers. Some form of censorship of the Internet exists in about forty-three nations. The most pervasive censorship is in China (see Chapter 7). The small, affluent, and authoritarian nation of Singapore thinks it can control the technologies of freedom that threaten its one-party rule. To control television, satellite dishes have been banned, and the country has been wired for cable television, thus enabling the government to screen out objectionable material. Controlling cyberspace is more difficult, but Singapore is trying. Schools are equipped with computers, and Singaporeans are urged to link up with the Internet by dialing a local telephone number. Thus, the government can monitor Internet usage through the local servers. Local officials concede that some users can bypass this system by dialing into the Internet through foreign phone systems. Singapore is not expected to be able to sustain such controls over the flow of electronic information that is so essential for the global economy.

Italy and other European nations have concerns about invasion of privacy and anti-trust aspects of Google and other Internet web sites. In France in 2010, the French Competition Authority officially declared Google a monopoly. That conclusion was hardly novel but appeared to go beyond any previous ruling in the United States or elsewhere.

## Implications of Rapid Change

To summarize, innovations in communication technology suggest certain broad trends for transnational journalism:

1  The unit cost of international communication of news will continue to drop as usage of the world news systems increases, and as the efficiency, speed, and reach of the hardware become greater. But "free" digital media pose serious threats to the viability of ink-on-paper media.
2  Technology is making it possible to send and receive news and other essential information from almost anywhere in the world and with increasing speed. The continuing integration of computers with telecommunication means much more interactive, or two-way, communication.
3  The two-way capability of cablevision, tied in with Comsats and personal computers on the Internet, means that information users can seek out or request specific kinds of information or news and not remain a passive mass audience. The two-way capability of telecommunications means that there will be more two-way flows of information, with consumers having more choice about what they receive. The trend toward such interactive communications systems is clear, as the rapid increase in the numbers of bloggers shows.
4  Because of continuing technical improvements, the potential numbers of channels and sources of information are virtually unlimited, and the possible varieties and kinds of future "content" stagger the imagination.

5   These personalized communications, typified by bloggers, the Internet, email, fax, videocassettes, and cablevision, present a challenge to authoritarian governments, which traditionally control their newspapers and broadcasting. How does Big Brother stop someone from watching a pirated videocassette, or from calling up distant information on the Internet, or picking up news from a satellite, or receiving email from a dissident group overseas? Battles over Internet free expression are replacing struggles over freedom of the press of global news media and will continue to be of international concern.

6   Finally, concern is growing about the effects of all this greatly expanded communication flow on its global audiences. Most people spend no more than an hour a day reading newspapers or getting the news from television or radio, but the news volume cascades on. David Shenk wrote that in the middle of the last century, "We began to produce information much faster than we could process it. We have moved from a state of information scarcity to a state of information surplus – from drought to flood in the geological blink of an eye." In his recent book, *Data Smog: Surviving the Information Glut*, Shenk argues that information overload is bad for your health, promoting stress, memory overload, compulsive behavior, and attention-deficit disorder. Shenk argues that the well-known global village, created by mass communication, is at the same time growing increasingly fragmented and fractionalized as people, despairing of being able to master a grand overview, retreat into their own special interests. He argues that cyberspace, including the Internet, promotes a highly decentralized, deregulated society with little common discourse and minimal public infrastructure.[16]

Concerned persons are pondering the implications of all this. Society, in short, faces the danger of computer/communications technologies advancing faster than our ability to develop methods of controlling and using them for the general welfare of humankind. This has always been true of technologies, but today that gap is becoming ominously wide. Nonetheless, innovations in media technology will continue to shape international news.

Finally, Pelton of INTELSAT saw much more to come: "New and perhaps totally different architectures for space communications are likely to evolve in the twenty-first century and the long-term growth and development of space communication seem relatively well-assured. In short, the twenty-first century should see the beginning of the true long-term road to space communications, making it truly the beginning of the "golden age" of space communications."[17]

## Notes

1. Nielsen Online report by *New York Times*, January 6, 2010.
2. "Most Online News Readers Use 5 sites or Fewer," *New York Times*, March 15, 2010, B2.
3. "In Animated Videos News and Guesswork Mix," *New York Times*, December 6, 2009, 1.
4. Ken Auletta, *Googled* (New York: Penguin, 2009) 302.
5. Auletta, *Googled*, 288.
6. "About Half of US Would Pay for Online News, Study Shows," *New York Times*, November 6, 2009, B6.
7. Martin Fackler, "Ink Gushes in Japanese Media Landscape," *New York Times*, June 21, 2010, A14.
8. Joseph Pelton, "Heading for Information Overload," *Inter-Media*, Autumn 1988, 19.
9. Pelton, "Heading for Information Overload."
10. Arthur C. Clarke, "Beyond Babel: The Century of the Communication Satellite," in *Process and Effects of Mass Communication*, W. Schram and D. Roberts, eds. (Urbana: University of Illinois Press, 1971), 952.
11. Pelton, "Heading for Information Overload."
12. "Old News and a New Contender," *The Economist*, June 18, 2005, 52.
13. Pelton, "Heading for Information Overload," 20.
14. Doreen Carvajal, "Europe Teems with Web Dailies That Twit the Mainstream Press," *New York Times*, February 21, 2005, sec. C, 7.
15. Richard Posner, "Bad News," *New York Times Book Review*, July 31, 2005, 1.
16. Michiko Kakutani, "Data, Data, Everywhere, and All the World Did Shrink," *New York Times*, July 8, 1997, sec. B, 6.
17. Pelton, "Heading for Information Overload," 21.

# 5

# The Whole World is Watching: Impact of Great News Events

*Real news is covered the same way that real wars are won: by putting enough boots on the ground.*
— Tim Rutten of the *Los Angeles Times*

*The Internet has certainly broken 30 years of state control over what is seen and is unseen, what is visible versus invisible.*
— Nartej Dhillon of Brookings Institution

Great news events of our times have given us insights into the role that global news plays in assisting and accelerating political and social change. Intensive television coverage of such an event as the air war over Kosovo and Serbia does not determine the political outcome of such crises, but reporting (or non-reporting) has a clear impact on public opinion, which in turn may well influence decisions made by government leaders of great nations.

Today, fast-moving changes are being shaped by transnational communication. Not only have speed and volume increased along with greater geographical dispersal of international news flow, but the nature and effects of the content have changed and diversified as well. Instead of the mere words and numbers of yesteryear's news, today vivid color video coverage of news events is now delivered to the world's news publics, greatly increasing the impact of the message. As a result, a new kind of audience involvement in world events has emerged. The propaganda maxim that the report of the event can be as important as the event itself has greater impact than ever in the age of media events.

*The World News Prism: Challenges of Digital Communication*, Eighth Edition.
William A. Hachten and James F. Scotton.
© 2012 John Wiley & Sons, Ltd. Published 2012 by John Wiley & Sons, Ltd.

America's local news has often become the world's local news. Ever since CNN brought the O. J. Simpson trial into Asian apartments and African villages, domestic dramas in American media have been part of the global conversation. After the massacre of thirty-two people in Blacksburg, Virginia, by a lone gunman British and Polish papers put the story on page one, France's *Figaro* and *Le Monde* wrote editorials. Overseas the story was not a foreign story but a local one. Britain's *Guardian* ran a list of the names of the slain students and teachers on its web site. This new internationalism is perhaps something Americans need to consider in their debates about immigration, the war in Afghanistan, education and foreign trade. Americans knowledge of the rest of the world does not seem to be growing at the same pace.

The following case studies illustrate how the audiences of great international events increasingly share their concerns with each other. In this chapter, we will look at journalistic aspects of several news stories: violent political protests in Iran, the devastating earthquake in Haiti, the Israeli sea raid near Gaza; the tsunami in South Asia, the 9/11 attacks on the United States, the collapse of Soviet communism, the 1991 failed coup in Moscow, and interactions between terrorist attacks and global television. Each provides instructive examples of the interplay between news and media

## Election Protests in Iran

After presidential elections in Iran in June 2009, many thousands of Iranians took to the streets to protest the results. In the past, the regime could block out such unfavorable news by shutting phone lines and restricting a few foreigners. But in this new area of social communication with cell phone cameras, Twitter accounts and other facets of the World Wide Web in play, governments cannot keep the outside world from learning what happened. In the riot, a young Iranian woman was shot and bled to death in a Tehran street and became a world wide martyr because a 40 second video of her death ricocheted around the world. The two megabyte video was emailed to a nearby friend who forwarded it to the Voice of America, the *Guardian* in London and to five other online friends in Europe with a message that said "please let the world know." Another friend posted it on Facebook. Copies of the video spread quickly to YouTube and were televised within hours on CNN.

Despite Iran's efforts to keep a lid on the violent street events, the victim, Ms. Agha-Sotan, was transformed from a nameless victim to an icon of the Iranian protest movement. It was easier for Iranian authorities to limit images and information within Iran than to stop them from spreading rapidly to the outside world. Iran has severely restricted Internet access for Iranians but a loose worldwide network of sympathizers has risen to maintain connections between activists and spontaneous film makers. The pervasiveness of the Web has made censorship[1] a much more complicated task for Iran and the three dozen other countries – as varied as China, Cuba, Singapore, and Uzbekistan – that extensively control their nations' use of the Internet.

From the start of the digital "disruption," governments and rebels have dueled over efforts to censor communication. Text messaging was used to rally support for a popular uprising in Ukraine in 2004 and to threaten activists in Belarus in 2006. Myanmar tried to silence protestors in 2007 by shutting down their Internet for six weeks. China blocked sites like YouTube at the twentieth anniversary of the Tiananmen Square riots.

In Iran censorship has been more sophisticated then most and it uses the latest spying technology to locate opponents. But Twitter and phone video can operate in limited ways to a world of online spectators. Because of this determination, hundreds of amateur videos have been uploaded to YouTube after the riots providing television networks with raw and unverified videos from the protests. Global news gathering benefits from the fact that video and tweets indicate to many that broadly based Internet devices and the spirit of young, tech-savvy people cannot be completely repressed by an authoritarian regime.

In addition to Twitter, YouTube had been an important tool to spread videos from Iran when traditional media have trouble filming protests or the ensuing crackdowns. The BBC's Persian-language television channel said that during one of the protests, it was receiving about five videos a minute from amateurs, even though the channel was largely blocked within Iran. One video showed pro-government militia members firing weapons at a rally. "We've been struck by the amount of videos and eyewitness testimony," said Jon Williams, the BBC World News Editor. Adding "The days when regimes can control the news are over." In Iran however, as new media proliferate, traditional journalists have been having a more difficult time. Journalists were told they could not cover protests without permission, effectively confining journalists to their offices.

## Earthquake Flattens Haiti

In mid-January of 2010, Haiti was devastated by an earthquake of 7.0 magnitude that shattered its impoverished and teeming capital of Port-au-Prince into rubble. The death toll was estimated at over 200,000. Global media became focused on the vast misery and helplessness of the small Caribbean nation. Television journalism was perhaps Haiti's greatest helper during the first days of dire need. Within 20 hours, two major US, networks were broadcasting from the scene followed by reporters and photographers of the major print media. CNN said it was its biggest deployment, short of a war, of news media since the tsunami in 2004. Network television expanded its coverage bringing vivid pictures in homes everywhere. At first, news networks and newspapers found themselves supplementing traditional reporting with Twitter and cell phone videos of witnesses in Haiti. The biggest challenge for the media was that the entire infrastructure of Port-au-Prince had collapsed. Reporters equipped themselves with satellite phones and clips that allowed them to draw power from car batteries for their laptops, cameras, and phones. Many of the press slept on the ground.

Yet Haiti's extreme distress remained mostly a network television story. Television quickly informed a mass audience globally of what had happened and, more importantly, helped to create a worldwide caring and sympathetic audience willing to help alleviate such unprecedented human misery – vividly shown right there on their television screens.

Critic Alessandra Stanley wrote, "Disaster is both one of the hardest and easiest sights to watch on television: the medium feeds on paradox, presenting extraordinary images that horrify and also comfort. Since the earthquake struck Haiti, network and cable news shows have organized the chaos with raw, graphic footage, as well as with beautifully edited vignettes, some scored to music, that calibrate the balance of hope and despair."[2]

In such a calamity, television reporters are the heralds of the fund-raising efforts. Television reporters repeatedly told people where and how to donate money for Haiti and allow viewers to feel that they can do something to help. They also help television news organizations by reminding viewers that journalists can do something to help. They also help the television organizations by reminding viewers that journalists serve as a pillar of the rescue mission – on the scene to do more than just report the news. Another function of television news is to remind government officials, UN groups, the Red Cross, Care and other aid agencies just how desperate Haiti was and how much must be done to rebuild this shattered country.

## Dueling Videos in Israeli Sea Raid

In June 2010, Israeli commandos attacked and boarded the so-called "freedom flotilla" ships at sea from Turkey carrying supplies to blockaded Gaza. In the mêlée nine activists were killed in a confusing conflict in which both sides were well armed – with video cameras. Both sides promptly released a blizzard of video clips "proving" the other side was the aggressor. The flotilla movies proved popular on the Internet. A video from the Israeli defense forces notched 600,000 views on YouTube. Digital views from both sides were shown worldwide on television news programs. But these views did not establish the sequence of events or who attacked first.

James Hoge, editor of *Foreign Affairs*, said there has been a gradual increase in the use of video clips to bear witness and shape opinion. "On a matter like this, public opinion is awfully important in terms of determining which image is going to last. First, it was people in crowds with mobile phones. Now, as so often is the case, governments catch up and begin to use the tools for their own purposes."[3]

The activists had intended to stage a "media event" and were webcasting live from the open seas as the confrontation started. They were using the services of Livestream, a New York-based firm that hosts free webcasts. On board was a full multi-camera production uplinked to the Internet and to a satellite that allowed news channels to rebroadcast live pictures of the raid in progress. Video images from the vessel were viewed by a quarter million people on Livestream and after the attack were watched by countless others on television. The episode again illustrated the propaganda maxim that what people believe happened can be more important than what actually happened.

## Tsunami Batters South Asia, Killing Thousands

After an underground earthquake off the coast of Sumatra on December 26, 2004, a giant wave radiated throughout the coastal areas of Indonesia, Thailand, Sri Lanka, India, numerous islands, and even to the coast of East

Africa. The death toll reached over 220,000, and the homes and livelihoods of millions were devastated.

The disaster rippled beyond South Asia, making it a tragedy of global proportions. Among the casualties were thousands of vacationers of fifty nationalities from outside the area. The missing included 1,500 from Sweden, 700 to 800 from Norway, and over 100 each from New Zealand, Denmark, the Czech Republic, Italy, Germany, and Israel. The disaster's reach was an unsettling reminder that globalization can bring the world together in tragic ways.

The world's news media responded quickly, as thousands of images from around the region poured out to television networks. Video compression technology, fed by digital cameras and enabled by satellite and videophones, along with laptops with uplink capabilities, meant that the world was viewing the deadly aftermath just hours after it had ended.

Soon after that, real-time video footage of the tidal wave striking the shore, much of it taken by tourists on or near beaches in Thailand, began appearing on network broadcasts. In this disaster, there had been a reversal of the news-gathering process. Usually, reporters would get a story and then commission a photographer to go and get the pictures. In this case, the reporters were chasing the pictures and trying to create some context for what the viewers were seeing.

Some saw the tsunami story as a kind of tipping point in so-called "citizen journalism," of which bloggers are a part. Digital technologies – the Internet, email, blogs, digital cameras, camera phones – have enabled people on the scene of a news event to share with professional journalists the capability to reach a wide audience, and show the world what they saw and experienced.

"Tsunami videos" proved a boon for bloggers trying to attract viewers. Dozens of locations on the Internet hosted amateur videos of the Indian Ocean disaster. Many video bloggers were deluged with requests to see more of the dramatic scenes. One blog created just after the disaster, Waveofdestruction.org, logged 682,366 unique visitors in four days. Another site, named "Cheese and Crackers," went from attracting about ten surfers a day to 640,000 visitors after showing the tsunami videos.

But the tidal wave and its follow-up stories of the relief and reconstruction efforts of the outside world were also a boon for the so-called "mainstream media." Tim Rutten, media critic of the *Los Angeles Times*, noted that the story vindicated the indispensability of the mainstream media. He said that in their response, "they have fulfilled the most basic of journalistic obligations – the duty of witness. They have placed the suffering and loss of millions before the conscience of the developed world, and the result has been a demonstration of human solidarity across national, religious and culture divides that seemed beyond reach just a month ago."[4]

Using front-page stories as a measure, in the first several days the *New York Times* published fifty-three stories on the tsunami, the *Los Angeles Times* thirty-eight, and the *Washington Post* thirty-one. In Britain, the BBC had audience increases of as much as 50% for its regular nightly news programming. CNN, with its extensive overseas staff, saw its daily audience increase by 38% and its prime-time viewers grew by 46%. CNN had eighty journalists on the scene within days of the disaster and the BBC had 100 people in the field. Rutten commented that "Real news is covered the same way that real wars are won: by putting enough boots on the ground."[5]

Most of the world responded generously with money and assistance for disaster relief. Finally, the tsunami story was a truly global drama that had victims and heroes but no villains – no human ones, anyway.

## The 9/11 Terror Attacks on the United States

The news of a single day has rarely had such a profound effect on modern history. December 7, 1941 – the date of the surprise attack on Pearl Harbor that brought America into World War II – was such a day. September 11, 2001 – the terrorist attacks by hijacked airliners into the World Trade Center towers in New York City and the Pentagon in Washington, DC – was another historic day that set off a global upheaval with still unforeseen repercussions. After the collapse of the two skyscrapers, the scarring of the Pentagon, the crashing of four airliners, and about 3,000 lives lost, Americans and many others worldwide no longer felt personally secure and safe from the threats of a dangerous world beyond their borders. The United States and its allies promptly embarked on a war against terrorism.

News coverage of the many facets of 9/11 was comprehensive and magnificent. In New York and Washington, DC, journalists reported a local story of great national and international import. Global color television – nonstop and constantly updated – carried unfolding details to every corner of the world. Supplemented by radio, print media, the Internet and cell phones, much of the world saw and heard nearly the same video images and news reports that Americans received. And the US audience was huge: 79.5 million viewers were watching news coverage on broadcast and cable television networks in prime time on September 11, according to Nielsen Media Research.[6]

On September 14, three days later, 39.5 million viewers tuned in to television news coverage in prime time. The Internet audience (which is international) was huge as well. The number of page turns (hits) on just www.cnn.com jumped to 162.4 million.

Moreover, that vast audience approved of the way both the US government and the media had responded. According to a poll by the Pew Research Center for the People and the Press, 89% of people felt the media had done a good or excellent job in covering the attacks.[7]

Professional journalists agreed.

So after more than a decade of looking inward and often ignoring the outside world, the news media, as well as thoughtful citizens, began showing a more serious interest in world affairs again; in particular, trying to understand radical Islam and the complex politics of the Middle East and Central Asia. The nature and motives of Osama bin Laden became a subject of intense public and media interest – at least for a while.

A Pew poll taken in October 2001 found that the terrorist attacks and the war in Afghanistan had created a new internationalist sentiment among the public. There was more support for a multilateral foreign policy than before 9/11, with roughly six-in-ten (59%) now saying that interests of the allies should be taken into account by US policy makers. By a two-to-one margin, the public thought that taking an active role in the world, rather than becoming less involved, would be a more effective way of avoiding problems such as terrorism in the future. And support for assertive US leadership also had grown.[8] These opinion shifts were dramatic, but did not last.

Since 9/11, the major national news media had been given a chance for redemption, reporting with great competence a global news story with many dimensions. Because of budget cuts and fewer overseas reporters and bureaus than earlier, the broadcast networks – ABC, NBC, Fox, and CBS – were the least prepared for this new "asymmetrical" war against terrorism, which has no standing armies to confront: its enemies are hidden, subversive, and of differing nationalities, but are found in "training camps" in remote areas of the developing world – in Afghanistan, and maybe in Iraq, Syria, Somalia, and Sudan. Or, probably some terrorists have been living in the West for many years in deep cover and waiting for the chance to strike – a new challenge for reporting as well as for governmental counter-terrorism efforts.

The 9/11 coverage on network television was important, unprecedented, and revealing about television news itself. Network news showed it could still mount a powerful system of news coverage; no US network or cable system performed badly. Viewers depended on Tom Brokaw, Dan Rather, and Peter Jennings (all three no longer anchors) not only for news but for reassurance and solace. In the first weeks, television coverage was unabashedly patriotic, with American flags much in evidence, but the public apparently did not mind. In those first days, television news ran up huge costs but carried few commercials. The major print media dispatched platoons of reporters and photographers to cover whatever could be found out in Afghanistan, Pakistan, or wherever. Similarly, many journalists from Europe followed suit.

Americans were also getting their news from other sources: BBC television reporters scored several major scoops in Afghanistan, because the British government was more forthcoming with news. Although the press received high marks for its initial war coverage, the news media still faced controversy when reporting news from the "homeland." Some thought that a few members of the press had forsaken their traditional skepticism and were too willing to be a pawn of government and accept only the official versions of events. But other critics argued that the press was unpatriotic at times – too sympathetic to war protesters, and tending to overplay stories about collateral damage to civilians and reports of atrocities by the US military.

All agreed this was a different kind of war – if, indeed, it was a "war." For the first time since the end of the Cold War, the press had a major international news story to focus on – one with staying power.

## Electronic Execution of Soviet Communism

The collapse of communism in Central and Eastern Europe in 1989, along with the end of the Cold War, were two of the most significant political events since World War II (some said since 1848), and were all the more dramatic because they were so unexpected. Certainly Western mass communication – going over, under, and around the Iron Curtain – played a role in raising expectations and in breaking the communists' monopoly on information and popular culture.

Critic George Steiner commented on the impact of television soap operas:
Once "Dallas" had come their way [it could be picked up several hundred kilometers east of Checkpoint Charlie], once tapes of Western soap operas

and rock jamborees could be multiplied and sold beyond the "Dallas line," the cataclysm and saturnalia were inevitable. Television sparked the great wild surge toward a consumer economy, and television packaged (brilliantly) the actual rush. Why live by bread alone when there is peanut butter? Why endure as a Soviet satellite when the word "satellite" means cable television?[9]

The dramatic and sudden collapse of communism in Eastern Europe came after a generation of communication interactions between the Western nations and the socialist nations of Eastern Europe, the USSR, and the third world – all set in the context of the Cold War. Recent economic successes of the West, along with the failures of socialist political economies, helped explain the media changes. Further, the sheer pervasiveness of Western communications accelerated modifications of and, in time, the abandonment of communism and its press theory.

Western journalism rode the crest of the technotronic revolution that had reshaped global mass communication during the past generation and created the information societies of the West. (One Russian general said that the USSR lost the Cold War because it was hopelessly behind the West in computer technology.) Communication satellites, computerization, global television, high-speed data transfers, and especially new media products such as videocassette and audiocassette players, all spurred by profit-making opportunities, has led to a vast flood of Western television programs, movies, videocassettes, CDs, and taped music recordings, moving inexorably from Western to Eastern Europe.

Grist for this vast mill has consisted of not only Western pop culture (movies, television shows, music videos, and rock and other popular music) but also newspapers, magazines, and books. Western versions of the news, along with Western methods of news reporting and presentation, became widely accepted and emulated. The AP, Reuters, CNN, the BBC and Radio Free Europe, Radio Liberty, and the *International Herald Tribune*, among other media, added diversity to the monolithic news structure of the communist regimes. Whatever their shortcomings, Western media had a crucial advantage over communist media: They were not government controlled and hence they achieved a wide credibility. Consequently, centralized communist governments lost their monopoly over their own information.

Western news media acted as catalysts for political change in communist nations in several ways. People in Eastern Europe did listen to Western broadcasts, which carried both world news and news about the satellite nations themselves.

Much of this news went by shortwave radio, some by AM and FM broadcasting and, for East Germany, via television from West Berlin and the German Federal Republic. German-language television was received all over the GDR (German Democratic Republic) except in low-lying Dresden, which was locally dubbed the "Valley of the Ignorant" because of the poor television reception there.

Some observers believe the beginnings of the breakup of the communist empire in Eastern Europe began with the successes of the Solidarity trade union in Poland. The Polish communist regime's monopoly on news was broken in two ways: first, by the rise of alternative newspapers that challenged the government and supported Solidarity goals; and, second, by a triangular communication flow between the alternative papers, foreign reporters, and international broadcasters. It worked this way. Foreign journalists reported news of Solidarity to their Western media; these stories were beamed back to Poland via international shortwave radio, particularly by the BBC, Deutsche Welle, and Radio Free Europe; then the stories were also picked up by the alternative papers in Poland.

This communication model was followed again and again. Michael T. Kaufman, who covered Poland for the *New York Times*, wrote:

> It turned out that a few dissidents using non-violent means, and exploiting the freedom of the press and airwaves beyond their borders, could in this increasingly interconnected world bring down autocrat after autocrat. Foreign correspondents wrote for their own papers, but their reports were translated and beamed back to countries where such information as they were writing was banned. The spread of portable radios and videos made such information much more accessible. The official press was forced to offer more information, more truth, as it was forced to compete for credibility with the outsiders. . ... Once informed, the people were mobilized. In most places, they marched and chanted and drew placards and with the world press watching such means proved sufficient to expose previous forbidden truths and to make revolutionary changes that had so recently seemed impossible.[10]

In the revolutionary events of 1989, the media played a variety of roles. One was to report that such things happen and that times are changing. Another was to show that the world was indeed watching and that the Berlin Wall could be turned into a sieve. A third purpose was to show potential demonstrators in other countries that the unthinkable was perfectly possible. So, uprisings in East Berlin, Budapest, Prague, and Bucharest all reinforced one another.

For William E. Henry of *Time*, the triumphs owed something to journalism but little to journalists:

> The function of news people was not sage or analyst but conduit, carrying the raw facts of an amazing reality to the startled citizenry in each revolutionary nation and to a waiting world beyond. . . . the most interesting part of the news business is, in fact, the news. For broadcast journalists, events proved anew that the chief element of their much discussed power is the simple capacity to reach many people quickly – and in cases of true turmoil, with a verisimilitude no other medium offers. television's basic function was as the great legitimizer.[11]

## The Failed Coup in Moscow

Communications was one of the major reasons why the right-wing coup d'état failed to topple the Soviet government in August 1991. The nine coup leaders arrested Mikhail Gorbachev, closed down all but a handful of Communist Party media, and held a television press conference proclaiming the new government. They assumed that the nation would passively accept the changeover. However, the coup masterminds failed to understand how much the Soviet Union had changed in six years of *glasnost*. With a more open communication system and a new taste for free expression, the resistance in Moscow rallied around Boris Yeltsin. They used fax, photocopying machines, and cell phones to let fellow citizens know it was not too late to resist the coup. Inexplicably, the plotters shut down neither international telephone lines nor the satellite relay station, and they did not jam shortwave radio. No actions were taken against the large foreign press in Moscow, which sent out a flood of words and pictures to a disapproving world. CNN was even received in some Soviet republics. It was as if the coup leaders became immobilized, like deer before car headlamps, by the television camera lights recording and transmitting the events within the parliament and the street barricades outside. Soviet journalists, emboldened by *glasnost*, refused to accept the coup restrictions. Blocked at the printing plants, dozens of independent publications ran off photocopies and passed them out on street corners. Moscow's subway was quickly papered with handbills. Interfax, the independent news agency, distributed underground reports along with its own stories.

The impact of Western radio was even more impressive. The BBC doubled its Russian-language program to eighteen hours, its largest increase ever. It also relayed the banned broadcasts of a Moscow station. Radio Liberty's twenty-four-hour broadcasts, in Russian and eleven other Soviet languages, reached an estimated audience of 50 million. Gorbachev later said he gratefully listened to the BBC, RL, and the Voice of America while under house arrest at his dacha in the Crimea.

As *Newsweek* commented, "The coup leaders apparently relied on popular indifference and fear of authority. But those are not the attributes of people in the know. And last week Russians proved that they have entered the information age."[12]

Ironically, the new communications openness that propelled Boris Yeltsin to political power after the failed coup also caused him severe political damage in the winter of 1994–1995, when he sent the Russian army into Chechnya to put down a rebellion. In Moscow and throughout the nation, millions of Russians watched television pictures of the brutal suppression of the revolt and the killing of thousands of civilians. And many Russians did not like what they saw.

## Terrorism and Television

The very nature of global television and telecommunications, that can bring people closer together while sharing the mutual grief of tragic events, such as the assassination of John F. Kennedy or the tsunami disaster in South Asia, also can be manipulated to capture the world's attention. Unquestionably, certain acts of international terrorism, such as jet hijackings, political kidnappings, and civilian bombings as in Oklahoma City, are perpetrated primarily to capture time and space in the world's media. Terrorism has been called "propaganda of the deed" – violent criminal acts, usually directed at innocent civilians, performed by desperate people seeking a worldwide forum for their grievances. Experts disagree over terrorists' motives.

Terrorism, of course, is not new. But the flare-ups of the phenomenon since the 1960s – especially in the Middle East, Northern Ireland, Latin America, Turkey, Italy, West Germany, Spain, and now the United States and Britain – have been facilitated in part, some say, by global television coverage that beams images of terrorist violence into millions of television sets around the world. Many terrorist groups have mastered a basic lesson of this media age. Television news organizations can be manipulated into becoming the final link between the terrorists and their audiences and, as with all sensational crimes, the more outrageous and heinous the terrorist act, the greater attention it will receive in the world's news media. Walter Laqueur said, "The media are a terrorist's best friend. . ... Terrorists are the super-entertainers of our time."[13]

In this age of global television, the effects of 9/11 and the 7/7 attacks in London were deeply felt in many lands. Whether in Madrid, Jerusalem, Shanghai, or Jakarta, the news and video were filtered through the prisms of differing cultures, ethnicities, politics, and religion. But the most important reaction was in Washington, DC, where the Bush administration, supported by US public opinion, vowed to strike back hard at terrorism.

After 9/11, international terrorism became a major concern at the top of the foreign news agenda as well as the global political agenda. After being downplayed by news media for years, terrorism was major news again; the "acts of war" on September 11 immediately triggered a new kind of war with Islamic terrorists and any states supporting them. The risk of future attacks of such a devastating nature was raised from "possible" and "unlikely" to "probable" and "likely" in the minds of editors and security officials alike.

A positive result was that the American public woke up to the importance of foreign news; the nation was reminded that we live inseparably in one world – a world that can be threatening and dangerous. The news media were reminded of the perils of neglecting foreign news since the 1989 fall of communism. Historians may be critical of American presidential leadership for failing to respond sharply to terrorist acts against America during the 1990s. And much of the news media, particularly local media and broadcast and cable television, can be faulted for not informing the public (and government) adequately about the growing dangers coming out of the Middle East conflicts: the bombing of Marine barracks in Lebanon; the bombing of Air Force living quarters in Saudi Arabia; the blowing up of US embassies in Nairobi and Dar es Salaam; and the attack on the USS *Cole* in Yemen – all precursors to 9/11.

For the first time since 1812, when the British burned down the White House, Americans realized that their two-ocean defensive shield could be penetrated. (In 1941, Hawaii was still a territory.) People realized we were now vulnerable to bioterrorism and even nuclear attacks as well as suicide bombings. In addition, airliner hijackings returned to the news as a major threat to the security of commercial aviation. The possibility of being hijacked by suicidal terrorists who used the airliner as a deadly missile attack, killing all aboard, had hardly been imagined.

No doubt the vivid television pictures multiplied the psychological impact of the terror – the depression, sense of loss, and insecurity – felt by so many people. This, apparently, is what the terrorists intended, but did global television assist the terrorists in achieving their aims? Perhaps, but there was no choice. Acts of terrorism are major news and, of course, have to be reported.

Be that as it may, terrorism and all its facets are news, and as such it poses worrisome questions for broadcast journalists: Does television coverage really encourage and aid the terrorists' cause? Is censorship of such dramatic events ever desirable? Raymond Tanter wrote, "Since terror is aimed at the media and not at the victim, success is defined in terms of media coverage. And there is no way in the West that you could not have media coverage, because you're dealing with a free society."[14]

Terrorism coverage is a journalistic problem of international scope, just as international terrorism itself is a transnational problem that individual nations cannot solve without international cooperation. Broadcast journalists argue about whether the violence would recede if television ignored or downplayed an act of terrorism. Most journalists doubt that self-censorship by news organizations is a good idea, or even possible, in such a highly competitive field. However, television organizations have established guidelines for reporting terrorism incidents in a more restrained and rational way.

As with much else in foreign news, a big story in one nation is not necessarily a big story somewhere else. And, further, actors in the same violent story can be called "terrorists" in one nation and "freedom fighters" in another. Yet, for Western news media, any terrorist attack will be an important news story.

## Notes

1. Mark Landler and Brian Stelter, "Web Pried Lid of Censorship," *New York Times*, June 1, 2009, A1.
2. Alessandra Stanley, "Haiti Broadcast Coverage: Compassion and Self Congratulation," *New York Times*, January 16, 2010, 3.
3. Brian Stelter, "After Sea Raid, Videos Carry On Fight," *New York Times*, June 2, 2010, A1.
4. Tim Rutten, "When Facts Trump Attitude," *Los Angeles Times*, www.latimes.com, January 8, 2005.
5. Rutten, "When Facts Trump Attitude."
6. "Add It Up," *American Journalism Review*," November 2001, 11.

7. "Add It Up."
8. "America's New Internationalist Point of View," Pew Research Center for the People and the Press, online report, October 24, 2001.
9. George Steiner, "B.B.," *New Yorker*, September 10, 1990, 113.
10. Bernard Gwertzman and Michael Kaufmann, eds., *The Collapse of Communism* (New York: St. Martins Press, 1990), 352–353.
11. William Henry, "The Television Screen is Mightier Than the Sword," *Time*, May 10, 1990, 51.
12. "How Resistance Spread the Word," *Newsweek*, September 2, 1991, 39.
13. Neil Hickey, "Terrorism and Television," *TV Guide*, August 7, 1986, 2.
14. Hickey, "Terrorism and Television."

# 6

# Globalization of Media and Language

*Mankind has become one, but not steadfastly one as communities or even as nations used to be, nor united through years of mutual experience. . . nor yet through a common native language, but surpassing all barriers, through international broadcasting and printing.*

— Alexander Solzhenitsyn

*The road signs on the informational Highway are in English. Eighty per cent of the world's Home pages are written in some kind of it.*

— Robert McCrum

*Parlez-vous Globlish?*

— Robert McCrum

If Jules Verne's adventurous Phineas Fogg traveled around the world in eighty days again today, he would find that as an Englishman abroad he would have little trouble keeping up with the news and entertainment. At almost every stopover, he would be able to buy a copy of the *International Herald Tribune* or possibly the *Financial Times*, and at his hotel's newsstand he would have a choice of *The Economist, Time*, or the *New Yorker*, among other English-language publications. In his hotel room, he would be able to watch the day's televised news either from CNN via cable and Comsat from Atlanta or BBC World. On the local television station, he could see a world news package of stories put together by Reuters Television outside London. And if he had a small shortwave radio, he would be reassured by listening to the BBC World Service from Bush House in London or the Voice of America. Also, on local television, he would likely find reruns of his favorite

*The World News Prism: Challenges of Digital Communication*, Eighth Edition.
William A. Hachten and James F. Scotton.
© 2012 John Wiley & Sons, Ltd. Published 2012 by John Wiley & Sons, Ltd.

British programs, and if he sought out a local movie theater, he likely would have a choice of current Hollywood productions. Chances are that a local bookstore or airport newsstand would have a wide selection of English-language magazines and paperback books.

Today, he is likely to have a laptop computer, a cell phone, or an iPad with which he would be able to keep up with the news and entertainment as well as stay current by email with personal and professional contacts.

The increasing availability of such Western publications and electronic media fare (most of it in English, the *lingua franca* of international communication) is an example of the way the major institutions of news communication – world news services, satellite services, broadcast systems, great newspapers and magazines – have become increasingly internationalized or globalized in recent years. Globalization offers business opportunities for media corporations to make money overseas. This is facilitated by innovations in media technology (facsimile printing and satellite distribution in particular) and a growing elite cosmopolitan audience, as well as other social and political realities. Whatever the cause, the fact is that more and more of the activities of the major news media now transcend parochial or national concerns and serve broader transnational purposes.

This Brave New World is mainly expressed in the English language or its varied modifications, according to writer Robert McCrum in his important 2010 book, *Globish: How the English Language Became the World's Language* (FN/W.W. Norton, New York, 2010). English speakers can travel anywhere in the world and often find that the "native" or local speakers already know English or some modified version of it such as "Manglish" (Malay and English), "Konglish" (English in South Korea) or in Mumbai (formerly Bombay) where people speak a mixture of Hindi, Urdu, Gujarati, Marathi – and English.

McCrum believes that alongside the Internet, the globalization of English and "of English literature, law, money, and values is nothing less than the cultural revolution of my generation." [1] McCrum says that English is the language of aspiration and the lingua franca of international culture and commerce. (including of course international journalism and popular culture).The most admired and imitated model of journalism is that which evolved in the United Kingdom and the United States. A leader of any nation who wants to be widely understood in today's world must be able to speak English in a televised or radio interview. The same is true for public figures and celebrities. And the new media of digital disruption are mainly in English. (There is more on English as a media language later in this chapter.)

Various media conglomerates have been arising out of the capitalistic West which some critics feel may dominate, if not unduly influence, much of international communication and entertainment in the near future. Frequently mentioned among these "media baronies" are those of Rupert Murdoch of Australia, Britain, and America; Silvio Berlusconi of Italy; Time Warner, Disney Company (ABC), and Viacom (CBS) of the United States; the Bertelsmann group of Germany; and Sony of Japan – all multimedia and multinational.

But in recent years, we are seeing that some of these media leviathans are not doing so well – being overshadowed or neutralized by digital media. However, in August 2010, two of the largest media companies, Time Warner and Murdoch's News Corporation, reported strong earnings and large increases in advertising revenue. Both firms saw big gains in their television and cable units.[2]

As recently as 1989, the world was still defined by the Anglo-American television networks like NBC, BBC, CBS, ABC and CNN or by international magazines like *Time*, *The Economist*, and newspapers like the *New York Times*, the *Washington Post*, But today for example, the digital Guardian Unlimited can record 29 million hits a day on the Internet.[3]

Today, the new media enable local cultures to define themselves in local terms through the local media. For the world's lingua franca, the stronger the local loyalty, the more urgent is the need for the supranational advantages of the world's English or Globish. And Globish, he asserts, is "fulfilling its destiny as the worldwide dialect of the third millennium." In China, for example, an official slogan is "Conquer the English language to make China strong."[4]

But the globalization of mass communication is proceeding in response to the needs and economic opportunities of a shrinking world. The transnational media are doing more than seizing the chance for greater profits from new markets, albeit those factors are obviously important. Whether viewed as another example of Western "media imperialism" or as a significant contribution to global understanding and integration, the international media are becoming increasingly cosmopolitan, speaking English and or Globish, and catering to an internationally minded audience concerned about world affairs.

## An American in Paris

The daily, ink-on-newsprint newspaper is still a major prop of global journalism because they still gather most of the world's news and because they serve as a check on excessive political and economic authority. Moreover, printed newspapers are still doing well in other major nations including Japan, China, and India. There are more than 8,000 dailies worldwide and many thousands more weekly journals. A few of the more serious "prestige" papers attract readers far beyond their national borders. Not many Westerners read foreign publications, so they are unaware of the extent to which people abroad depend on newspapers and magazines published in other countries. The intellectually demanding *Le Monde* of Paris, famous for its analyses of world affairs, is widely read in the Arab world and francophone Africa. The London-based *Financial Times* uses a plant in Frankfurt to print nearly 53,000 copies daily of an edition described as "Europe's business paper" and has a US edition printed in New York City for American readers. Gannett distributes in Europe copies of *USA Today* printed in Switzerland; the only difference is that the weather maps are of Europe and Asia. Britain's *Guardian, Independent,* and *Daily Telegraph* are found on many foreign newsstands, as are Germany's *Frankfurter Allgemeine* and Switzerland's *Neue Zürcher Zeitung.*

But the newspaper that has evolved furthest toward becoming a truly global daily is the *International Herald Tribune* of Paris. The IHT is the sole survivor of several English-language papers, including the *Chicago Tribune,* the *Daily Mail* (of London), the *New York Herald,* and the *New York Times,* that earlier published Paris or European editions for English speaking travelers. Started by James Gordon Bennett in 1887 as the Paris edition of the *New York Herald,* the IHT has outlived its parents and today is fully owned by the *New York Times* company. As of recently, much more of the paper is staff written. This marvel of distribution appears daily on some 8,500 newsstands all over Europe, supplied by editions printed in Paris, London, The Hague, Marseilles, Rome, and Zurich; and more recently in Hong Kong and Singapore. African and Middle Eastern subscribers are served by mail; distribution in North America, Latin America, and the Caribbean comes from a Miami printing plant. The IHT thus has become the first newspaper in history to publish the same edition simultaneously on all continents.

Although it remains an American newspaper in outlook and perspective, it has gradually acquired an important non-American readership. Nearly half its readers are an elite group of European internationalists – business people, diplomats, and journalists fluent in English. These non-American readers are part of an "international information elite" who, regardless of geographic location, share a similar rich fund of common experience, ideas, ways of thinking, and approaches to dealing with international problems.

Numerous other publications, particularly magazines, have reached and helped shape this international information elite. Hearst Magazines International has successfully published magazines abroad, with sixty-four foreign language editions of eight magazines. Its leaders, *Cosmopolitan*, *Esquire*, *Good Housekeeping*, and *Popular Mechanics*, were distributed in fourteen languages to sixty countries.[5]

Another success, *Reader's Digest*, established its first foreign edition in Britain in 1938. By 1995, there were forty-seven international editions printed in eighteen languages. Almost 13 million copies a month are sold abroad. In some countries, including nearly all Spanish-speaking countries, the *Reader's Digest* is the most popular magazine. So successful has been its adaptation to foreign soil that many readers are unaware that the *Digest* is not an indigenous publication.

*Time* and *Newsweek*, besides spawning such notable imitations as *Der Spiegel* in Germany and *L'Express* in France, have been successful as transnational publications, and both can claim strong appeal to that internationally minded readership.

Weekly news magazines have been hurt by the rapid 24/7 increase of the news cycle due to the digital media. *Time* still has three international editions – Europe, Asia, and South Pacific – with more stress now on commentary and features rather than hard news. Newsweek which was sold 2010 to a 92-year old stereo equipment billionaire for virtually nothing after the *Washington Post* said it could no longer afford to keep losing money on the magazine. Newsweek has slashed its circulation to 1.6 million from about 4.1 million in 2000. *Time*'s circulation has been cut to 3.3 million from 4.1 million in 2000.[6] Several top staffers at *Newsweek*, – Fareed Zakaria, Howard Fineman, and editor Jon Meachem – have moved to other publications.

A major competitor of the news magazines abroad is *The Wall Street Journal*. With a satellite-assisted leap across the Pacific, the highly successful *Journal* launched, in 1976, an Asian edition in Hong Kong that covers a sixteen-country business beat from Manila to Karachi. Smaller than the domestic edition, *The Asian Wall Street Journal* tries for the same mix of authoritative business and political news, a risky experiment for a region with so little press freedom. And pressures have been applied, mostly by Singapore's authoritarian ruler, Lee Kuan Yew. In November 1985, the editor of *The Asian Wall Street Journal* apologized to a Singapore court for

any possibility of contempt of court raised by a *Journal* editorial commenting on Singapore politics. The incident prompted questions about the
appropriate responses when a foreign court challenges the editorial freedom
of an American newspaper published abroad. By mid-1990, after three years
of harassment and a lengthy legal dispute with Lee, the *Journal* announced
that it was ending circulation in the island republic.

The Wall Street Journal also has a European edition, printed in the
Netherlands and written and edited in Brussels, Belgium. The paper, which
can be purchased on the day of publication throughout Britain and
continental Europe, is edited for the international business executive doing
business in Europe. Major competitors are two highly regarded British
business publications, *The Economist* and the *Financial Times*.

In Latin America, following the invasion of cable television, American
newspapers and magazines have been gaining many new readers in the
region. Magazine publishers have launched Spanish-language editions of
Glamour, *Discover, People, National Geographic*, and *Rolling Stone*. The
*Miami Herald* has become the international English newspaper of Latin
America, with ten regional printing plants and an overseas circulation of
about 35,000 to 40,000. Brazilian sales of *Reader's Digest* in Portuguese
jumped from 35,000 to 600,000 in two years.

## Changes in World News Services

The subtle changes in the world news services as they have expanded abroad
are further evidence of this growing globalization of transnational media.
Although they claim to "cover the world," the agencies historically have
tended to serve primarily their own national clients and those in their
spheres of influence; that is, Reuters serviced British media and the British
Commonwealth, AFP worked mainly for the French press and overseas
French territories, and UPI (in its prime), in addition to its US clients, long
had strong connections in Latin America. But these world agencies have
become more international in scope, selling their services to whoever will
buy, wherever they may be.

In addition, the personnel of world agencies have become significantly
internationalized. Formerly, the AP, for example, boasted that its news from
abroad was reported by American AP correspondents who had experience
in running an AP bureau in the United States The agency would not depend
on foreign nationals to provide news from their own countries for AP use in

the United States. That has changed. With the increased professionalism of journalists abroad, news agencies not only find it more useful to use qualified local journalists, but also may get better reporting from staffers who know their own country, its language, and its social and political traditions. In late 2005, the AP planned to introduce an Internet database system called eAP that will deliver news photos, and video and sound clips, with identifying codes that will enable the AP to track how many times articles are used by a client.

Another facet of internationalization is foreign syndication of news by major daily papers. The New York Times News Service sends more than 50,000 words daily to 550 clients, of which 130 are newspapers abroad. Its close competitor is the Los Angeles Times/Washington Post News Service, which transmits about 60,000 words daily to fifty nations or about 600 newspapers, half of which are outside the United States. This total includes papers in Germany and elsewhere that receive the DPA (Deutsche Presse Agentur), with which the service is affiliated.

As noted previously, there is syndication as well of television news film and videotapes, especially those of America's NBC, CNN, CBS, and ABC, and Britain's BBC and ITN, most of it distributed by two Anglo-American firms – Reuters Television and Associated Press Television News – via videotape and satellite (and sometimes by airmail) to almost every television service in the world. There is probably more international cooperation than competition in the transnational video news business, in part because most nations have only one government-controlled television service. Unlike the print media, which usually carry a credit line on agency reports or syndicated material, syndicated television news is usually presented anonymously. Whether watching news from Cairo or Shanghai, the viewer is rarely informed who supplied the foreign video.

## Advertising Goes Worldwide

Advertising, too, has followed the global trend. "Megamergers" among advertising and marketing services companies point up how internationalized Madison Avenue, the symbolic home of American advertising, has become. The biggest merger in advertising history took place when Saatchi & Saatchi of London agreed to buy Ted Bates Worldwide for $450 million. Saatchi & Saatchi thus became the world's biggest agency, with US billings of $4.6 billion and world billings of $7.6 billion. The second largest advertising empire was created with the amalgamation of three other major concerns – the Doyle Dane Bernbach Group, BBDO International, and Needham Harper Worldwide – which, combined, had world billings of $5 billion and US billings of $3.7 billion.[7] Later, the United Kingdom's WPP agency bought out two American giants: J. Walter Thompson and Ogilvy and Mather.

Agency executives involved in these mergers cited the industry's understanding of the need to offer clients worldwide service as a primary motivation. As an executive of Young & Rubicam pointed out, "There is a trend toward global assignment of agencies. If you don't have a complete set of worldwide resources, you're in danger of being left out in terms of getting the best clients."[8]

Implied is the view that transnational advertising agencies would be in a position to channel standardized advertising from transnational corporations into transnational media with minimum effort. The same commercial – whether for Coke or McDonald's – could just be translated into many languages and placed in media anywhere in the world. However, this "global sell" theory has not worked out, according to Alvin Toffler, who wrote, "What's wrong with the global sell theory is that it makes little distinction between the world's regions and markets. Some are still in a pre-mass market condition; others are still at the mass-market stage; and some are already experiencing the demassification characteristic of an advanced economy."[9] Due to cultural preferences, widespread consumer differences about products persist, as do attitudes toward food, beauty, work, play, love, and politics. Toffler concluded that "globalization is not the same as homogeneity. Instead of a single global village, as forecast by Marshall McLuhan, we are likely to see a multiplicity of quite different global villages – all wired into the new media system, but all straining to retain or enhance their cultural, ethnic, national, and political individuality."[10]

## Media Changes in Europe

The increasing economic integration of the European Union plus the demassification and deregulation of broadcast media are rapidly internationalizing much of mass communication in Western Europe. Although Europeans, like people everywhere, prefer to read, view, and listen to news and entertainment in their home or native languages, the push toward transnational communication is still strong. This is due to the rapid expansion of cable and satellite options for viewers, as well as increased numbers of private or commercial television and radio channels and the increasing popularity of VCRs, DVDs, and the Internet.

As noted previously, major American and British print and broadcasting organizations are each trying to increase their readers and audiences in European nations. And other media conglomerates in France, Germany, Italy, and Japan are buying up media properties abroad. Deregulation and privatization of radio and television and the expansion of cable and pay television, assisted by satellite distribution, also have added potentially important new daily news outlets in English as well as many more entertainment options for Europeans. Europe's broadcasting systems, formerly run by governments or by public corporations (paid for by special taxes or fees), have heretofore generally offered high-quality programming but with limited choices. But Western Europe is now following the deregulated American models, with greatly increased choices. As a result, there has been a rush for the huge profits to be made. Adherents of Europe's tradition of public service broadcasting feel that programming quality will be sacrificed by deregulation and commercialization. The money to be made from advertising, viewer fees, and revenues from movies and video programs is expected to run into the billions.

Western Europe nations, particularly France, are concerned about the influence and popularity of American movies and television shows with European audiences, and have established quotas on imports and subsidized their own productions. However, another quieter invasion has taken place: American companies have infiltrated nearly every corner of the European television business. Time Warner, Viacom, Disney/ABC, Cox Cable, NBC, and others are getting involved in European-based television programming, in broadcast stations, in cable and satellite networks, and in the coming convergence of telecommunications and entertainment. And they see a huge market: 350 million people in twelve major Western European nations and 650 million overall west of Russia, many of them hungry for televised news and entertainment.

## Expanding Media Baronies

Many of the innovative changes in European media, as elsewhere, are being made by the transnational media conglomerates, themselves a by-product of rapid changes in international communication. There is growing concern as well about the economic, and potentially political, influence wielded by these powerful forces in global communication. The prototype of the media barons is Rupert Murdoch with his News Corporation. With 150 media properties in Australia, the United States, and Britain, Murdoch has been carefully assembling a vertically integrated global media empire. In the United States, he owns the Fox television network, *The Wall Street Journal*, and the *New York Post*. In addition, he has a significant share of Twentieth Century Fox Broadcasting, which produces television shows and owns thousands of hours of films and television programs. In Europe, he has pioneered in satellite broadcasting and owns 90% of the British Sky Broadcasting channel (a satellite television system), a new sports network, and a twenty-four-hour news channel that draws from his two London papers, *The Times* and *The Sunday Times*. He owns direct broadcast satellite services in Britain, Italy, Hong Kong, Japan, and Mexico; he owns two-thirds of daily newspaper circulation in Australia; and he owns HarperCollins Publishers, and *Seventeen* magazines, and other British papers, including *The Sun* and the *News of the World*. Constantly juggling his properties (and his considerable debts), his News Corporation, which had revenues of less than $1 billion in 1980, had expanded its revenues to $14 billion in 2000.[11]

Murdoch's media acquisitions have apparently influenced several major US media mergers, all of which have had implications for the future of international communications. In August 1995, the Walt Disney Company announced its purchase of Capital Cities/ABC, in a deal valued at $19 billion. The merger brought together ABC – then the most profitable television network, including its highly regarded news organization (Peter Jennings then as anchor) – and its ESPN sports cable service with an entertainment giant: Disney's Hollywood film and television studios, cartoon characters, theme parks, and so on, and the merchandise they generate. (In one recent year, the Disney Company sold more than $15 billion worth of Disney merchandise worldwide, a total more than seven times the global box-office receipts for Disney movies.) Disney is more interested in content, especially game parks, movies, and consumer goods, than in conduits (cable or satellites). For 2000, Disney's total revenue was $25.8 billion, putting it in second place among media giants.

The real giant among the mega-media companies was AOL Time Warner, whose 2000 total revenues hit $36 billion, well ahead of

Disney. Viacom (CBS) stood in third place at $20 billion, followed by Vivendi/Universal at $18 billion, Bertelsmann at $16 billion, and Murdoch's News Corporation at $14 billion. However, the bursting of the dot com bubble in late 2000 hit AOL Time Warner hard, wiping out almost $200 billion in shareholder value. Time Warner shed AOL and has since come back. However, the French-controlled Vivendi/Universal conglomerate went under.

Another major merger began with Westinghouse's takeover of CBS Inc., creating the nation's largest broadcast station group, with thirty-nine radio and sixteen television stations reaching 32% of the nation. About the same time, Viacom, a hot cable company, bought a legendary Hollywood studio, Paramount Communications, for $8.2 billion. Several years later, Viacom bought the CBS Corporation for $37.3 billion, creating the world's second-largest media company. In May 2000, the FCC approved the Viacom/CBS merger and for its money CBS brought to the merger $1.9 billion in radio properties, including 190 radio stations; $4.4 billion in television holdings, including the CBS network, CBS Entertainment, CBS sports, and seventeen television stations; and $546 million in cable properties. However, CBS and Viacom separated into two different entities in 2006.

These megamergers positioned the resulting giants – Time Warner, Disney/ABC, and Murdoch – to better penetrate and dominate the growing international markets for television, movies, news, sports, re-cords, and other media programs. At the time of its merger with ABC, Disney president Michael Eisner spoke glowingly of India's huge middle class of 250 million as a great potential audience for Disney movies, cartoons, news, and sports programs. NBA and NFL games have been gaining large audiences overseas; hence the importance of the ESPN networks. Critics noted that news organizations (and journalists), such as *Time* magazine and CNN, or ABC News or CBS News, were just small players within these entertainment giants.

The keen competition among CNN, MSNBC, and Fox News Channel (FNC) to dominate a twenty-four-hour cable news channel in the United States. has strong international potential as well. Broadcast networks have been looking to international markets as a way of gaining hundreds of millions of new viewers. NBC's international holdings currently are about 20% of the network's worth of $10 to $20 billion; in the next ten years, half of the network's value is expected to come from international holdings. As predicted, Asia is becoming the main area of global audience growth, because about 25% of the continent's vast population is expected to receive cable before long. By contrast, the US market, with cable in 65 million of its 97 million households, is nearing saturation. Numbers of cable viewers are expected to rise abroad in time for the startup of NBC Europe as well as related NBC services in Latin America. Since 9/11, the war on terrorism for a while gave an impetus to twenty-four-hour global news, and competition has become much more intense.

## Other European Baronies

Among European media groups with far-reaching holdings is Bertelsmann AG of Germany. From a Bible-publishing house, Bertelsmann grew into a media giant with book and record clubs in Germany, Spain, Brazil, the United States, and eighteen other countries. Bertelsmann owns Bantam, Doubleday, and Dell publishing in the United States, and Plaza y Janes book publishers in Spain, in addition to thirty-seven magazines in five countries, record labels such as RCA/Ariola, and a number of radio and television properties. In 1998, Bertelsmann shocked US book publishers by buying Random House for an estimated $1.4 billion, consolidating its claim as the world's largest English- language publisher of trade books. Considered the crown jewel of American book publishers, Random House had $1.1 billion in sales in 1996. With the sale, half of the top twenty US publishing firms, with a 28% share of the total US market, were in foreign hands. With $15.5 billion total revenue in 2000, Bertelsmann ranked as the world's fifth largest media conglomerate.

Possibly the most swashbuckling of the media barons has been Italy's Silvio Berlusconi, who built a multibillion-dollar media television and newspaper empire, Fininvest, of unusual power and influence. With 42% of Italy's advertising market and 16% of daily newspaper circulation, he has concentrated his power more into a single market than any of the aforementioned barons. He owns Italy's three main private television channels, Rete 4, Canale 4, and Italia 1, as well as *Il Giornale*, a leading Milan paper, two leading news weeklies, thirteen regional dailies, and a large book publisher plus television holdings in France and Germany. Using his extensive media power, Berlusconi became Prime Minister of Italy in 1994. He has been in and out of political power since but has continued to be a dominant political force in Italy.

## Diffusion of Mass Culture

A major impact of these global media giants comes from their diffusion of the popular culture of the West to all – literally all – corners of the world, with profound influences that can only be described as revolutionary. The world is beginning to share a common popular culture. Much of the diversity of the world's cultures and languages is being lost forever. This trend is part of a long-term historical process that predates modern media, but in recent years the pace has accelerated.

American films regularly acquire more than 50% of the French market; about 50% of the Italian, Dutch, and Danish markets; 60% of the German markets; and 80% of the British markets. Recently, among the world's 100 most attended films, eighty-eight were American. Seventy-five percent of all imported television programs come from America. Millions in Europe watched *Oprah Winfrey*, subtitled or dubbed. American basketball, played in 192 countries, may become the world's most popular sport. The NBA finals have been broadcast in 109 countries in twenty languages. Here are random examples of US mass culture abroad: *Dallas* has been seen in ninety-eight countries; 40% of television programming in New Zealand is American; Mickey Mouse and Donald Duck, dubbed in Mandarin, have been seen weekly in China; *Sesame Street* has been seen in 184 countries; and the hottest game show on French television is *La Roule de la Fortune*. Popular culture also conveys life styles. Like their Russian counterparts, young Chinese prefer American jeans and T-shirts as well as rock music. Young people in Germany are using such slang terms as "rap music," "body building," "windsurfing," and "computer hacking" – and, what is more, they are doing these activities.

One of the most powerful influences on global youth culture has been Music Television, or MTV, which first appeared on US cable in 1981. Since then, it has grown into a global phenomenon reaching into about 250 million homes worldwide. Despite criticism and unease from some members of the older generation, the recording business, by hitching would-be music hits to television, has found a marketing tool that has brought it unprecedented profits. Much of MTV's success was based on adapting the musical programming to the musical tastes of the teenagers of the region receiving it. In 2010, MTV bowed to cultural change and scrapped the legend "Music Television" off its corporate logo and adopted the name Syfy. The change was a belated recognition of what had been obvious for years,

MTV had evolved into a reality channel that occasionally runs programs that have to do with music.[12]

The West, it has been said, won not only the Cold War but also the battle for the world's leisure time. Popular culture has been one of America's most lucrative exports, but observers say that the worst, instead of the best, of American culture seems to be flooding the world. Critic Michiko Kakutani commented, "Some of America's culture exports are so awful that you suspect that we are using the rest of the world as a vast toxic waste dump and charging for the privilege."[13] Chinese pop singers produce songs so similar to those in the West that you have to listen carefully to find that the lyrics are in Chinese. But the West has been greatly influenced by popular culture produced by the rest of the world.

## The Videocassette and DVD Revolution

The global dissemination of popular culture, especially movies and music videos, was first greatly facilitated by the rapid spread of videocassette recordings and videocassette recorders to play them on. (The VCRs have been largely replaced recently by digital video disks (DVDs), but the impact and effects are similar.) The terms "explosion" and "revolution" have been used to describe this phenomenon. In less than a decade, the VCR and videotape penetrated remote areas that the printing press and other information devices had not successfully reached after centuries. The spread has been to poor nations as well as the affluent West, but for different reasons. Depending on culture and political traditions, VCRs can have profound effects not only on viewers but also on broadcasting and other media. Widespread use of VCRs can challenge the usual system of government control of television by providing diversity of views and variety in entertainment. (The use of audiocassettes has done much the same thing to radio broadcasting.) VCRs circumvent the utilization of broadcast television for development and political control by bringing about a de facto decentralization of media. People in poor countries, including youth, now often have the freedom to view what they want to see – not what Big Brother, or even their parents, think is best for them. And apparently what they want are movies, pop music, and videos from the West. In Saudi Arabia, the only choice for viewers of over-the-air television has long been the puritanical, heavily censored and dull programming of government television. (For example, religious orthodoxy requires that a Saudi woman's face may not be shown on television.) As a result, VCRs and DVDs have proliferated by showing much of the forbidden fruit of Western movies, including X-rated videos, most of them smuggled into the country.

In India, many people, annoyed by the inadequacies of state-run broadcasting, have turned to private enterprise "alternative television" news on videocassettes. The producer of "Business Plus," a monthly tape on political and economic issues, said India has the only private-view news magazines in the world. The tapes, made in English and Hindi, rent for about 60 cents a day or sell for about $8. The audience, though small, is composed of middle-class, cosmopolitan Indians dissatisfied with the vacuity of official news and documentaries. The trend toward news-oriented videotapes began earlier with "Newstrack," a fast-paced monthly video of investigative reporting with a segmented format like that of "Sixty Minutes."

Throughout emerging nations, small shops renting or selling videotapes (and later DVDs) from the West have become commonplace. In the remote nation of Bhutan, on India's northern border, people had been watching videos on television sets for years before the nation had an over-the-air television service. To a Westerner, the VCR is an easy way to watch a movie or record a television program for later viewing, but to many millions in developing nations, VCRs and DVDs are a means of gaining alternative news sources or viewing sometimes prohibited Western entertainment shows – activities that authoritarian countries have largely failed to censor or control.

## English as the Media Language

Effective communication across national borders, regardless of other cultural and political differences, certainly requires that sender and receiver communicate in a mutually understandable language. More and more, that language is English, which is clearly the leading tongue of international communication today.

Among the "Big Ten" world languages, English usually ranks third, with about 300 million native speakers in twelve countries, after Mandarin Chinese, with about 885 million, and Spanish, with 332 million native speakers. English is ahead of Russian with its 282 million speakers, Arabic, with 220 million, and German, with 118 million. Furthermore, English is the most widely used geographically. Several hundred million have some knowledge of English, which has official or semi-official status in some sixty countries. What is more, this number includes most of the world's leaders. (If a leader wants to get on global television, he or she had better know English.) In all, there are about 4 billion English speakers including those using Globish (a modified form of English) in the world, and the number is rapidly increasing, according to Robert McCrum.

Unquestionably, English has become the global language of science and technology. More than 80% of all information stored in 100 million computers around the world is in English, and 80% of all scientific papers are published first in English. English is the language of the information age: Computers talk to each other in English. The Internet today reverberates with many languages, many of which can be translated into English by computer programs. English is the most-taught language in the world; it is not really replacing other languages but, rather, supplementing them.

In many developing nations, English is the language of education, providing an entrée to knowledge and information. But one unfortunate result is that many native English speakers, especially Americans, have much less incentive than, say, Israelis, Dutch, or Swedes to learn other peoples' languages. Currently, the US government has an acute shortage of Arabic speakers. Few Americans even learn to speak Spanish, although it is widely spoken here. The nation's Hispanics numbered 35.3 million in 2000, and to inform and entertain them were thirty daily newspapers, 265 weeklies, 352 magazines, and 594 radio stations – all in Spanish.

Globally, English has also become the leading media language for international communication. Most of the world's news is carried in English. Most news agencies carry some of their news in English. Six of the world's biggest broadcasters – the BBC, CBS, NBC, ABC, CNN, and CBC – reach a potential audience of about 300 million people through English-language broadcasting.

The imperialism of nineteenth-century Britain was a major reason that so many people from Singapore to India to Kenya to Nigeria to Bermuda converse today in English. Not unrelated is the phenomenon of numerous English-language daily newspapers flourishing today in countries where English is neither the official nor even the most widely used language. Beginning with the *Chronicle of Gibraltar* in 1801, English-language dailies, catering to expatriates, the foreign community, and local educated elites, have long survived, if not always flourished, in such diverse metropolises as Mexico City, Caracas, Paris, Jerusalem, Taipei, Rome, Athens, Cairo, Beirut,

Manila, Bangkok, Singapore, and Tokyo, as well as throughout India and Pakistan and the former British territories of Africa, such as Nigeria, Ghana, Sierra Leone, South Africa, Uganda, Kenya, Tanzania, Zimbabwe, and Zambia. In parts of polyglot Africa, English has almost evolved into another African language because of the role it plays in education, commerce, and mass communication.

Most of the "content" of mass culture that moves across national borders is in English. Jeremy Tunstall has said that English is the language best suited for "comic strips, headlines, riveting first sentences, photo captions, dubbing, subtitling, pop songs, billboards, disc-jockey banter, news flashes, and sung commercials."[14] One appeal of English as an international language is that it is easy to speak badly.

This thrust of English as a world media language has become self-generating, and any educated person of whatever nationality who wishes to participate in this shrinking and interdependent world finds it useful to know English. In fact, because English is now spoken as a second language by more people around the globe than by the British and the Americans combined, it must now be considered as belonging to the world, as indeed it does. For when two persons of differing linguistic backgrounds are able to converse in person or through computers, the chances are they will be using English.

## Notes

1. Dwight Garner, "English as a Juggernaut Conquers the World with Glee and OMG," *New York Times*, May 26, 2010, 8.
2. Joseph Plambeck, "Profits Up at Time Warner and News Corporation Helped by Ad Rebound," *New York Times*, August 5, 2010, B4.
3. Robert McCrum, *Globish* (New York: Norton, 2010), 246.
4. McCrum *Globish*, p. 26.
5. Deirdre Carmody, "Magazines Find Green Pastures Abroad," *The New York Times*, March 20, 1995, sec. C, 5.
6. Jeremy Peters, "The Economist Tends its Sophisticated Garden," *New York Times*, August 9, 2010, B1.
7. Richard W. Stevenson, "Ad Agency Mergers Changing the Business," *The New York Times*, May 13, 1986, 1.
8. Stevenson, "Ad Agency Mergers Changing the Business."
9. Alvin Toffler, *PowerShift* (New York: Bantam Books, 1990), 340.

10. Toffler, *PowerShift*, 341.

11. Ken Auletta, "Leviathan," *New Yorker*, October 29, 2001, 50.

12. Scott Collins, "MTV Broadening its Brand," *Wisconsin State Journal*, February 11, 2010, C5.

13. Michiko Kakutani, "Taking Out the Trash," *The New York Times Magazine*, June 8, 1997, 31.

14. Jeremy Tunstall, *The Media Are American: Anglo-American Media in the World* (London: Constable, 1977), 128.

# 7

# China: New Media In An Old Political World

*China wants only "healthy, civilized news and information beneficial to the nation."*
                                                    – Ministry of Information official

*He's totally crazy he kept asking questions again and again.*
    – Provincial official on questions from artist and citizen journalist
                              Ai Weiwei about the Sichuan earthquake.

*China is changing; it is no democracy but it's no longer a totalitarian state.*
    – Nicholas Kristof, *New York Times* China Correspondent

China is changing, reaching out to the world to show a "harmonious society" with peaceful intentions. In mid-2010 Xinhua (New China), the national news agency, the world's largest by some measures and the official voice of the Communist Party, launched CNC World, its twenty-four-hour English-language television channel. China Central Television (CCTV) is also expanding overseas with broadcasts in English, Spanish, French, Russian, Arabic and Japanese. "Our principle is to be real, to be objective, to be accurate and transparent," said Zhang Changming, CCTV deputy president in launching the Arabic channel. "CCTV will present the world with the real China."[1] At the same time China is presenting its culture through more than 300 Confucius centers in eighty countries. The centers, primarily to showcase Chinese culture and promote Chinese language learning, are often attached to universities in the United States and

*The World News Prism: Challenges of Digital Communication*, Eighth Edition.
William A. Hachten and James F. Scotton.
© 2012 John Wiley & Sons, Ltd. Published 2012 by John Wiley & Sons, Ltd.

elsewhere.[2] Inside China there is also a new English version of the official *Global Times*, which at times seems willing to present viewpoints that differ from government policy. And *China Daily*, the English-language sister paper to the government's flagship newspaper, *People's Daily*, has had an expensive makeover to attract a wider audience at home and perhaps abroad in print and on the Internet.

This is the new media face of China, carefully crafted and developed at enormous cost to show a new face to the world. But at the same time it is difficult to ignore the old face that keeps appearing whenever the Chinese authorities are rattled by events within or outside the country. When protesters in Egypt flocked into Cairo's largest public square in January 2011, the word "Egypt" disappeared from Sina.com, one of the most popular Chinese web sites. Echoes of China's 1989 student uprising in Beijing's huge Tiananmen Square were no doubt felt in that city's corridors of power. Two months later when Chinese dissidents tried to mobilize "strolling protests" of citizens along Nanjing Lu, Shanghai's main shopping street, foreign journalists who tried to find out what was going on were detained and harassed.

Almost all the media in China – Xinhua, CCTV, some 2,100 newspapers, 9,000 periodicals, nearly 400 television stations, 200 radio stations and every book publisher – are owned by the government in China. The exceptions are some Internet search engines which are privately owned but kept under close government surveillance.

While trying to move into the international media world to compete with the Associated Press, CNN, and the BBC, the Chinese regime has made it clear that it is not loosening its grip on China's media, including Internet sites and even personal blogs. All media, even foreign media entering China, are subject to censorship at any time.

At the same time they have reached out to foreign audiences, Chinese authorities have not hesitated to crack down on dissent and curb any medium or journalist that could threaten their rule. A journalist working for a Chinese radio service received a life sentence for translating a call for protests by Uyghurs in northwest China where there was ethnic rioting in 2009. One of China's best-known dissidents, Liu Xiaobo, was given a long prison term in December 2009 on the vague charge of "incitement to subvert state power." Ai Weiwei, an internationally famous artist and also a citizen journalist, was barred from leaving the country and his Shanghai studio was demolished by authorities in January 2011. Hu Shuli, an internationally famous magazine editor, was forced in 2009 to leave *Caijing*, which had irritated business and political leaders for years with exposés of corruption and incompetence. Google gave up its mainland China operation in 2010, rejecting Chinese censorship rules. Media mogul Rupert Murdoch, who sold his last assets in China in 2010 after years of negotiating with Beijing, had noted earlier that the Chinese government was "quite paranoid about what gets through."[3] And even when President Barack Obama's 2009 inaugural address mentioned communism and fascism in the same sentence, CCTV cut him off. Yet, Obama's entire address showed up the next day on Xinhua's web site and in the *People's Daily*, the official Communist Party newspaper. Such a recent history does not suggest that China's international media ventures will escape censorship. Reporters Without Borders consistently ranks China near the bottom in its world survey of press freedom. Yan Lieshan, a columnist for China's *Southern Weekend*, which has battled censors for years to report corruption and incompetence, warned that any sign that international reports by Xinhua or other Chinese media are censored, will doom what he calls "the great external propaganda campaign."[4]

In the twenty-first century China continues to be a nation that wants the benefits of an open, capitalist economy for its 1.3 billion people, while still tightly controlling its media. For the past thirty years, the Chinese leadership – nominally still Communist but in fact strongly committed to a capitalist economy that it calls "market socialism" – has been unsure about how to carry this off. After a visit to China, one American editor asked, "Can China run a free market economy without a free market in ideas?"[5] Many suggest it is impossible to do so. It is, some insist, just a matter of time before the Chinese people add democracy to the list of modern life styles imported from the West.

The Chinese government officially accepts press freedom, but the constitution includes a list of situations in which government can restrict this freedom. The Chinese call this "a pragmatic approach" to freedom of the press that includes strong opposition to the notion of press "freedom to spread lies and rumors."[6] This "pragmatic approach" to press freedom has meant that China's leaders have alternately encouraged its media to be independent – at least economically independent – but then cracked down when that independence seemed to threaten those in control.

The confusion showed when two respected news organizations presented conflicting reports on China's media in the same week. The BBC reported "sweeping changes across the media industry," including "hard-hitting investigations" of corruption.[7] That same week, *The Economist* reported on

"China's Media: Back on the Leash."[8] Both reports agreed on the cause of the apparent contradiction. The Chinese government has transformed almost all the nation's subsidized media from being a huge financial drain into a profit-making global industry. This means advertising, which implies popular content that attracts lots of readers, listeners, and viewers. But Chinese Communist officials do not want any content, popular or not, domestic or foreign, that could threaten their grip on power. Foreign media conglomerates can, for example, bring sports or entertainment programs into China via satellite and even run fashion magazines. But China forced media mogul Rupert Murdoch's STAR-TV to drop all BBC news reports when they criticized China's human rights record. This move came after Murdoch angered Beijing by predicting that satellite television would put totalitarian regimes out of business. In August 2005, the Chinese government denied approval for that channel, for a Viacom plan to co-produce children's programs with a Chinese company, and for a Disney channel that was to follow the opening of Disney's theme park in Hong Kong.

Western media conglomerates try hard to satisfy Chinese authorities. This is a major reason the Chinese think it is safe to allow some foreign television channels in the country, or at least some parts of the country. When AOL-Time Warner got permission to start a Mandarin-language channel in a limited area of southern China, it agreed to carry CCTV's English-language channel on its cable systems in New York, Los Angeles, and Houston. For China, AOL chose to pick up a Singapore TV channel. Its motto was: "No sex, no violence, no news."[9]

## Television

The allure of Hong Kong forced China to let Western television into its southeast, mainly into booming Guangdong province, just next to the former British colony. Hong Kong's Western values, including democracy and independent media, are apparent on Hong Kong television. Large numbers of people in southeast China were watching Western-style Hong Kong television programs, since their antennas and illegal satellite dishes could easily pick them up. By 2005, China authorized six foreign companies to beam twenty-four-hour channels to southeast China. Government officials hoped these television channels would lure Chinese viewers from Hong Kong television, while the channel owners would protect their licenses by carefully avoiding any anti-government programs.

Television reaches 95% of the people in China with Central China Television's programs from Beijing dominating. In recent years, programs from provincial and large city stations have provided serious competition. Entertainment dominates with news taking up about 12% of air time. That news is carefully controlled by the Chinese government. All stations, for example, must carry Xiwen Lianbo, CCTV's 7 p.m. thirty-minute newscast. This provides a daily Chinese view of world events.

CCTV is burdened by the huge bureaucracy that surrounds it. In 2009 a fire at CCTV's almost completed new headquarters building lit up Beijing's night skies, but the Ministry of Information ordered no coverage until it readied a report. Internet bloggers, who spread the news quickly, joked that CCTV employees looking out their office windows could see the biggest story of the year but could not cover it. Like audiences everywhere, Chinese television viewers will abandon channels that block important news. When New York's World Trade Center was destroyed by suicide bombers in 2001, CCTV kept the tragedy off China's television channels for nearly an hour, while awaiting the Ministry of Information's guidance. But the news was out via the Internet, telephone, and other channels. People near Hong Kong quickly switched to its Phoenix channel. In Shanghai and other cities, Chinese students and others pooled their money to rent rooms at tourist hotels where they could get international channels such as the BBC and CNN. By the time CCTV got on the air with a muted report it had lost much of its audience. Anthony Fung, who has written extensively about China's media, said Phoenix TV is still so far ahead of CCTV in news that even Chinese government officials consider it an important information source.[10]

Increasingly, Chinese citizens are getting access to foreign television programs. Some believe that television has become the main source of information from outside China. One survey found Chinese adolescents were watching, on average, two American movies or television programs a week. Foreign films and television programs screened by the censors are available on many channels, dubbed in Chinese or with Chinese sub-titles. But most Chinese get their foreign movies from street vendors and small shops selling pirated copies. They come with a choice of Chinese-language tracks, such as Mandarin or Cantonese. US industry experts estimate that 85% of DVDs, videotapes, and CDs sold in China are pirated copies that the censor never gets to review. This influx of foreign ideas has drastically reduced the power of China's rulers to isolate and dominate society. Television has, in fact, forced changes in China's economic and political policies. As one media executive said, "Even if the Chinese tried to keep foreign cultural icons out, piracy would make them available."[11]

## Dating, Talent, and Contest Shows

Despite all the media controls, even some television shows produced in China can upset government officials. In 2010 authorities ordered the end to live dating shows after a female contestant on "If You Are the One" said the main quality of a husband for Chinese women was how rich he was. In summer 2005, a wildly popular singing contest attracted record audiences and a rebuke from *China Daily*, the official government newspaper. *Super Girl*, a Chinese version of *American Idol*, had more than 400 million viewers for its finale. Most viewers, no doubt, just saw this as television entertainment, but some people said the show made a political statement as well, because of how the winner, a singer from rural Hunan province, was chosen. The winner, Lu Yuchin, was popularly elected by 3.5 million cell phone voters. In a nation where most public meetings are banned, fans formed clubs to collect votes for their favorites. The contest originated with a provincial television station in rural Hunan, far from the watchful eyes of the Ministry of Information, and was sponsored by a local dairy – thus the official name of the show: *The Mongolian Cow Sour Yoghurt Super Girl Contest*. CCTV was startled by the huge numbers of viewers that the program drew, an audience larger than CCTV gets even for its Chinese New Year extravaganzas. It said the show had "debased Chinese culture." *China Daily* commented: "How come an imitation of a democratic system ends up selecting the singer who has the least ability to carry a tune?" Some thought Beijing was upset because the program introduced a huge Chinese audience to the idea of an election with numerous competing candidates. Others said CCTV was upset because the show cut into its own advertising revenues. Either way, *Super Girl* could be a threat to China's official mass media. CCTV's ratings share has been falling as provincial broadcasters have grown with dating, talent, and contest shows.

## China's "Oprah Winfrey"

Another very popular television program is *A Date with Chen Luyu*, a Chinese Oprah Winfrey. All sorts of celebrities and ordinary people share her sofa and talk about their lives on the Phoenix satellite channel, the first foreign-funded station authorized to reach mainland audiences. Chen Luyu insists that her program: "is not about politics. My viewers don't want to listen to things like that, so I don't do shows like that."[12] Her program is, however, a window on what concerns Chinese citizens. Inevitably, the talk includes comments on such topics as crime, corruption, and even AIDS, formerly taboo subjects. Chinese officials and perhaps the hostess herself want to avoid controversial topics. But she and even Chinese officials know that if all controversial topics are kept off the air, programs will soon lose their audiences.

## Newspapers

Despite their desire for tight media control, China's rulers want to create at least the appearance of transparency and more openness to the public and the media. In 2005, the State Information Office told Communist Party officials to start holding news conferences. This is a big change. In China, journalists can be severely criticized for seeking even routine information from Party officials. A Hong Kong reporter who asked when the Premier would hold a planned news conference was told it was "secret information." And almost anything can be declared a state secret in China. When scores of children died from poisoning at a school near Nanjing in 2002, Chinese officials ordered the death toll be kept secret. Instead, they insisted that the media report on the arrest of the suspect and official efforts to prevent a similar tragedy in the future. Official media followed the rules, but foreign journalists traveled to Nanjing with and without permission to get the facts. Only in September 2005 did China announce that the death toll, at least in natural disasters, would no longer be considered a "state secret." The announcement was made by the National Administration for State Secrets, a government agency that oversees the vast amount of information considered secret, at a news conference. No foreign journalists were invited to the conference.[13]

Even though the print media are directly owned by the government, controlling Chinese journalists has not always been easy. There are probably 100,000 people in China who say they are "journalists" and the number is growing. In 2003, one Chinese journalism professor found more than 300 schools in China claiming to have a journalism program although, as in many countries, most of the graduates will not end up as journalists.

The top requirement for Chinese journalists, according to the Communist Party's *Handbook for Journalists*, is "faithfully propagating and carrying
out the Party's principles and policies." But a major survey found many
journalism students in China still thought they could fill the classic
"watchdog" role and report government corruption.[14] And this role is
actually recognized in the Chinese media system. Back in 1986, Communist
Party Secretary Hu Yaobang told editors that they should include stories on
problems in China, but 80% of their articles should focus on China's
achievements.[15] In 2004, the Communist Party listed the press as one of the
eight major means for overseeing party and government officials. Despite
such official pronouncements, however, being a "watchdog" journalist in
China can be very risky.

## "The Best Journalist in China"

An example is Zhao Yan, who identified himself as "the best" journalist in
China.[16] That may explain why he was whisked off to prison from a
Shanghai Pizza Hut in September 2004 and charged with leaking state
secrets. Zhao was arrested shortly after he turned on his cell phone, a lapse
that he thinks led State Security police to him. Zhao worked for a decade for
*China Reform*, a newspaper with a reputation for exposing official corruption. While there, Zhao called himself "an anticorruption warrior." But
government officials began pressuring *China Reform* to tone down its
exposés and its chief editorial writer was detained by the police. Zhao
decided it was time to move on and took a job with the Beijing bureau of the
*New York Times*. Zhao's arrest may have been caused by a single sentence in a
*Times* story that suggested two top Party officials were having a dispute over
promoting a general. Suggestions of any disagreements within the Chinese
leadership always bring strong reaction from officials. Editors are routinely
warned before Communist Party meetings that they are not to speculate on
who might end up in leadership positions. China's leaders believe they can
handle the social and economic strains that are testing them, as long as there
is no sign of disunity.

Working for a foreign publication can be dangerous for any Chinese
journalist. The government has sometimes charged these journalists with
being spies. Ching Cheong, a reporter for Singapore's *Straits Times*, was
charged with spying for Taiwan in August 2005. He apparently obtained
documents showing discord among the Chinese leadership over Tiananmen

Square. Two decades later, Chinese officials remain very sensitive to any reference to this 1989 student protest that the Chinese military brutally suppressed. Another journalist, Shi Tao, was sentenced to ten years in prison for emailing a dissident in the United States that his paper, the *Hunan Business News*, could not report on any demonstrations on the anniversary of the Tiananmen Square student protests. Chinese censors spotted Shi's message when someone posted it on a web site.

While continuing to label as much information as possible "secret," the government is also cracking down on journalists who want to find information on their own. Chinese journalists have found that their newspapers were much more willing to print exposés if their stories exposed distant corruption. But in 2005 the Chinese government officially banned all "yidi baodao," or "reports from nonlocal places." Now, Chinese journalists have to stick close to home.

Foreign journalists in China have faced restrictions on their own travel, but have regularly evaded them. The *New York Times*, London's *The Guardian*, and other foreign publications reported regularly from all over China. Some of their stories came from tips from Chinese journalists who were not allowed to report the story. The *South China Morning Post*, published in Hong Kong, frequently was able to break stories that Chinese papers were forbidden to report, because their reporters could travel to cities and towns all over China. The *Oriental Daily News* of Hong Kong was a regular source of information about the mainland because of its contacts and it frequently reported news that was blacked out by mainland media. *Apple Daily*, a popular, pro-democracy Chinese-language tabloid in Hong Kong, that carried lots of news from mainland China, said its reporters were being denied visas for China because of its anti-corruption articles. It also said advertisers reported they were under pressure to withhold advertising.

## Exposing Corruption

Stories exposing corruption can be published even in China if editors are careful in choosing the right targets and the right time. In 2009 *Outlook* magazine detailed secret Beijing detention centers that provincial officials used to prevent citizens from lodging complaints with the central government. Xinhua spread the story across the nation, a clear sign that Beijing officials supported the exposé. Provincial papers have published their own exposés and soon found that these stories boosted readership. When the corruption campaigns threaten to get out of control, Party leaders tell the editors to cut back on the exposés. This pattern of government supporting anti-corruption exposés and then shutting them down has continued for decades. In 2003, for example, the *Southern Metropolitan Daily* reported the death in police custody of a graphic designer arrested because he lacked the proper identification. It became a national story and within two months the Chinese government replaced regulations that allowed police to make such arrests. Soon after this, however, three senior editors of *Southern Metropolitan Daily* were arrested. The charge was embezzlement, but many journalists believed the editors were being punished for pushing their criticism too far.

## Magazines

Of the more than 9,000 magazines only about 25% are profitable. The rest are Party publications, mostly journals with revenue coming from those government offices that believe they must subscribe to them. The most profitable are "story magazines" for migrant workers. They are cheap, usually pocket size, and are full of short, easy to read human interest articles. *Bosom Friend* specializes in love stories to attract the millions of lonely women who moved to the cities in search of jobs. It also has its tragedies, such as the story headed: "Boss and His Secretary: A Game Ends in Blood."[17] *Reader* claims its circulation of 10 million tops any magazine in China. It is similar to the American *Reader's Digest* with family stories and moral lessons.

The biggest money makers are fashion magazines with advertisers paying high rates to reach their affluent readers. There are Chinese editions *of Elle, Cosmopolitan, Harper's Bazaar, Esquire, Men's Health* and the British *HFM*. Most are jointly owned with foreign publishers but content is left to European and American editors. Digital magazines are growing fast. Fashion magazines are most popular online and half the online readers do not buy the printed copy.[18]

Most of China's magazines stick with safe topics such as sports, fashion, entertainment, and accounting but some have found that they are well placed to play the role of government critic with relative safety. *Caijing*, a business magazine published in Beijing, regularly exposed government as well as private corruption. While Hu Shuli was editor there were articles on stock market manipulation, corruption at government-owned banks, and government attempts to cover up the 2003 outbreak of SARS (Severe Acute Respiratory Syndrome). *Caijing* Editor Hu actually got her start writing for the Communist Party's *Workers' Daily*. Even there, she wrote and got published stories about corrupt local officials. She joined journalists who demonstrated to support the 1989 student protests in Tiananmen Square, but found her paper would not publish anything on them. Shortly after, she moved to the *China Business Times* and then to *Caijing*. As editor of *Caijing*, Hu exposed so many corrupt private and government officials that a magazine profile called her "the most dangerous woman in China."[19] *Caijing* first reached a broad national audience with an exposé of backroom dealings by some of China's leading fund managers in 2000. Another major story involved accounting fraud at a blue-chip Chinese company. The mainstream media would not touch the story even though an insider provided all the information necessary to verify the fraud. *Caijing* broke the story along with *Southern Weekend*, a muckraking newspaper that is read all over China. Only when the company came forth with a formal announcement of an internal investigation did the mainstream media run the story.

In China, even during times of relative media freedom, only a handful of media outlets will venture to report on corruption or other sensitive matters even within government limits. The rest of the media follow after explicit government approval. Because of *Caijing*'s reporting, it has became required reading in the Chinese business community. But it is not just reporting on sensitive business stories that earned *Caijing* its reputation as one of the most important publications in China. When the World Health Organization reported in March 2003 that the SARS epidemic had crossed from Hong Kong to the mainland, *Caijing* leaped on the story as a major threat to business and people in China. Ignoring government denials, *Caijing* produced four special weekly issues on SARS. For these and other stories, the World Press Review in 2003 named Hu International Editor of the Year. This international recognition and *Caijing*'s owner, Beijing's Stock Exchange, may have shielded Hu from government crackdowns. Also, from her early years on the more directly government-controlled *Workers' Daily*, she knew the limits on journalism in China. "I know how to measure the boundary lines," she said. "We go up to the line and we might even push it. But we never cross it."[20] But sometimes that line was difficult even for Editor Hu to see. In June 2002, *Caijing* lost a defamation suit to a company for reporting alleged financial irregularities. The head of the company was the niece of former President Deng Xiaoping.

"*Caijing* is about as good as it gets in China," said Orville Schell, Dean of the Graduate School of Journalism at the University of California at Berkeley. "And, they've picked the perfect niche – business – which gives them the maximum latitude to do investigative work in China."[21] But some see even *Caijing* becoming more cautious. After all, although owned by the Beijing Stock Exchange, it is still a government publication. Some staff members have been called in for "self-criticism." When Hu was forced out as editor, many staff members left with her. The future of *Caijing* is clearly in doubt. Meanwhile, Hu is developing another magazine that will undoubtedly cause problems for some Chinese authorities.

## A Muckraker in the South

Any magazine or other media located in Beijing are going to be closely watched by the state censors. Being distant from Beijing does give editors some advantages. *Southern Weekend*, 2,000 miles to the south in booming Guangdong province, has a national reputation for aggressive reporting and exposing government corruption. *Southern Weekend* says it has to be aggressive to compete with the nearby Hong Kong media. Time and again, it has tested the limits of reporting and thus gained a national audience. You can find *Southern Weekend* on newsstands all over China. A news vendor in Lanzhou, more than 2,000 miles away in northwest China, said he could sell more copies of *Southern Weekend* if he could get them from the state news agency.[22] *Southern Weekend* has made a few missteps. In 2002, the paper was ordered to pull a story about alleged corruption at Project Hope, a charity run by the Communist Youth League. Officials did not deny there was corruption, but feared that the exposé would dry up contributions for some important charities.

Another publication known for aggressive reporting on farm protests is *Freezing Point*, a supplement to the widely read *China Youth Daily*. The government shut down *Freezing Point* early in 2006. There were so many protests, however, that *Freezing Point* was allowed to start publishing again, but Chinese officials refused to reinstate *Freezing Point*'s nationally known editor, Li Datong. Li was already in trouble because six months earlier he had posted a letter on the publication's web site criticizing the Propaganda Department for planning to dock reporters' salaries if they strayed from the Communist Party's line. Joseph Kahn, *New York Times* Bureau Chief in

Beijing, said strong editors like Li will still keep pushing the limits in China and may eventually win the battle for more press freedom.

Even if journalists are unable to report stories in their own publication, the news often gets out anyway. When a flood in central China killed eighty miners, local officials tried to cover it up with bribes and threats. Local media were afraid to report it. Journalists who covered the story, however, quickly leaked the information to distant publications and Internet web sites. The major Communist Party publications recognize that they will lose their readers if they do not do some hard reporting of their own. After the mine disaster news got out to the public, the *People's Daily* jumped in with a series of articles. But the Xinhua news agency ignored the story.

All the Chinese media ignore serious public protests, even when they turn violent and people are killed. The Chinese media were silent about a violent demonstration in December 2005, against construction of a power plant, which left twenty or more people dead. Four days later, Xinhua released a story reporting three deaths after villagers in the southern town "assaulted the police."[23]

## China's Tabloid Press

Some Chinese newspapers still get subsidies. These include the Party's flagship papers, *People's Daily* in Chinese and *China Daily* in English, both published in Beijing and circulated nationwide. Nearly 400 other Party newspapers are published by provincial and local governments, some of them no doubt requiring subsidies in various forms such as official advertisements. Some 80% of the newspaper market is held by the urban evening tabloids. The Communist Party or the local government still owns the papers, but editors can publish almost anything they think will attract readers. The editors quickly adopted the same content that Western tabloids use to attract city readers: crime, sex, entertainment, features, color, short but graphic articles, and even some stories about corruption. Since most sales are by street vendors, editors provide such sensational headlines as "He Insulted Her; She Axed Him."

The tabloids are generally evening papers, while the morning papers remain tightly government controlled and contain official reports that interest few readers. As a result, the evening tabloids surged ahead of the morning papers in circulation and advertising revenue. Even the Party's flagship *People's Daily* lost 75% of its circulation in the 1990s. Trying to fight back, some Party morning papers mix official news with more of what the readers seem to want. In Shanghai the *Jiefang Daily* put the Party messages in a front section then added popular content, including society columns. The *Shanghai Daily* switched to a tabloid size and popular content and began making a profit. Tabloid editors are constantly frustrated with Xinhua with its constant emphasis on "good news" that must show a "harmonious China."[24] Some set up their own exchange networks to get news about crime, violence, and tragedy that they believe their readers want but Xinhua won't provide. Xinhua has its own dilemma. Since the government provides the subsidies that it lives on, the Party publications and not the tabloids have to be its priority. To survive, Xinhua must have "a mixture of party logic and market logic."[25]

Some journalists despair that the tabloids spell the death of "serious" journalism in China and suggest editors will not risk their economic success by challenging any but the most corrupt local officials. This is a "new opium for the masses," say some critics, who also charge that the low paid tabloid journalists take bribes or charge fees to get stories into their newspapers. In 2009 ten journalists and forty-eight officials were charged with taking bribes to cover up a mine disaster.

The Party finds it increasingly difficult to dictate to the editors of the self-supporting publications. One Shanghai newspaper editor said he never reads Ministry of Information material. Still, there are limits on all these editors, who get reminded at times that they are running government-owned publications. In 2003, the top page one story in one issue of the English-language *Shanghai Daily* was the Academy Awards from Hollywood, while it ignored a Communist Party declaration that *China Daily* headlined. Party leaders reportedly called from Beijing and the Party report was in the next day's paper – but not on page one.

## A New Cultural Appeal

Perhaps the most dramatic example of a Chinese publication shifting from the government subsidy model to going after readers on its own is *China Culture Gazette*. It changed from a boring and money-losing Ministry of Culture magazine to a hot-selling industry leader, *Culture Weekend*. The secret was celebrity interviews and nudes, most of them Westerners. *Culture Weekend* even changed color from red to yellow. A "yellow" publication or film in China is X-rated. The Ministry was furious, but the editor pointed out that the huge sales were the only thing that prevented the magazine from closing since the government had chopped its subsidy. *Culture Weekend* kept publishing and other publications started providing a diet of girls in bikinis, movie stars, and pop singers. Again, editor Zhang Zuomin knew the limits: "I will not run anything antiparty in my paper," he said, "and I will not run pornography."[26]

## Radio

The rapid rise in car ownership and the increased hours spent in commuting has boosted radio listening in China's cities. The Beijing Traffic program revenue jumped 50 times in 10 years. Radio reaches 95% or more of the Chinese people. Much of it is the usual mix of music, weather, official news, and various special programs for farmers, women, children, and other groups. Some radio stations have their own staff for reporting local news but most rely heavily on Xinhua.

Competing with the tabloid press for the audience in China's cities is another Western import, talk radio. Talk radio is one of the few channels available to most Chinese for giving their opinions in public. It also sets up a different relationship between the media and the audience, since call-in listeners can often pick the topic and set the tone and direction of the discussion.

These programs generally focus on local issues (complaints about pot-holes, broken street lights, etc.), social issues (improper behavior on sub-ways and buses), and the inevitable personal problems (inattentive husbands and unfaithful wives). Competition from Hong Kong got talk radio started in mainland China. Hong Kong radio talk shows were attracting large audiences in southeast China, so in 1986 the government set up a mainland station to compete for listeners. The Chinese call-in programs proved hugely popular and soon won back the audience from the Hong Kong stations, winning official praise for "breaking the domination of foreign radio." Other talk radio stations were soon on the air in China's major cities and one other effect was soon clear. The new talk radio stations attracted far more listeners than the traditional stations that were filled with official propaganda and dreary programs. And talk radio hosts soon learned that some provocative dialogue on a sensitive issue could push up listen-ership in hurry. These hosts soon became local celebrities and advertisers clamored to buy time on their programs.

Programs to deal with special problems soon developed. Some hosts regularly helped dissatisfied customers get refunds from merchants, others collected complaints about the health system. Public officials, including city mayors, were invited on to answer citizen complaints. Late-night programs brought on physicians, psychologists, and other specialists to deal with personal problems of callers. Among the most popular programs was *Secret Whispers*, a late night show on Shanghai East Radio. The program tried to answer callers' questions about sex, a topic virtually ignored in both families and schools in China. A survey of callers found that, in Shanghai at least, sex and money were the most popular topics. One Shanghai talk show reportedly attracted 400 calls a minute. Inevitably, some callers want to talk about sensitive topics, such as government corruption or the gap between rich and poor in China. Since most shows are live, hosts have to be ready to redirect the discussion but still not discourage other callers. And some topics are just not open for discussion, at least not on China's radio stations: a Beijing host quickly cut off callers who wanted to talk about legalizing prostitution and easing the policy of one couple, one child. Program hosts fend off critics by arguing that their programs are educational and also frequently bring on guests who support official policies. The call-in radio programs suggest a different level of public participation in public issues in China. They are channels for public debate and discussion that are essentially beyond government control.

## New Threats: The Internet and Cell Phones

Perhaps even bigger threats to China's rulers are the Internet and cell phones. China has more than 400 million Internet users and more than 350 million cell phone users. They represent, in fact, an instant communication network. Internet cafés with rows of computers are found in China's cities. The government reportedly has 50,000 people constantly monitoring web sites for any political threat. Young people, especially in China's cities, use their mobile phones for both email and text messaging. Government tries to monitor messages that go to large groups, but the speed of cell phone messaging makes it very difficult. In April 2005, huge crowds gathered for anti-Japanese demonstrations, despite government efforts to mute the protests. The Chinese authorities have been aggressive in their efforts to block and counter web sites they consider unfriendly. They are especially on guard against the cult movement Falun Gong In March 2002, Fulan Gong supporters hacked into a city cable network in Changchun, the birthplace of the movement, and broadcast an hour of Fulan Gong material and attacks on the Chinese government to an estimated 300,000 homes. China also pressured Internet providers, including Yahoo and Google, to identify the sources of any messages officials consider subversive and to block unwelcome sites or information. A Google search outside China for photos of Tiananmen Square, for example, produced images of the 1989 student uprising, but a Google search within China showed tourists taking photographs.

Most Chinese on the Internet are just looking for entertainment and chatting with friends. Internet servers in China are privately owned and are expected to look out for subversive activity. Baidu.com has the largest market share and has grown since Google left China in July 2010. It is trying to attract more young users via Baidu Post Bar, an online community it calls the "water cooler" of the Internet. Students doing research papers routinely "Baidu it" to find the information they want. Baidu's video sharing site has been censored by Chinese authorities for excessive sexual content and has a daily poll to find the ten most beautiful women in China.

Other Internet search engines, all privately owned, are Alibaba, 40% owned by Yahoo and specializing in e-commerce; TenCent QQ, the most popular chatting tool for young people; Sina, the leading news site although all its news comes from Xinhua or other official sources; Sohu, news and sports and NetEase, an online games site. Also online are YouKou (like YouTube), Foufou (Twitter) and YuPoo (Flickr). YouKou and Tudou have some of the most popular US television shows on just hours after they are broadcast. The Chinese government is setting up its own search engine that will compete with the privately-owned companies.

Despite their efforts, Chinese authorities find it impossible to monitor all web sites. A BBC journalist in Beijing found the BBC Chinese Service and the main BBC web site blocked. But when he switched to other international news web sites, he quickly got access. An American journalist also found that a carefully worded message can get by the censor. He posted a message calling for multiparty elections. The censor erased it within ten minutes. But then the journalist changed the tone to suggest that China's Communist leaders might allow multiparty elections "in 20 years." The censor either missed this message or let it pass. In fact, there are so many Internet messages to monitor that the censors reportedly only delete messages that seem to represent a serious threat. One indication of the problem is that even though China tries to suppress evidence of homosexuality in the country, one study reported 250 gay-themed web sites in China.

But even though Chinese authorities are constantly alert to keep the Internet under control, they will encourage Internet use when it serves their purposes. The Internet has, for example, become an accepted channel for dissent, because it is much preferable to more threatening public demonstrations. In 2000, the government ordered all government agencies to set up web sites to receive complaints. The Ministry of Foreign Affairs web site got 1.2 million complaints in three years, mostly saying that China was not acting strongly enough in world affairs. After many years of Western dominance, Chinese will rally to support the government against any perceived foreign threat. Bringing Hong Kong back into China, the crackdown in Tibet and the claim that Taiwan is part of China are all supported by the vast majority of Chinese. As C. C. Lee, a long-time China scholar, has pointed out, Party leaders will use the media to rally Chinese nationalism against any challenge to China's sovereignty or international status.[27]

"Policy-makers can't make decisions based on public opinion, but they can't ignore it either," said Li Minggang, Ministry of Foreign Affairs web site director.[28] And even non-government web sites can have a place under China's media policy at times. When China's Railway Ministry let a Japanese company bid to build a new Beijing–Shanghai express train, a Patriots' Alliance web site sprang up to protest dealing with China's former enemy. Within ten days, its online petition had 87,320 protesting signatures, reflecting anti-Japanese feelings that remain strong more than sixty years after the end of Japan's World War II occupation. The Chinese government quickly rejected the Japanese proposal. But the government's attitude changed when the Patriots' online rhetoric turned to Taiwan. Chinese officials feared that the Patriots' anti-Taiwan messages would help the most anti-Communist candidates in the upcoming election on that still-defiant island that China hopes to integrate peacefully with the mainland just as it did Hong Kong. Meanwhile, the Patriots' Alliance web site, attracting 80,000 visitors a day by 2004, branched out and even received a local government commendation for leading a clothing drive for the poor. Web site owner Lu Yunfei believed he deserved government support: "We're doing this for the public good," he said, "so how could the government oppose it?"[29]

## New Internet Controls

Overall though, Chinese authorities want to control the Internet just as they control all other media in China. They have had the "Great Firewall" (the Kung Fu Net to Chinese bloggers) in place for years to block unwanted Internet messages. In 2009 authorities proposed adding a "Green Wall" by requiring all new computers to be equipped with filtering software. This censorship plan was dropped only after massive resistance by Internet users. Twitter is particularly annoying to the censors because it is virtually impossible to monitor the millions of short messages much less trace their origin. And it is Twitter that is increasingly being used to organize online protests as in the 2009 campaign that forced the government to release a waitress who had fatally stabbed a Party official as she resisted his advances. Microblogs, which are very difficult to censor or even monitor because the message is sent in fragments, are another threat to government control of the Internet. Leading Chinese microblogger Deng Fei of *Phoenix Weekly* exposed contaminated blood supplies in Henan Province. Reporters used microblogs to send the story of Chinese citizens blocked at the Beijing airport when they tried to present a petition to the government.[30]

In 2005, the government did decree that newspaper and magazine web sites must "give priority" to news and commentary from official sources. The government ordered search engines Sohu and Sina, which had been posting private criticisms of government in their chat rooms, to block such comments. "The foremost responsibility of news sites on the Internet," the regulations stated, "is to serve the people, serve socialism, guide public opinion in the right direction, and uphold the interests of the country and the public good."[31] Foreign Internet providers were ordered to reveal the identities of users and popular student bulletin boards were told to block access by off-campus computers. Despite student protests, bloggers were now required to register their real names. The new rules were seen as helping officials track down the authors of anti-government statements.

Students, of course, are quick to seek and often find ways to outwit the Internet censors. In 2005, China banned Wikipedia, the online encyclopedia that users can edit. But a Chinese hacker in North Carolina, came up with a program called Freegate that links computers inside China with servers in the United States. At least temporarily, this made Wikipedia available via Chinese computers. Students know how to use proxy servers to find information on almost everything including the Tiananmen Square demonstrations but most are after entertainment. They use "Verycd," also known as the "Electric Donkey," to reach blocked movies.

But the Chinese authorities keep trying to limit Internet access, and have even tried some "Internet cops," Jingjing and Chacha. These are animated icons used in the southern city of Shenzhen, a hotbed of unauthorized Internet activity just across from Hong Kong. Xu Qian, one of the 100 staff of Shenzhen's Internet Surveillance Center, says of Jingjing, "He is just like a policeman, interactively moving along with you. Wherever you go, he is watching you."[32]

## The Bloggers

Government officials have become increasingly annoyed with bloggers. They include individuals who have no connection to traditional media and some suddenly appear and disappear before authorities can find out who they are. Li Xinde traveled around the country with a digital camera and a laptop computer looking into reports of corruption. He then posted his stories on his web site and left town before local authorities could find him. There are millions of bloggers in China and at one time 2 million had accounts with Bokee (Chinese for "blog). By mid-2005, Bokee had a staff of 200 with advertisers including IBM. Bokee ran into financial problems in 2008 and founder Fang Xingdong brought it back as an e-commerce site. A very popular blogger is "Aggressive Little Snake" whose "The Dog Newspaper" web site won a German prize for best blog. Chinese officials strongly discourage public discussions of human rights so "The Dog Newspaper" campaigns for the rights of canines.

## Sex and Politics

One of the attractions of Bokee was a lurid sex diary posted by its own marketing director, Mu Zimel. It attracted millions until it was banned by the government. Another top Internet attraction was sex columnist Li Li on Sina.com. Her "Ashes of Love" book had huge preorders until the government banned it along with her blog.

Chinese officials have always tried to keep explicit sexual material from the public, but over the centuries have failed. Mian Mian's 2003 novel

*Candy*, promoted as "a blast of sex, drugs and rock 'n' roll" among modern China's youth, was banned by the government and as a result had a huge black market sale. She became a celebrity among Shanghai's young people to the amazement of her quiet, middle-class parents. The Chinese government banned the film *Farewell My Concubine* and was embarrassed by its worldwide success. To the Chinese government, the film is doubly disturbing. It paints a stark picture of the turmoil of the 1966–1976 Cultural Revolution and its main character is a homosexual Chinese opera star. Still, Chinese officials give great leeway to the top film producers in China probably because they are well known to international audiences who can influence decisions that affect China. The ban on *Farewell My Concubine* was lifted during the Chinese campaign to have the 2008 Olympics staged in Beijing. Meanwhile, Chinese filmmakers went to Hong Kong and elsewhere to escape the Beijing censors. Chinese authorities get upset when these unapproved and uncensored films win international prizes as "Chinese films." But when there are no politics involved, Chinese censors seem to have become more willing to let sex into public view. Fashion magazines with scantily clad women on the covers plus "candid talk about sex" on the pages between fill city newsstands throughout China. "We court the metrosexual," said Jin Jin, editor of *FHM* magazine.[33]

## Future of the Media

Despite the sometimes anti-government bravado, however, there is little chance of any revolutionary change in China's media. The Tiananmen Square protests and their tragic end frightened many Chinese. They saw the abyss of civil war again opening up, and many Chinese believe radical political change is too dangerous. Editor Chen Xilin of *China Business Times* said of the student protesters who died: "Tragic, yes, but that's history. The new elite is a lot smarter, and one thing is certain about the future of China: it belongs to smart people."[34] China's economic boom is muting the most serious protests and most people, especially the younger generation, see this as more important than rapid political change. Some of the Tiananmen Square student protesters are now wearing business suits and are part of China's middle class. Even Mian Mian, denounced less than a decade ago as "a poster child for spiritual pollution" by the Chinese government, is fitting into the new China. Her latest novel, *Panda Sex*, uses the notoriously sex-shy bear as a symbol to suggest that getting ahead in life may be more important than either politics or sex. China's media leaders and foreign media moguls seem to agree on the political point, but sex is likely to continue to be a headache for Chinese censors, since newsstand sex sells well. China's media seem to be accepting a period of continued economic boom, but very gradual political change, in the country. But Chinese officials fear the Internet could push political change too rapidly and therefore see it as the big challenge to their rule and will increasingly try to control it. "Whether or not we can actively use and effectively manage the Internet," said China's President Hu Jintao, "will affect national cultural information, security and the long-term stability of the state,"[35] A long-time American correspondent in China also sees the Internet as the "beating heart" of change in China"[36]

Because of China's economic success and growing international status and power, most Chinese accept the Communist Party's authoritarian rule and its control of the nation's media. China will change and its media may well lead the way, but the change will be slow. "China is on the move," said former US ambassador Winston Lord. "But the speed of its pace and the rigors of its course will require it to apply the brakes often."[37]

The economic boom and a cautious approach to political issues seem to be the compromise that most Chinese accept. Perhaps this compromise is symbolized by a best-selling music cassette, "Red Sun." It features old hymns praising Communist leader Mao Tse Tung set to soft rock rhythms.

# Notes

1. David Barboza, "China Puts Best Face Forward in New English-Language Channel," *New York Times*, July 2, 2010, A8.
2. Nick Young, "The Cultural Crusades," *New Internationalist*, June 2009.
3. Howard W. French, "Fashion Magazines Rush to Mold China's Sense of Style," *New York Times*, October 3, 2005, A10.
4. Yan Lieshan, "When in Rome ... A Few Thoughts on External Propaganda," *China Digital Times*, March 20, 2009.
5. Max Frankel, "Word and Image: A Great, Irrelevant Wall," *New York Times Magazine*, October 25, 1998, 36.
6. Tsan-kuo Chang and Zixue Tai, "Freedom of the Press in the Eyes of the Dragon: A Matter of Chinese Relativism and Pragmatism," in *International Communication: Concepts and Cases*, K. Anokwa, C. A. Lin, and M. B. Salwen, eds. (Belmont, CA: Wadsworth, 2003), 24.
7. Dan Griffiths, "China's Breakneck Media Revolution," http://news.bbc.co.uk, August 20, 2005.

8. "China's Media: Back on the Leash," *The Economist*, August 18, 2005, 50.

9. John Jirik, "China's News Media and the Case of CCTV-9," in *International News in the Twenty-First Century*, C. Paterson and A. Sreberny, eds. (Eastleigh, UK: John Libbey/Luton Press, 2004), 133.

10. Anthony Y. H. Fung, *Global Capital, Local Culture: Transnational Media Corporations in China* (New York: Peter Lang, 2008), 114.

11. Geraldine Fabrikant, "Media Executives Court China, but Still Run into Obstacles," *New York Times*, August 29, 2005, C1.

12. "China's New Faces," BBC World, http://news.bbc.co.uk, September 17, 2005.

13. Joseph Kahn, "China's State Secrets Will Guard One Less: Death Tolls," *New York Times*, September 13, 2005, sec. A, 5.

14. Wei Win and David Weaver, "Making Chinese Journalists for the Next Millennium," *Gazette*, 60(6), 1998, 513–529.

15. "China: The Media," Section 15 in *Library of Congress Country Studies*, October 3, 2005.

16. Jim Yardley, "Secrecy Veils China's Jailing of a Journalist," *New York Times*, August 31, 2005, A1.

17. Li Pin, *Report on the Development of the Magazine Industry in China (No. 2)*, Beijing Social Science Academic Press (2007), 57.

18. Chen Gang, Chen Jinchao, Song Wenjie, and Zhou Shao, "Research on the Readers of e-Magazines," *New View of Advertising*, February 2008, 24.

19. "International Editor of the Year," *World Press Review*, October 2003, 20–21.

20. David Barboza, "Pushing (and Toeing) the Line in China," *New York Times*, April 18, 2005, C, 3.

21. Barboza, "Pushing (and Toeing) the Line in China."

22. Author interview, October 24, 2002.

23. Howard W. French, "Beijing Casts Net of Silence over Protest," *New York Times*, December 14, 2005, A3.

24. Charles W. Eliot, "Flows of News from the Middle Kingdom: An Analysis of International News Releases in Xinhua" in *The Global Dynamic of News: Studies in International News Coverage and News Agenda*, Abbas Malek and Anandam P. Kavoori, eds. (Stamford, CT: Ablex Publishing, 2000), 348.

25. Xin Xin, "A Developing Market in News: Xinhua News Agency and Chinese Newspapers," *Media, Culture and Society*, 28/1, 2006, 60.

26. Jianying Zha, *China Pop: How Soap Operas, Tabloids, and Bestsellers are Transforming a Culture* (New York: The New Press, 1995), 107.

27. Chin-Chuan Lee, "The Global and the National of the Chinese Media: Discourses, Market Technology and Ideology," 1–31 in *Chinese Media, Global Contexts*, Chin-Chuan Lee, ed. (London: RoutledgeCurzon, 2003).

28. Charles Hutzler, "Yuppies in China Protest Via the Web – And Get Away With It," *The New York Times*, March 19, 2004, A4.

29. Hutzler, "Yuppies in China Protest Via the Web – And Get Away With It."

30. Ying Chan, "Chinese Journalists Circumvent Government's Tight Restrictions," *Nieman Reports*, 65/1 (Spring 2011), 53–57.
31. Joseph Kahn, "China Tightens its Restrictions for News Media on the Internet," *New York Times*, September 26, 2005, A9.
32. Mure Dickie, "China's Virtual Cops Pinpoint Web Dissent," *Financial Times*, February 18, 2006, 3.
33. French, "Fashion Magazines Rush to Mold China's Sense of Style."
34. Zha, *China Pop*, 108.
35. Mure Dickie, "China President Urges Party Officials to 'Purify' the Internet," *Financial Times*, January 26, 2007, 1.
36. Howard W. French, China's Chess Match," *Columbia Journalism Review*, November/December, 2010, 41–45.
37. Quoted in Guo Ke, "Newspapers: Changing Roles," 43–60 in James F. Scotton and William A. Hachten, eds, *New Media for a New China* (Oxford: Wiley-Blackwell, 2010).

# 8

# The Middle East:
# Media Storms in the Desert

*Merci Facebook!*
  – Wall graffiti in Tunisia, "60 Minutes" television program,
February 20, 2011

*We made a revolution in the Arabic media.*
 – Muhammad Jasmin al-Ali, General Manager, Al Jazeera Television

*I wanted to talk about pure sex, and I did it.*
  – Zaven Kouyoumdjian, host of a long-running talk program on
Lebanon's Future TV channel

Revolutions in communications are hurtling the people of the Middle East into the twenty-first century. The signals of these revolutions are Al Jazeera television, the Internet and above all the explosion among the new Arab generation of social media – cell phones, Facebook, and Twitter. They are challenging traditional Arab media and threatening the authoritarian regimes that have ruled the Middle East for decades. Rulers in Tunisia and Egypt were ousted in uprisings that reached the world in dramatic photographs and video that overcame attempts of the old regimes to block them. Rulers in Egypt made a belated attempt to stop the images, at one point cutting the country off from the Internet for five days despite the damage it did to its economy and its credibility but it was too late to halt growing protests. Other Middle East regimes such as Syria learned to move quickly to halt Internet protests and even used the technology to track down dissidents.

*The World News Prism: Challenges of Digital Communication*, Eighth Edition.
William A. Hachten and James F. Scotton.
© 2012 John Wiley & Sons, Ltd. Published 2012 by John Wiley & Sons, Ltd.

Al Jazeera, the independent satellite broadcaster based in the tiny Arab nation of Qatar, is credited by many for setting off the first modern communication revolution in the Arab World. Called by some "The Al Jazeera Phenomenon," it has taken audiences away from government television stations across the Arab world and forced major changes in traditional mass communication and even the way the people of the region view their rulers.[1]

At the same time Internet use in the Middle East has exploded, growing four times faster than in the rest of the world. From 2000 to 2010 the Internet in the Arab world grew by an astounding 1,800%, four times the rate of the rest of the world. Thirty percent of the population in the Middle East, many left out of the main stream of twentieth-century progress, now has access to the Internet, the same proportion as in the rest of the world.[2]

But growing even faster in numbers are cell phones. They may represent the greatest threat to the authoritarian traditions of the Arab world. Cell phones, through calls and texting, provide young people with ways to connect undetected in their closed societies. Cell phones are also being used to mobilize people such as the Kuwaiti women who used mass texting to successfully campaign for voting rights. In another Arab country cell phones and other social media such as Facebook and Twitter helped mobilize the thousands of young people who took to the streets in January 2011 to protest an oppressive Tunisian regime and force the President from office. The social media have become the channels for younger Arabs to vent their economic and political frustrations and to organize protests. And increasingly they are being used to transmit photos and videos of Arab governments using violence in attempts to repress their own people.

## Al Jazeera

Al Jazeera, which has been attacked by just about every Middle East government, appeared in 1996 when the Qatari ruler decided to establish a satellite television station. Qatar (population 800,000) is a small peninsula jutting off the northeast coast of Saudi Arabia (population 25.7 million), considered one of the most conservative states in the Arab world. The new Qatari ruler, Emir Sheikh Hamid bin Khalifa Al-Thani, overthrew his elderly father in a peaceful coup and announced he wanted to modernize Qatar. Two of his early steps were unheard of in the Arab world: he abolished both censorship and the Ministry of Information. He announced that

Al Jazeera ("The Island" in Arabic) would get a government loan (a reported $137 million) to start but be free of government control. Al Jazeera would have enough funds to send reporters and camera crews to cover important stories and to staff bureaus in London, Paris, Beijing and even Kabul. It gained a world audience in 2001 as the only satellite channel in Afghanistan when war broke out there following the attacks on New York's World Trade Towers. At its start Al Jazeera had the good fortune to inherit a trained news staff from a BBC channel that shut down because the Saudis, a major funder, insisted on censorship. Then Al Jazeera got a coveted position on a Saudi satellite because a technician at another channel mixed up a foreign porn show with a children's program. For the first time viewers in the Middle East would have a twenty-four-hour apparently independent Arabic news source that could compete with the BBC and CNN, thus breaking the Western news channel monopoly over the Arab audience.

The Emir hoped that Al Jazeera could survive on eventual advertising revenue, but the Saudis and other Middle East governments have pressured advertisers away from it. The Emir kept funding Al Jazeera and the channel soon was capturing viewers from the government-controlled broadcasters. Its audience of perhaps 50 million, 75% in the Arab world, is heavily male and also young, with more than 70% under 35. Al Jazeera viewers tend to have non-traditional views and even Middle East Christians consider its news programs trustworthy.[3] "We made a revolution in the Arabic media," said Muhammad Jasmin al-Ali, general manager of Al Jazeera.[4]

One reason Al Jazeera gathered a huge audience in a short time was that Arabs had learned to distrust government media. Government-controlled television stations not only slant the news but also distort or just omit it. In the 1967 Arab-Israeli war Arab audiences listened to days of reported victories only to learn from foreign news sources that the Israelis had routed their armies. In 1990 Saudi media waited two days to report that Iraq had invaded neighboring Kuwait. Perhaps the cruelest blow came in 2004 when the Egyptians were told they would host the World Cup soccer matches only to learn Egypt did not get even one vote from the selection committee that awarded the tournament to South Africa. A 2010 study put it bluntly: Middle East viewers do not trust television stations run by the government but give high credibility to Al Jazeera.[5]

Al Jazeera also gained viewers with investigative programs and provocative panel shows. On "The Opposite Direction" panelists got into shouting matches and even walked out over controversial topics that were taboo on other channels: human rights, political dissent, government corruption and women's role in Arab society. Phone calls and emails showed that the programs had an audience all over the Middle East. Arab leaders were not happy with these programs since they raised issues they do not want in the public dialogue. Algerian officials cut off electricity in an attempt to block reception of one program.

Al Jazeera's broadcasts have brought attacks from all sides. Critics said Al Jazeera producers too often seek emotional topics to boost audience numbers and stir up viewers. Others charge Al Jazeera never questions Qatari policies but the station's directors cite programs that have criticized Qatar's support for the United States in Iraq and even questioned whether Qatar should host the US airbase there.

The Palestinians closed Al Jazeera's bureau for "unbalanced" coverage. Israel has frequently accused the channel of emphasizing Palestinian casualties but ignoring Israeli killed and wounded. Kuwait has closed Al Jazeera's office in that country three times. Somalia and even Spain have objected to Al Jazeera reporting. Egypt's official *Al-Ahram* newspaper said its reporting was "deceptive."[6] In the United States Al Jazeera reporters were expelled from the New York Stock Exchange after it showed captured US soldiers in Iraq. Showing a tape from Osama bin Laden brought attacks from US officials and some American media.

The Saudis finally decided to compete with Al Jazeera, setting up their own satellite news channel in 2003 with a reported $300 million, much of it from the Arabian government. It was clearly meant to be a moderate alternative to what Arab governments see as Al Jazeera's unsettling influence over Middle East audiences. But many Arabs see Al Arabiya following the American political agenda too closely. President Obama made his first media appearance in the Arab world on Al Arabiya just days after his inauguration. Its general manager called Iran's nuclear ambition "the most dangerous threat that is facing the region in a hundred years."[7] Iran has expelled three different Al Arabiya bureau chiefs.

Al Arabiya's format is similar to Al Jazeera's but its Arabic news avoids disturbing topics and pictures and its panel shows are closely scripted to avoid on-air explosions. It had no on-air English channel as of 2010. The English-language channel of Al Jazeera, launched in 2005, covers the Middle East conflicts but tries to compete with CNN and the BBC by emphasizing world news. In fact, during its English-language news program, with its Western news anchors, Al Jazeera is sometimes recognizable as an Arab channel only because of its "tear-drop" logo at the corner of the screen. Al Jazeera's careful on-air neutrality in its English-language reports has produced a marketing problem. "If it looks like BBC, why should we add it?" asked one US cable producer.[8] Al Jazeera is gradually spreading into the United States, Canada, Australia and Europe via subscription television or free channels.

Al Jazeera and Al Arabiya have web sites in Arabic and English. Al Jazeera's English web site has more text than its Arabic web site, perhaps recognizing the low Arabic literacy level in some parts of the Middle East. Some of the images on Al Jazeera's Internet Arabic web site and on its Arabic-language channel are not found on BBC, CNN, or most other television channels including Al Arabiya. Al Jazeera does not shy away from showing graphic pictures of dead soldiers or civilians from the Palestinian-Israeli conflict, Afghanistan or Iraq. Because of this, some suggest that CNN viewers in the United States and Al Jazeera viewers in the Arab World are, in effect, watching different wars. Al Jazeera's producers say they owe it to their audience to show these conflicts as they are. Al Jazeera tries to have journalists at the scene of all the serious conflicts in the Middle East. It is the only news organization that regularly has reporters on both sides of the Israeli-Palestinian conflict.

The United States has been very disturbed by Al Jazeera's coverage of the Iraq war. In 2004 Secretary of State Colin Powell tried to persuade the Qatari ruler to interfere.[9] That summer the Iraqi government temporarily closed Al Jazeera's Baghdad office. The Iraqis have at times suspended both Al Jazeera and Al Arabiya over broadcasts it did not like. But even American officials recognize Al Jazeera's influence in the Arab World. While US Defense Secretary Donald Rumsfeld was calling its Iraqi war coverage "vicious, inaccurate and inexcusable," a top US general appeared on Al Jazeera's "No Limits" interview program to defend US policy.[10] Although Al Jazeera remained largely unseen by most of the American public, by 2011 it had become prime source of information by the US President's staff.[11]

Sometimes journalists find the opposition to covering Middle East conflicts goes beyond words. An Afghan correspondent for Al Jazeera spent three days in prison because US soldiers thought he had contacts with the Taliban. US missiles, by accident the United States military said, hit both the Kabul and Baghdad headquarters of Al Jazeera, killing one journalist. An Al Arabiya reporter was killed by a US missile and three other Al Arabiya staff members were kidnapped and killed in Iraq while covering a mosque attack. In 2008 Al Jazeera's Nour Odeh was honored for her bravery in reporting from the volatile Gaza Strip. Other Middle East conflicts largely ignored by the media have taken their toll of journalists. A 2010 International Press

Freedom Prize from Reporters Without Borders went to a Somali radio station where five journalists were killed in the previous three years in that nearly forgotten war zone.

Arabic news channels from outside the Middle East have failed to capture much of the Arab audience. Entertainment programs on Al Hurra ("The Free One"), an official US channel, get an audience but it has little credibility as a news source.[12] Some suggest that one problem might be that none of Al-Hurra's senior managers speak Arabic. A mix of Arabic and modern music on its sister US-funded radio station, Al Sawa, has Middle East listeners but its news broadcasts do not. Al-Alam, Iran's attempt to reach a Middle East audience via television has some influence among Shi'ite Muslims but its reach is not known. Rusiya Al-Yaum started broadcasting from Moscow in 2007, providing Arabic translations of Russia's English-language channel. The BBC again started an Arabic television news channel in 2008 following the demise of the Saudi-backed effort that ran into censorship problems. Also in 2008 Euronews added news programs in Arabic, one of many languages from that organization.

But if foreign news channels have difficulty getting an Arab audience, foreign entertainment programs do not. Soap operas from Turkey dubbed in Arabic have a huge audience in the Arab world with one episode of "Noor" attracting 80 million viewers. The episodes have a mix of passion and infidelity and even a hero who treats his wife well, which brought adulations from Arab women.[13] More entertainment and less news and other controversial material is the goal of the increasingly powerful media owners in the Middle East. This group of business moguls copies Western formats, buys Western programs and focuses on pop culture to capture the young viewers that advertisers traditionally prefer. Huge audiences watch the entertainment programs made for Ramadan when most Muslim families are up late feasting and watching television after their sunrise to sundown fast during the Muslim holy month. Satellites allow lots of choices with the Egyptians and Syrians producing most of these Ramadan series for decades. Plots carefully mix secular themes with Islam, and terrorism is definitely not supported. Much of the funding has come from conservative Gulf states where 40 to 50% of daily programming is religious, rising as high as 80% during Ramadan.[14]

But the Turkish soaps and other satellite programs that have been stealing the Arab audiences have brought changes even to these Ramadan programs. A new Syrian Ramadan program ventured into such taboo subjects as homosexuality, extra-marital sex, and corruption and quickly won a large audience. Perhaps even more daring, the program takes its name from a Koran verse, translated as "What your right hand possesses." The program is, surprisingly, on a government-owned channel. It has been denounced from Muslim pulpits. The Syrians also produced a Ramadan satire series, "Spotlight," that pulled in a large youth audience by ridiculing the country's Ministry of Education.

The Middle East country with the freest television industry is Lebanon, even ahead of Israel. Its first privately-owned station (LBCI) started in 1985 while Israel's first truly independent television station was not licensed until 2002. There are fifteen television stations and more than forty radio stations in Lebanon. Only some are licensed to broadcast news. At one time there were sixty television stations and 150 radio stations in Lebanon, reflecting the wildly diverse political, religious and social divisions in the society.

Lebanon's Future TV, with both local and satellite broadcasts, is one of the most successful of the "Family" stations. Perhaps its most popular show is Superstar, the Arabic version of American Idol, bringing calls and emails from all over the Middle East from viewers who want to vote for their favorite performer. El Halaka Al Adaaf is the channel's Arabic version of "The Weakest Link." Future TV's most famous talk show is Sireh infatahit ("Open Discussion"). Its host, Zaven Kouyoumdjian, makes it clear that ratings rather than politics are his concern. He shocked his audience with a program on "The technicalities of sexual behavior" in 2004. "If we want to talk about sex in the Arab world, we always talk about it under the umbrella of education," he said. "I wanted to talk about pure sex, and I did."[15] The program's ratings went through the roof. Future TV tries to balance programming to make it a "family channel" so it interviews artists and authors on Khalleek bil eit ("Stay at Home") and covers Lebanese football.

Clearly the most popular television program for women in the Arab World is also Lebanese. MBC-TV's Kalam Nawaem ("A New View") is modeled on the American program "The View." On the Lebanese version four Arab women discuss problems they see for Arab women, such as the rising divorce rate and sex education for children. Since starting in 2002 it reportedly has captured half the women in the Arab world in its audience.

Future TV has ventured into news and attempted to compete for Al Jazeera's audience without much success. The station has wanted to produce talk shows on the Al Jazeera model but the Lebanese government has resisted this as a sure source of controversy in its carefully balanced society. In 2008 its news and commentary brought an attack from

Hezbollah, whose militia broke into its fortress-like building, wrecked the station and put it off the air for several days. LBC, a Christian station, set off riots in 2006 when a commentator mocked the Hezbollah leader. Hezbollah has its own television station, Al Manar, which has an audience all over the Middle East estimated by Beirut's *Daily Star* newspaper as 200 million. Hezbollah ("Party of God") is dedicated to the destruction of Israel and at times seems a stronger supporter of Syria than the Lebanese government. Hezbollah's leader Hassan Nassrallah sometimes takes over the station and speaks to his followers for hours. Al Manar was the first television station to be designated a "terrorist entity" by the US government, but an American professor at a Lebanese university found its news presentation very good. "Many people tune into Al Manar whether they are Christian, Druse, Sunnis or what because Al Manar has very good reporting," said Dr. Judith Hark. "Their analysis is very precise and very well thought out. They're very shrewd, forthright and are taken very seriously."[16] Al Manar even has an audience in Israel where its graphic images of Jewish casualties in Lebanon aroused Israel public opinion to demand a withdrawal in 2000.

Another popular but mostly movie channel is Dubai One. It has some news but features American films, some carefully censored to avoid problems in Saudi Arabia and some other Arab countries. Dubai's Media City has developed into a Middle East media center with advertising agencies and other media offices moving to that tax-free zone.

Dream TV was set up in 2002 as Egypt's first private commercial television station with programming aimed at affluent Egyptians. It had no news staff but did venture into talk shows. Guests on one program charged officials were incompetent in dealing with a train fire that killed 400 people and there was no apparent government reaction against the station. But the government did react when the most popular talk show, "Editor in Chief," strayed into politics, with one program suggesting that President Hosni Mubarak's son would not be acceptable successor as President. The talk show host, Hamdy Kandil, simply disappeared from Dream TV.[17]

There have been efforts elsewhere in the Middle East to set up local television stations to broadcast the news, sometimes under American protection. But there is little advertising available except from the government and factions that do not agree with the station's broadcasts make staff security a problem. In Afghanistan Saad Mohseni owns the country's most popular television (Tolo) and radio (Arman) networks. In 2009 he partnered with Rupert Murdoch to set up a Farsi satellite network to send entertainment programs dubbed in Farsi in Dubai's Media City into Iran.

Mohseni was planning Tolo News, a twenty-four-hour Afghan satellite news channel, but has hesitated since even his non-news programs bring threats. A woman singer on "Afghan Star," based on "American Idol," was threatened with death for appearing. Armed police raided Tolo TV's offices and dragged off employees because the attorney general disagreed with some broadcast remarks. The future for locally generated television news in the Middle East does not look bright.

## Internet

The huge surge in Internet use in the Arab world has come since 2008 when only 11% of the people there were using the Internet even once a month. By mid-2010 that figure, at least for the Middle East countries, had leaped to nearly 30%.[18] Even allowing for some measuring differences, the growth was astounding. The greatest Internet use was in Bahrain where 88% of the population had Internet access, followed by the United Arab Emirates at 76%. Both of these surpassed Israel at 72% (75% of Jews have access but only 50% of Arabs in the country). Even in Iran and Saudi Arabia, where Internet use is controlled and sometimes dangerous, large proportions of their citizens were on the Internet and some were using social media such as Facebook, Twitter, and Flickr (see Table 8.1) And two-thirds of these social media users were in the 15–29 year age group, which makes up a third of the Arab population. These young people drove Facebook use in the Arab World up a phenomenal 78% just in 2010.

Middle East rulers resisted what they saw as a new threat to their control of information and to their regimes. In 2009 the OpenNet Initiative reported fourteen out of eighteen countries in the Middle East and North Africa filtered entering Internet messages. Substantial blocking or filtering was found in seven Arab countries: Oman, Saudi Arabia, Sudan, Syria, Tunisia the United Arab Emirates and Yemen. No evidence of blocking web sites was found in Algeria, Egypt or Iraq in 2009. Another study found Saudi Arabia, Iran, Syria and Tunisia were most active in the Middle East in blocking Internet messages.[19]

Access to the Internet cannot be totally blocked for long since banking and other vital economic interests rely on it to do business globally. Government developments such as Dubai's Internet City and Egypt's Smart Village try to attract companies with Internet links. Arab countries also subsidize computers for schools and even for homes to help modernize their

**Table 8.1**   Internet Use in the Middle East (2010).

| | Population (Millions) | Internet Users (Millions) | Population Usage | 2000–2010 Growth |
|---|---|---|---|---|
| Middle East | 212.3 | 63.2 | 29.8% | 1,825% |
| Rest of World | 6,632.3 | 1,903.3 | 28.7% | 432% |

| | Population (Millions) | Internet Users (Percentage) | Facebook Users (Percentage) |
|---|---|---|---|
| Bahrain | 0.7 | 88 | 34.2 |
| UAEmirates | 5.0 | 76 | 45.4 |
| Israel | 7.4 | 72 | 44.0 |
| Qatar | 0.8 | 52 | 33.9 |
| Iran | 76.9 | 43 | 3.6 |
| Oman | 3.0 | 42 | 7.6 |
| Kuwait | 2.8 | 39 | 20.6 |
| Saudi Arabia | 25.7 | 38 | 12.2 |
| Jordan | 5.4 | 27 | 17.1 |
| Lebanon | 4.1 | 24 | 23.1 |
| Egypt | 66.6 | 21 | 5.5 |
| Syria | 22.2 | 18 | 1.1 |
| Palestine | 2.5 | 14 | 10.8 |
| Sudan | 42.0 | 10 | 0.7 |
| Tunisia (2007) | 10.3 | 9 | 17.6 |
| Algeria (2007) | 33.5 | 6 | 4.0 |
| Libya | 6.5 | 6 | 4.0 |
| Yemen | 23.5 | 2 | 0.7 |
| Morocco (2007) | 30.5 | 2 | 7.6 |
| Iraq | 29.7 | 1 | 1.3 |

English remains the dominant world Internet language with more than 25% using it. About 3.3% use Arabic, putting it behind Spanish (5.0%) and German (3.8%) but ahead of French (3.0%) and Russian (3.0%). Developing rapidly is Iran's Farsi, now one of the Internet's top ten blogging languages.

Sources: www.internetworldstats.com; www.startuparabia.com; www.pogar.org; www. ArabSocialMediaReport.com (Dubai School of Government)

societies. And Internet sites can change so rapidly that a government intent on blocking must devote huge resources to do it effectively. This is the basic dilemma for the Internet blockers when they try to set up a system to filter out the messages they do not want but leave those they do want.

Saudi Arabia may have the most elaborate Internet filtering process, routing all Internet messages through a government control point in Riyadh. The Saudis were mostly blocking sites concerned with pornography, drugs, gambling and religious conversion. They seemed less interested in sites on politics, homosexuals, alcohol or even Israel. No major news sources were blocked. The Saudis have been very public about their Internet blocking, some suggest to quiet traditionalists who resisted having any Internet access in the kingdom. Earlier conservatives had fought against allowing television in Saudi Arabia. It is relatively easy to get around the Saudi system through a proxy server outside the country. And 2010 saw a huge increase in Twitter users in Saudi Arabia of 240%, far above the global average.[20]

Many Arab states have had an elaborate system of rules governing what could and could not be viewed on the Internet, usually barring, as Saudi Arabia did, "Anything contrary to the state or its system."[21] Iran became much harsher in its Internet control after the 2009 elections and the riots that followed. All Internet traffic in and out of Iran goes through one government-controlled portal. Again, cautious and tech-savvy users can set up Internet Server addresses outside the country as proxies to hide their own computer's IP address. This is to be expected, said James Cowie on the Renesys Internet intelligence blog. "If you put 65 million people in a locked room, they're going to find all the exits pretty quickly," he said, "and maybe make a few of their own." There are an estimated 70,000 active bloggers in Iran.[22] Iranian women journalists, after the closing of all print magazines for women, turned to the Internet. "We use social media as a news tool," said Parvin Ardalan, who established the web site "Change for Equality" in 2006. Ardalan, sentenced to jail several times, received Reporters Without Borders first "Netizen" Prize in 2010.[23]

Since public protests in many Middle East countries risk police crackdowns and heavy punishment, activists have increasingly turned to the Internet. Activists all over the Middle East have used the Internet to get their message out to the people. In Egypt the 6th of April movement used Facebook to organize people in support of industrial strikers who were planning to strike on April 6, 2008. It became a key organizer of the Tahrir Square protests that forced Egypt's President Hosni Mubarak from office. By January 2009 online membership in the organization had grown to 70,000, mostly young people who broadened their protests into a cyberspace political movement through Facebook, Twitter, Flickr, and other social media. "The Internet is our battlefield," said Ahmed Maher, who was using

Facebook to rally opposition to Egyptian authorities by coordinating the 6th of April Youth movement. "The regime controls the streets, the parties are ineffectual and there are no places to gather." Maher said the movement agreed on only general principles, such as democracy and fighting corruption. Occasionally, they try to carry out street protests but generally keep within cyberspace. "They let us say what we want online," said Maher. But passing into action on the street is a no no." Maher was apparently not involved in street protests related to the movement, but was still arrested and jailed.[24] But even jailing does not silence some bloggers. Alaa Abdel-Fattah, considered by many to be Egypt's most famous blogger and pro-democracy dissident, managed to write notes from jail that his supporters posted on the Internet.

In Saudi Arabia Waleed Abu Alkhair used his Facebook site to publish news about human rights victims. He reported on a young journalist denied entrance to a women's shelter after she was beaten by her father on returning from an overseas human rights program. The shelter then decided to admit her. "We would love to do grassroots campaigning but it is impossible here," said Alkhair. "Websites are the only reasonable way to spread a message locally and internationally without risk." Alkhair also led a twelve-day Internet media blitz to get a thirty-two-year-old Saudi woman released after six months in jail for disobeying her father.[25] One study found that the Saudis tried to block many Internet sites related to women, even the "Women in History" section of the Encyclopedia Britannica.

In the United Arab Emirates political expression has appeared on the Internet despite resistance to any questioning of UAE rulers. Even a former crown prince deposed in a 2003 palace coup has been using the new media to promote his restoration. Disturbed authorities can, however, deal out harsh punishment to cyber dissidents. In September 2010 an Iranian court gave Hossein Derakhshan a twenty-year prison sentence, the longest ever for a blogger. Derakhshan, an Iranian-Canadian, earlier published a guide to blogging in Persian and is sometimes called Iran's "blogfather." He was a government critic and even visited Israel, forbidden by most Arab governments. The court said his sentence was for cooperating with a hostile state and insulting Islam. Derakhshan is not alone in paying the penalty for using Internet to oppose Iranian authorities. Reporters without Borders in February 2010 counted sixty-five "netizens" and journalists imprisoned in Iran. A month earlier the organization said Iran was the "world's biggest prison for journalists."[26] Iran has also organized a citizen "cyber-army" and called on members to stop "destructive" online networks.

Iran was not the first Middle East country to pursue its bloggers. In Tunisia Zouhair Yahyaoui, founder of the satirical TUNeZINE, one of the first Internet open discussion forums, was imprisoned. Yahyaoui used a pseudonym but authorities tracked him down after the web site brought up issues such as human rights and freedom of expression.

Bahrain's most prominent blogger, Ali Abdulemam, was arrested in September 2010 after years as a government critic. A computer engineer, Abdulemam regularly overcame government efforts to block his web site. Egypt, Syria, and Bahrain have all moved to discourage blogging through arrests and even police beatings. Even after President Mubarak was forced out the Egyptian blogger "Son of Ra" was sentenced to three years in prison for criticizing the military.[27]

A major Islamist web site, IslamOnline, founded in 1997 by an Egyptian cleric, was caught up in the ongoing struggle over who will control the Internet in the Middle East. In March 2010 hundreds of IslamOnline editorial staff members in Cairo walked out, accusing conservative Qatari home office administrators and financial supporters of seeking editorial control. IslamOnline, originally established in Cairo, has been one of the largest Islamic web sites with considerable editorial independence, unusual for the Arab World. In October 2010 the editorial staff launched a separate site, OnIslam.

The Internet is, of course, open to anyone with a computer and the Middle East with its years of volatility has produced many kinds of bloggers. An Arab women living in Belgium, Maika El Aroud, is one of the most prominent supporters of Al Qaeda. Writing in French, she couples messages of hatred toward the West with support for women to take a larger role in global jihad. In Cairo Gamal al-Banna, a newspaper columnist and former member of Parliament, is at eighty-eight reaching a broader audience with his message of pluralism by moving to the Internet. In New Jersey, Jane Novak, who speaks no Arabic and has never been to Yemen, campaigns to free the Yemeni journalist Abdul Kari al-Khaiwani "while the kids are at school." Her blog, www.armiesofliberation.com, a steady critic of Yemeni policies, is banned in Yemen but is so well known that newspaper editors there say her picture boosts sales.[28]

A citizen journalist in Palestine with a video camera documented an Israeli woman cursing her Arab sister in both Hebrew and Arabic. A human rights organization in Jerusalem posted the video, causing outrage in both Israel and Palestine and bringing an Israeli government investigation.

An Iraqi dentist named "Zeyad" has built a large following throughout the Arab world with vivid reports and comments about life in that war-torn country. A critic of religious fundamentalists, security concerns keep him away from Internet cafés and he talks with other Iraqi bloggers only by email. The *Washington Post* and the *Guardian* in London have published his material. "He brings the kinds of perspective you can't get unless you're there," said a *Guardian* blog editor.[29]

Publishing citizen blogs, photos, and even videos has become routine for even major media organizations reporting on the Middle East. The *New York Times* relied heavily on citizens in Syria for coverage of the April 2011 protests and violence there since the regime blocked all foreign journalists from entering the country.[30]

There is a risk in this, of course. As Marc Lynch has pointed out, only a fraction of the Arab public blogs even if blogging is bringing new voices to the public dialogue in the Middle East. Lynch, Director of the Middle East Studies Program at George Washington University, also warns that relying on English-language blogs, as those in the West typically do, is likely to provide an unbalanced sense of what is going on. Another problem with blogs submitted to the mainstream media from the Middle East is inability to check the material. This has proved a problem for major news media in the West. During the 2009 Iranian election protests, CNN, the *New York Times*, London's *Guardian* and other media published many English-language blog reports containing unverified videos and anonymous Twitter messages. Fox News anchor Shepard Smith showed a YouTube video of police beating people but admitted to viewers, "We do not know when or where this video was from." The sheer volume of material is a major problem. CNN received 5,200 pieces related to Iran and approved 180 for television.[31] The Internet and blogs will play roles in developing a real public sphere where ideas can be freely discussed in Arab society. But Lynch, a blogger on the Middle East himself as "Abu Aardvark," questions whether it will become a "liberal public sphere" tolerant of opposing views and free of state interference.[32]

## Cell Phones

By some counts the Middle East had more cell phones (300 million) than people (212 million) in 2010. In 2009 one study found six Middle East countries where there was already more than one cell phone subscription per person. A Gallup survey about the same time found it difficult to locate any people without a cell phone in the oil-rich states of Kuwait, Saudi Arabia, Qatar, Bahrain and the United Arab Emirates.[33]

Cell phones are more popular than computers in the Middle East for many reasons. The most important, perhaps, is the long history of poor but expensive government-run phone services there. Also, a cell phone is much less expensive to buy and use than a computer, especially since many street corner entrepreneurs will rent you one to make a call. To use a cell phone, unlike a computer, you do not have to know how to read and write, a consideration in Middle East areas where education levels are low and much written material comes in the formal Arabic that only the well-schooled understand. Cell phones have also been more acceptable for religious reasons since they could not access Internet pornography and other unacceptable material, at least until the new Smart Phones appeared. And a cell phone represents individual freedom, especially for young people, much as a car does in the more affluent West. Almost every university student in the Middle East has a cell phone. As one article put it, a cell phone has become "as essential to human functioning as a pair of shoes."[34]

Regardless of how many cell phones there are in Middle Eastern countries, they are creating new freedoms for the people and new concerns for government authorities. In the Middle East countries with probably the strictest government controls on public communication, Iran and Saudi Arabia, more people own cell phones. Iran tried to establish a "telephone police" to keep watch on cell phone messages but they were soon overwhelmed by the volume of calls.

Cell phones are a way for young people to connect with their outside world and each other in the closed Arab societies. Millions use them to vote for their favorite on "Star Academy," the region's most popular television show. Since no dating is allowed in most of these countries, young people go to shopping malls, parks and cafes to contact each other using cell phones and wireless Bluetooth. But there are always dangers – governmental, parental and even criminal – in using technology to develop new social relations. Some men have used the new technology to get photos of women whom they then threaten to "expose" unless paid large sums. Saudi women have been fighting back, even training as technicians to keep men away from their computers.

Cell phones are also used to mobilize people for social and political protests. Kuwaiti women used mass text messaging in 2002 to organize a successful campaign for voting rights. Egyptian and Lebanese activists have used cell phones to organize pro-democracy protests. In Saudi Arabia and Bahrain Shi'ites used text messaging seeking political participation in those largely Sunni societies. Iranian demonstrators used cell phones to upload photos of clashes with security forces and of injured students.

"It is a very excellent device to mobilize the people, especially in making social gatherings, demonstrations," said Ibrahim Abu Argoub of the University of Jordan. "In elections they use it very often in exchanging political messages in Jordan and all Arab countries."[35]

Cell phones have become so common in the Muslim world that religious leaders are being asked how to use them properly. It was decided that Koran verses can be used as ring tones but users were cautioned not to confuse people into thinking it was time for prayer. A Muslim man may even divorce his wife via a cell phone text message but it is not acceptable proof of divorce.

Saudi Arabia has been especially active in trying to control cell phones, especially camera phones. Saudi Arabia jailed youths who filmed a rape and sent the images to the Internet. The Saudis tried to block further importing of camera phones, but there was widespread smuggling. A Saudi teenager who smuggled a camera phone to school and assaulted the teacher who tried to take it from her was sentenced to a lashing in front of her schoolmates as well as jail. At the same time Saudi television stations called on their citizens to use their cell phones to support the country's candidate in the "Star Academy" contest. That program is so popular in the Arab World that much of the region's activities come to a halt as people watch the show.

Mobile phone growth in the Middle East has seriously threatened the government-owned fixed line services. Cell phones are more reliable and in some countries less expensive than fixed-line phones. Cell phones represent a threat to Middle East governments in many ways but they are clearly not going to be stopped or even limited effectively.

## Print media

There are countless publications in the Middle East, mainly in Arabic but also in English, French, Hebrew and many other languages including Farsi and Turkish. Newspapers vary enormously throughout the Middle East, ranging from Lebanon's wildly free dailies in Arabic, English, and French to Iran's tightly controlled publications, mainly in Farsi. Two widely read Saudi Arabian-supported dailies are *Al Nayat al-Hayat (The Life)* and *Ashraq al-Awsat (The Middle East)*, edited in London but printed in several Middle East cities. *Ashraq al-Awsat* has an English-language edition. Both papers are editorially moderate but support Saudi Arabia policies.

The Arabic versions can be read by people throughout the Middle East and the Arab world. Although spoken Arabic varies greatly throughout the Arab world, there is one basic written form, Modern Standard Arabic. This is taught in schools and understood by educated Arabic readers across the Middle East.

The remarkably diverse society of Lebanon is credited with giving it the freest press in the Middle East. A Christian island in a Muslim sea, Lebanon had its first weekly newspaper, *Hadiqat al-Akhbar" (Garden of News)*, by 1858. Its diverse press, cited as "a unique development in the Arab world," reflected its fractured and highly volatile society.[36]

Perhaps the most daring newspaper in the Arab world is Lebanon's *Al Akhbar*, which embarrassed many of the region's leaders in 2010 by publishing US State Department cables from Wikileaks. The paper supports gay rights and feminism and has exposed abuse of domestic workers and prison overcrowding. It is a strong supporter of Hezbollah in its anti-Israeli crusade. "Our project is basically anti-imperialism," said Managing Editor Khalaled Saghieh, who has a US university education. Funding from a London banker keeps the paper free of the tangle of Lebanese politics. In 2010, just five years after it was launched, *Al-Akhbar* had a reported daily circulation of about 12,000, close to that of *Al Nahar*, which was founded in 1933. *Al-Nahar*, for years the leading daily in Lebanon, supports US policy and is a fiery critic of Syria.

The four leading Lebanese dailies are in Arabic followed by the French *Orient de Jour* and the English *Daily Star*. Lebanon's newspapers are free of government control but political party subsidies and ties to various sects tend to restrict their independence.

There is also the problem of journalists taking bribes in Lebanon and in many other Middle Eastern countries because of low salaries. Journalists justify the bribery by citing their difficult economic situation, although some have called for reforms. Paying newspapers to cover stories, ignore stories or report them in a certain way is a long standing practice, according to Magda Abu-Fadil of the Journalism Training Program at The American University of Beirut.[37] There have also been efforts to counter this problem with sessions on media ethics in training programs within the media and at universities.

In nearby Jordan, the press is relatively free with little direct censorship although editors do often practice "self-censorship." There are newspapers that challenge the regime, often referred to as Jordan's "yellow press." The main conflict has been between the press and parliament, which has prosecuted journalists and tried to impose a special tax on the media. Jordan was the only Muslim country where a newspaper reprinted the Danish cartoons of the Prophet Muhammed that set off riots in several cities. Two editors were fired, but not jailed. In 2009 King Abdullah II issued a decree forbidding the jailing of journalists, but critics say journalists remain unsafe from law suits that could jail them or close publications in Jordan. Jordanian journalist Naseem Tarawneh said government officials were just not able to accept being told that "they were doing a bad job."[38]

Israel, across Lebanon's southern border, also has a multilingual press, with about twenty newspapers in Hebrew, Arabic, English, German, Yiddish and four in Russian. *Haaretz*, in Hebrew and English, and *The Jerusalem Post*, in English and French, are widely read and considered authoritative and reliable. *Haaretz* (The Land) sent its own correspondent to report on the Egyptian protests of January 2011 and when the Internet was shut down he continued to file stories "in the ancient manner," by fax or telephone. *Haaretz* has lost thousands of readers by consistently questioning Israeli policies towards the Palestinians. It once published only in Hebrew but since 1997 has become an important English-language source in print and on the web.[39] There is no direct censorship in Israel and government officials and policies are routinely attacked. Matters involving the military are handled cautiously because of the ongoing conflicts with Palestinians and with Hezbollah, just over the border in Lebanon. A new threat to Israel's established newspapers has recently appeared in the form of free daily papers, such as *Israel ha-yom*, which depend totally on advertising revenue.

Palestine has three Arabic daily newspapers and for a time had an influential English-language paper, *The Palestine Times*. It was founded in 1996 but financial difficulties closed it in 2007, though it hoped to return. It was not publishing in 2010. Two Arabic newspapers were started in 1995 after the Oslo peace meetings that eased relations for a time between Palestine and Israel. *Al Hayat al Jadida* is published by the Palestine government while *Al Ayyam* is independent, although internal conflicts have threatened its future. *Al Quds* (Jerusalem) is the oldest Palestinian newspaper and probably has the highest circulation. It has angered Israeli authorities for anti-semitic comments and has also been criticized by the Palestinian Authority for working with the Israelis on some issues.

Lebanon's northern neighbor, Syria, allowed private media in 2001 for the first time in forty years. *The Lamplighter*, a satirical weekly, was the first private publication to appear and gained a large audience with its attacks on government ministers. The government first withdrew all official advertising and then cancelled *The Lamplighter's* license. Ten years after Syria's privatization decree some claim it was a fraud, enabling wealthy businessmen close to the regime to control the country's media.

In Iraq there was an explosion of newspapers after the overthrow of Saddam Hussein. Many of them closed from lack of readers, advertising, and security. In 2007 the BBC estimated there were still about fifty publications, almost all in Baghdad, battling for revenue and readers. By 2011, there were nineteen listed by one Internet site as still publishing with many more counted as online publications. *Al-Sabah*, a daily backed by the US coalition, is widely read for its sports and cultural coverage but has low credibility among Iraqis. *Al-Bayan*, the publication of Prime Minister's Nour al-Maliki's political party, has also had credibility problems. Although there is little direct censorship, lack of advertising revenue is a problem. In 2008 the government curbed its advertising which had contributed 40 to 70% of revenue for newspapers. Some claimed this was done to promote *Al-Bayan*, the ruling party's newspaper.

In neighboring Iran the government has kept tight control over all publications and runs the major news agencies. In 2009 it closed at least six newspapers, accusing them of lying about election protests and violent government suppression. Hundreds, including journalists and photographers, were jailed, and many fled the country to avoid arrest.[40]

A major barrier to publishing throughout the Arab world is licensing laws. The publications, the printing presses and even the journalists can require licenses from the government. An Egyptian editor trying to start a weekly news magazine learned that in the previous ten years only five licenses had been issued for political publications. Most of those licenses went to people connected to the government. The editor, Hisham Kassem, decided to publish his magazine, the *Cairo Times*, in Cyprus, flying printed copies back to Egypt. A censor had to approve each issue of this "foreign" publication before it could be sold in Egypt. Censorship laws are always vague. Editors usually exercise a great deal of self-censorship to avoid expensive last-minute problems with the censor. Middle East defamation laws greatly restrict criticism of royal families, presidents, ministers, and other government officials. In 2008 Saad Eddin Ibrahim, an Egyptian democracy activist, was sentenced to prison for "defaming Egypt."[41]

Egypt's *Al-Ahram* has long been one of the most influential newspapers in the Arab world. *Al-Ahram* (The Pyramid) was government run but still considered reliable. Its Friday English-language edition was read throughout the Middle East and in Europe because of its thorough coverage of cultural activities. *Al-Ahram*'s long-time editor, Mohammed Hassanein Heikal, was famous throughout the Middle East but inevitably his outspoken columns landed him in trouble with Egypt's political rulers. He left *Al-Ahram* and has been an Al Jazeera commentator for more than a decade.

The efforts of government-owned newspapers to please officials has sometimes proved embarrassing. In September 2010 *Al-Ahram* was caught doctoring a photograph to show Egyptian President Hosni Mubarak at the head of a group of Middle East leaders at the White House when he actually was walking at the back. A software engineer caught the photo manipulation and alerted the public on his blog. Al Ahram's staff was so angry at the newspaper's suppressing news about the anti-Mubarak protests that they tried to prevent the editor's entry to his office and called for an investigation of his finances.[42]

More English-language newspapers are appearing in the Middle East. Like the *Tripoli Post* in Libya, they tend to avoid domestic politics and focus on business plus wire agency news from outside the country. An English-language newspaper that has taken on local government while not questioning political authority is the *Saudi Gazette*, which circulates throughout Saudi Arabia. After serious 2009 flooding in the city of Jeddah, the *Gazette* denounced the mayor for incompetence. Similar examples of what could be called civic journalism can be found more often in Middle East publications as rulers realize the press has to be given a better face or the readers will abandon it for Al Jazeera and the Internet.

English-language newspapers are seen as a sign of modernization and Arab governments want to have them, but are wary of their threat to the existing order. Foreign editors are sometimes imported to develop a publication which can lead to conflicts. Martin Newland, who has edited papers in England and Canada, came to Abu Dhabi in 2007 to start *The National*. It is a government-owned newspaper but the deputy editor, Hassan M. Fattah, said he expects *The National* "to set a standard" for other regional newspapers. "There are no ministers sitting in my office," said Fattah, a former *New York Times* reporter. He was the only Arab among the paper's top editors.[43] But Newland is not so sure how much freedom the paper has, at least at this stage. The paper has done its share of investigations and exposés, notably bucking both school officials and the police to discover that a young boy died because he was locked in a hot bus for four hours. But as Newland told his staff at the outset, "Understand that we are not here to fight for press freedom. We are here to produce a professional, commercially viable newspaper. Press freedom is a byproduct of this."[44]

Al Jazeera, the Internet, blogs, twitter, Flickr and even the old print media are changing the media scene in the Middle East. Whether they can also change the political scene remains to be seen. Arab journalists surveyed in thirteen countries in 2007 cited political reform of anti-democratic regimes and human rights as their top missions.[45] The Internet especially can "provide a new tool of expression" for new voices in the Arab community, said Hussein Amin, chair of the Journalism and Mass Communication Department at The American University in Cairo.[46] But most of the Arab Middle class is much more interested in being entertained by the media than reformed by it. And while activists have used the Internet to bring some changes, many of those who use it are voting for their favorites on television shows or chatting with friends via Twitter or on podcasts. Newspapers, while still alive and influential, reach the comfortable elite who are not likely to be agents of change. Change is coming to the Middle East, change in the media and change in social and political institutions. To what extent each will change the other is not clear.

# Notes

1. Mohamed Zayani (Ed.), *The Al Jazeera Phenomenon* (Boulder, CO: Paradigm Press, 2005).
2. www.internetworldstats.com.
3. Philip Auter, Mohamed M. Arafa and Khaled Al-Jaber, "Who Is Al Jazeera's Audience?" *Transnational Broadcasting Studies*, Spring 2004.
4. Hugh Miles, *Al Jazeera: The Inside Story of the Arab News Channel that is Challenging the West* (New York: Grove Press, 2005), 82.
5. Thomas J. Johnston and Shahira Fahmy, "Who is Winning the Hearts and Minds of the Arab Public?" *International Communication Research Journal* (45/1–2), Spring 2010; Rasha A. Abdulla, *The Internet In the Arab World* (New York: Peter Lang, 2007), 4.
6. "Al Jazeera sues Al-Ahram in Egypt and UK courts," *Qatar Review.com*, July 29, 2010.
7. www.aawsat.com/english/news.asp?section=2&id=2159.
8. Eric Pfanner, "Al Jazeera English Tries to Extend Its Reach," *New York Times*, May 19, 2008.
9. Jacqueline E. Sharkey, "Al Jazeera Under the Gun," *American Journalism Review*, October/November 2004.
10. "Interview with 'Brigadier General Mark T. Kimmitt, US Central Command," *Transnational Broadcasting Studies*, 2006.

11. Brian Stelter, "Al Jazeera Renews Case To Air in US," *New York Times*, February 1, 2011.

12. Thomas J. Johnston and Shahira Fahmy, "Who is Winning the Hearts and Minds of the Arab Public?" *International Communication Research Journal*, 45/1–2 (Spring 2010).

13. Nadia Bilbassy-Charters, "Leave It to the Turkish Soaps to Conquer Hearts and Minds," *The Middle East Channel*, April 15, 2010.

14. Ali al-Hail, "The Age of New Media: The Role of Al Jazeera Satellite TV in Developing Aspects of Civil Society in Qatar," Transnational Broadcasting Studies, Spring 2000.

15. Nour Malas, "Democratizing the Arab Screen." *Middle East Broadcasters Journal*, January/February 2008.

16. Trish Schuh "Free Speech "Marked for Death:" Lebanon's Al Manar TV Targeted," *Global Research*, July 17, 2006.

17. Ahmed Osman, "Rude Awakening: Dream TV Drops Top Talkers," *Transnational Broadcasting Studies*, Spring/Summer 2004.

18. www.internetworldstats.com.

19. "The Web Police," *The Atlantic* (May 2006), 50–51.

20. Badr Al-Qahtani, "Saudi Arabia: Twitter Use Skyrockets in 2010," A*sharq al-Awsat* (London), January 4, 2011.

21. Abdulla, *The Internet In the Arab World*, 44.

22. Ian Black, "How Iran is filtering out dissent," *guardian.com.uk*, June 30, 2009.

23. Dominique Soguel, "Women Online in Iran brave heavy Web Surveillance," *Womens eNews*, April 12, 2010.

24. Heba Saleh, "Arab dissent finds voice in cyberspace," *Financial Times*, July 2, 2009, 3.

25. "Saudi Woman Who Spent 6 Months in Jail for Disobeying Her Father is Released," *Instablogs.com*, October 27, 2010.

26. "Iran is world's biggest prison for journalists," *Reporters Without Borders*, January 6, 2010.

27. Lim Stack and Ethan Bronner, "Egypt Sentences Blogger to 3 Years," *New York Times*, April 11, 2011.

28. Robert F. Worth, "A Blog Banned in Yemen, But Written in New Jersey," *New York Times International*, May 20, 2008.

29. Yochi J. Dreazen, "Iraqi's Blog Chronicles Daily Life of a Nation in Turmoil," *The Wall Street Journal*, April 6, 2006, B1.

30. Robert Mackey, "Syrian Women Demand Release of Detainees," *New York Times*, April 13, 2011; Anthony Shadid, "Syria Escalates Crackdown as Tanks Go To Restive City," *New York Times*, April 26, 2011.

31. Brian Stelter, "Journalism Rules Are Bent in News Coverage from Iran," *New York Times*, June 29, 2009.

32. Marc Lynch, *Voices of he New Arab Public: Iraq, Al Jazeera and Middle East Politics Today* (New York: Columbia University Press, 2006), 247–248.

33. Victoria Stodden, "Global Information and Communication Technology and Democratic Tendency," Paper presented to International Conference on Information Technology and Development, Doha, Qatar, April 18, 2009; Steve Crabtree, "Cell Phones Outpace Internet Access in Middle East," *Gallup.com*, July 13, 2009.

34. "The apparatgeist calls," The *Economist*.com, January 6, 2011.

35. Aida F. Akl, "Cell Phones Open New Vistas in Middle East," *VOANews*.com, May 7, 2010.

36. Ami Ayalon, *The Press in the Arab Middle East* (New York: Oxford University Press, 1995), 73–106.

37. "Problems of the Arab Press," December 21, 2010, *al-bab.com*.

38. Oula Farawati, "Jordan's new websites running for legal cover," *menassat.com*, January 7, 2011.

39. David Remnick, "The Dissenters," *New Yorker*, February 28, 2011, 47–59.

40. "World's biggest prison for journalists," *Reporters Without Borders*, December 20, 2010,

41. "Problems of the Arab Press," December 21, 2010, *al-bab.com*.

42. Matt, Bradley and David Luhnow, "Egyptians Take on 'Mini-Mubaraks'," *The Wall Street Journal*, March 10, 2011, A1.

43. Heather Timmons, "A New Mideast Paper Vows to Be Different," *New York Times*, April 29, 2008.

44. Timmons, "A New Mideast Paper Vows to Be Different."

45. Lawrence Pintak, Jeremy Ginges and Nicholas Felton, "Misreading the Arab Media," *New York Times*, May 25, 2008, WK 12.

46. Abdulla, *The Internet in the Arab World*, ix.

# 9

# India and Africa: Contrasts in Development

*There is always something new out of Africa.*
> – Pliny the Elder (A.D. 23–79)

*Five billion people can now make mobile phone calls. Fewer have access to a good toilet.*
> – International Telecommunication Union

On the Indian subcontinent and the continent of Africa great masses of diverse peoples are moving toward modernization and media development at different rates and in different ways. India, as the world's largest democracy and now the world's most populous nation (estimated at over 1.6 billion people) has benefited from its free press which has played a crucial, if abrasive, role in its amazing modernization. Indian democracy is remarkable for the amount of freedom of expression it permits its citizens. Indians can and do organize political parties, trade unions, chambers of commerce, student and civic groups and caste, religious, and ethnic organizations. Despite occasional clashes with politicians, Indian newspapers and publications are generally free from government interference and are multiplying in numbers and circulations in all the Indian languages. Much of the press speaks out on public affairs and has been critical of its prime ministers. Its recent explosive growth in traditional and digital communication is related to the industrial boom that as brought comparative affluence along with consumer goods including television sets, personal computers, and digital media to an expanding middle class.

*The World News Prism: Challenges of Digital Communication*, Eighth Edition.
William A. Hachten and James F. Scotton.
© 2012 John Wiley & Sons, Ltd. Published 2012 by John Wiley & Sons, Ltd.

This media expansion while maintaining free expression stands out in marked contrast to the media stagnation of Africa. Yet India has been and continues to be a deeply troubled and problem-ridden sea of humanity. Writer V. S. Naipaul called it a "wounded civilization" and John K. Galbraith, once a US ambassador there, referred to it as a "functioning anarchy." Further, any perceptive visitor to India can see that there is much that is troubling and deficient about the press and broadcasting. Free newspapers are not necessarily good newspapers. But India's problems are not hidden away; they are out in front for all to see. The press corps, foreign and domestic, is free to roam the vast subcontinent of 3,287, 263 square kilometers and report what it sees and hears. There are no secret gulags or closed areas forbidden to journalists as in China.

India and Africa share similar third world characteristics. Both are large regions with heterogeneous and diverse peoples, numerous languages, and conflicting religions – all marked by deep historic cleavages and communal strife. But India is one nation while Africa is a cluster of forty plus nations. The main Indian languages are Hindi, Telegu, Bengali, Marathi, Tamil, Urdu, Gujarati, Malayalam, Kannada, and Oriya. (There are vibrant newspapers in all these languages.) These principal languages separate the major regions, and within each linguistic region, there are vast dialect differences. Hindi, the official language, is spoken only by a fraction of Indians and is heard mostly in the North. Mumbai (formerly Bombay) residents claim twenty-two mother tongues and twenty-four linguistic groups of 1,000 or more in this one city. As mentioned before, many people in Mumbai speak a mixture of English and four Indian tongues called "Globish."

A great plus is that the educated class speaks English – a link language that connects Indians from different regions and different mother tongues. English is a major asset as well for India's role in the new world of digital communication. These English speakers support over two dozen major media including the great dailies inherited from the British Raj such as the *Times of India, The Statesman, The Hindu,* and *The Tribune.*

About 30% of the one billion plus Indians live in poverty but due to recent economic gains another 350 to 400 million Indians have standards of living ranging from adequate to lavish. India has a much broader cultural base than Africa – more educated people, more doctors, more engineers and scientists. India's scientific and technological development is clearly related to India's impressive expansion of education over the years. There have been over 3 million students enrolled in 135 universities, 1,500 professional colleges and 3,500 arts and/sciences colleges. The centerpiece of India's transcendence is at Bangalore (or Bengaluru) in Kannada state which has rightly been called the Silicon Valley of India, and is home to the most recognized colleges and research institutes in India. With 6.1 million people, Bangalore is the fastest growing major metropolis in India. Not only is it the center for much of the global outsourcing media services but is also a concentration of firms specializing in research and development as well as electronic and software production.

Today's thriving, pulsating society owes much to the Raj – the long period of British rule – when British trade and commerce had a deep impact. English law and the traditions and practices of British journalism including freedom of the press and independent journalism had a lasting impact. Printing technology came to India over 300 years ago The first daily newspaper was published in 1790 in English and called the *Bengal Gazette*. The great English-language papers of today go back to the nineteenth century. After independence came in 1947, the English-language papers were acquired from British owners by Indian capitalists and were completely Indianized while retraining the practices and traditions of British journalism including a strong feeling for freedom of the press. This was respected by law and grudgingly accepted by politicians. So, despite its diversity and complexity, India has had the critical mass to develop a truly national media system. National newspapers and magazines and nation-wide radio and television broadcasting including cable (augmented by the Insat I-B communication satellites system) became possible and in time jumped over linguistic and cultural barriers. At the same time, regional papers in vernacular languages have flourished.

The press has serious shortcomings and sometimes lends itself to government manipulation and is subject to pressures from official advertisers and suppliers of newsprint. The press is not generally noted for investigative reporting and neglects important areas of news coverage. One critic said the press prefers to discuss rumors or gossip instead of facts and hard news. But India's press is unfettered and some papers have not been reluctant to criticize, even excoriate, its prime ministers.

India's media system today is impressive; it has the largest number of daily newspapers in the world with over 1,795 publications. Each great city has its own English language daily. For Delhi, it is the *Hindustan Times*; for Mumbai (Bombay), the *Times of India*; for Madras, *The Hindu*; for Bangalore the *Deccan Herald*; and for Calcutta, *The Statesman*. The *Indian Express*, with ten editions, is not identified with any of these cities but circulates in all of them. These major dailies are available in other cities as well. The Times of India

with over 650,000 circulation (325,000 in Mumbai) is the largest organization, putting out nineteen other publications as well. In addition,
there are twenty-six more regional English papers. As central as the English
language press has been for India, the most impressive growth of the press
in recent years has been in regional vernacular publications which are
thriving. Further, some 50 dailies have online editions in English and
other languages.

Since television was introduced in 1959, India has been one of the largest
television markets in the world. Television is estimated to reach 60% of
all Indians (rural and urban). Doordarshan ("distant vision" in Hindi) is
a government-run national television network established in 1957 that
reaches more than 90% of the population. Doordarshan produces its own
soap operas: a television drama series depicting the Hindu epic, Ramayana,
attracted great interest and television critics estimated that more than
100 million viewers watched the show each Sunday morning.

The advent of the Insat I-B satellite, placed in orbit in 1983 by the U.S
shuttle Challenger, made possible nationwide and direct television broadcasting. Credit goes to Indian scientists and engineers who developed the
Indian National Satellite (INSAT) at a cost of $130 million. The cost of
developing a comparable land-based telecommunication system was estimated at $1 trillion. But the major growth in electronic communication has
been taking place in urban areas, where video cassettes, CDs, and motion
pictures have been expanding. India has long been one of the leading motion
picture producers in the world, turning out over 700 feature films a year
mainly in Bombay or "Bollywood." Most of those films found their way
onto television and CDs. The media usage habits of a significant number of
educated, urban Indians is similar to that of their counterparts in Europe
and North America.

India's extensive and sophisticated media system has attracted the interest of Western media moguls. In August 2008, Rupert Murdoch, chairman
of the News Corporation, announced in Mumbai that his company would
invest $100 million in six new regional television channels. The six channels
would operate in regional languages and start within a year. Through its Star
satellite television, unit, News Corp is already a major owner of television
channels in India and is a minority owner of Tata Sky, a major satellite
television provider in India. As another indicator of India's growing economic power, Murdoch also introduced a new Dow Jones index to track the
Indian stock market. The new index, called Dow Jones India Titans, has
started tracking thirty stocks in one of the world's fastest growing economies.[1]

## Africa Flirts with the New Media

In the fifty years since the beginning of political independence from colonialism, the forty plus new nations of Africa have lagged behind the West in acquiring daily newspapers, radio and television broadcasting stations, motion pictures, magazines and book publishing, and news agencies as well as telecommunications generally. However, during this new century and in numerous places, Africans – despite their enormous problems and the difficulties of their harsh environment – have begun to adopt and adapt such media as cell phones, FM radio, VCRs and DVDs, and computer-assisted global communication. Though modest in scope, these activities contribute to individual and national development and may have important long-term consequences.

## Cell Phones in Rural Africa and India

Cell phones, have proliferated throughout the Western world in recent years and, for journalists, have proved to be exceedingly useful tools to file stories from remote places, or to keep in touch with their editors or colleagues. But the use of cell phones has grown even faster in developing nations and contributes to economic development.

For example, sales of cell phones have been increasing rapidly in rural India, where unexpected uses have been found for them. In the seas off Kerala state, crowded with fishing boats, fishermen use cell phones to keep in touch with the dozen-odd seafood markets, checking prices at different ports. Since acquiring the mobile service, fishermen have markedly increased their profits and efficiency. The 5,000 fishermen who work off the coast are not alone in embracing wireless technology. From garment workers in the south to farmers in the Punjab, rural India has discovered the convenience of doing business on mobile phones. Many people in rural areas have no alternative. Half of India's 660,000 villages have never been wired for fixed-line service, and those connected have had outdated equipment and long waits for service.

In Africa, lack of telecommunications has sorely frustrated the rise of television broadcasting and landline telephone service. Lately, we have seen how the videocassettes and CDs have largely bypassed television, which, like telephone service, has been confined to urban areas, often only in the country's capital. And now, rather unexpectedly, cell phones have catapulted rural Africa into the twenty-first century. During recent years, from 1999 through 2004, Africa has become the fastest growing cell phone market anywhere. Africa's mobile subscribers jumped an average of 58% annually, from 7.5 million to 76.8 million. The next fastest expanding region was Asia, which grew annually at 34% in the same period.

Africans, most living on about $2 a day, were not considered rabid telephone users. But when African nations began to privatize their telephone monopolies in the mid-1990s, the use of cell phones exploded after competitive operators began to sell air time in smaller, cheaper units. Africa has an average of just one landline for every 33 people, but cell phones are enabling millions of people to skip a technological generation and go straight from letter writing to instant communications. The technology is, for many, a social and economic godsend. One program in South Africa allows about 100 farmers in a remote area to learn the prevailing prices for produce in major markets, which is crucial information for dealing with middlemen. Health-care workers elsewhere in South Africa summon ambulances to distant clinics by way of cellphones.[2]

In India, cell phone handsets are sold for less than $25 with 1 cent a minute phone bills across India and on1-cent text messages and no monthly charges – while earning fat profits. For the first time, millions of Africans are able to communicate with people who are beyond shouting distance. The simple cell phone has enabled people to seek work via text messaging; borrowing, lending, and receiving salaries on cell phones; employing their phones as flash lights, televisions, and radios.

The number of mobile subscriptions in the world is expected to pass five billion in 2010, according to the International Telecommunications Union. That would mean that more human beings have access to a cell phone than the United Nations says have access to a clean toilet.[3]

## FM Radio and Political Change in Ghana

In sub-Saharan Africa, radio has long been the most potent mass medium, reaching far more people than newspapers or television. But in most African countries, AM radio has been a heavy-handed government monopoly. However, in Ghana, a West African nation of 26 million, a significant change took place in 1995 when the previous government, led by President Jerry Rawlings, gave up its monopoly on the airwaves and permitted the establishment of private FM radio stations. After that, more than forty

FM stations cropped up around Ghana, broadcasting in English and Ghanaian languages. The stations offered local music and their own news, and most importantly, they broadcast hours and hours of live talk radio, during which Ghanaians could tell government and anyone else what was on their minds.

The resulting national dialogue that took place over FM radio enabled presidential challenger J. A. Kufuor to win an election over Rawlings, whose tired and corrupt party had controlled the country for twenty years. This was the first-ever peaceful transition from one elected civilian government to another in Ghana. Observers said that when people saw something that concerned them, they called in to their FM station, which gave the public a voice. Politicians could hear ordinary people talk about many problems – unemployment, corruption, food prices. People were fed up and they told each other about it. Of Ghana's ten provinces, eight had these flourishing FM stations, and in all these provinces, Kufuor won. In the two provinces without FM stations, the incumbent Rawlings won. Since the election, the FM stations, all run by young Ghanaians who had worked or been educated in the West, have been trying to force more transparency on the new government. One official said, "The minute people were able to talk freely – and anonymously – on the radio and ask what officials were up to was the beginning of accountability for government in Ghana."[4] Finally, the four most democratic nations in West Africa today – Ghana, Mali, Senegal, and Benin – all have flourishing FM radio stations.

## Job Outsourcing and Satellite Channels

Africa has taken two small but significant steps to participating in global communication: telemarketing jobs and contributing to US cable programming. Kenya's international call center – KenCall – has about 200 telephone operators, who are kept busy dialing customers in Britain and the United States This is a growth industry in Africa, and in 2005 there were an estimated 54,000 call-center jobs in Africa out of a total 6 million such jobs worldwide, most of them in India. But the prospects for growth are good, because so many Africans are educated in either English or French. So far, South Africa is ahead of the others, with an estimated 500 call centers employing about 31,000 people. In West Africa, Ghana has lured an outsourcing company based in Dallas that employs about 2,000 Ghanaians to process health claims for Aetna and other insurers.

Another international connection for Africa with the greater world has been the launching in 2005 of the Africa Channel on cable television in the United States. A purpose of the project is to overcome some of the many stereotypes about Africa in the West. The backers have secured rights to 1,200 hours of movies, music, and reality and variety shows that have already been broadcast in Africa, principally in South Africa. Some features, including a daily current events program, "Africa Today," will be produced specially for the twenty-four-hour channel.

## Africa In and Out of the News Spotlight

For twelve days American newspapers and television news were full of stories and video about Ghana, Uganda, Rwanda, South Africa, Botswana, and Senegal – all stops on President Bill Clinton's tour of Africa, with an entourage of 800, including more than 200 journalists. For that brief time, the public was deluged with considerable information about that complex and troubled region. But after Clinton returned to Washington, DC, the news spigot from Africa was abruptly shut off. This reaffirmed a journalistic truism about Africa: the continent usually makes news when a famous personage comes calling, such as President Carter or as Pope John Paul II did later. Africa gets our attention as well when American soldiers' lives are at risk in Africa, or when US Marines landed in Somalia.

Yet most of the time, sub-Saharan Africa, except for South Africa, continues to be the least reported region of the world. One reason is that Africa's own news media, which are weak and usually government controlled, have not been effective in reporting reliable news to Africans, much less to the outside world, and generally are not much help either to foreign journalists trying to report from Africa.

During the 1960s and 1970s, independent black Africa received special attention in the Western press as some forty new nations with promising futures stepped onto the world's stage. But as many of these countries foundered and regressed, and as the Cold War waned, the global media's interest in Africa dropped sharply. There is a grudging consensus among journalists that Africa is badly neglected in global news. David Gergen of *US News* commented, "The history of American media has been one of general inattention to Africa, except when there's been a major famine or conflict."[5]

*Africa's Media Image*, a book edited by Beverly Hawk, with contributions by Africanists and journalists with African experience, gives detailed analyses of shortcomings of Western reporting of major African news stories over the past generation, confirming a near-unanimous view of African specialists that Western news media need to do better. News flows out of Africa to Europe and America in much the same ways that it does from other developing nations in Latin America, Asia, and the Middle East, with many of the same traits.

## Parachute journalism

A story breaks that captures the world's attention: widespread famine in Niger or Ethiopia, genocidal warfare in Sudan or Rwanda, civil war in Congo. The foreign press arrives, often in large numbers, covers the story, shoots pictures and video, and then abruptly leaves. This kind of reporting, typically seen on television, fails to provide needed context and follow-up that such stories require for public understanding.

## Declining coverage

Since the end of the Cold War, much less news has been coming out of Africa, as many civil wars and upheavals have ended. Many small nations, among them Benin, Botswana, Burkina Faso, Mali, Burundi, Guinea, Niger, Lesotho, and Togo, not only have rarely had resident Western correspondents but also are seldom visited by Western reporters passing through the region. A few years ago, armed conflicts were going on at the same time in Angola, Chad, Djibouti, Ethiopia, Liberia, Rwanda, Somalia, Sudan, and Western Sahara, but little reporting about these wars appeared in the US news media. When Nigeria's military dictator, Sani Abacha, died unexpectedly, this major story from Africa's most populous nation received only brief mention on the evening television news. The next day, the *New York Times* and the *Washington Post* both gave the story several pages of coverage.

## Barriers to reporting

Journalists in Africa face barriers not found elsewhere. Few foreign correspondents know the many local languages, although knowledge of English and French is usually sufficient for dealing with news sources. Distances are greater, communications less reliable, and air travel inconvenient and often haphazard. Reporters sometimes have to fly through

London or Paris to get from one African capital to another. African governments often treat reporters badly; some at times just bar all foreign reporters. Often, reporters may be allowed to enter, but access to news sources or officials is severely limited.

### Failures to report bad news

By gathering news that authorities do not want reported, correspondents face the threat of expulsion. Over the years, many Western reporters have been forced out of Africa and refused visas when they sought reentry. Because of this possibility, some journalists believe that sometimes the bad news does not get reported. A British journalist, Ian Smiley, suggested that such self-censorship was a standard feature of reporting throughout the developing world and was nowhere more rigorously observed than in Africa.

Because of this reluctance to report fully, a darker side of Africa may be ignored. True, the coverage has been thin and violence prone, but the need may not be just to provide more positive, cheerful, and sympathetic coverage. The need may be for more realistic and thorough coverage of the continent's deepening crisis. Not much of this gloomy scenario gets into daily news reports.

Two respected journalists have sounded warnings. Robert Kaplan painted a disturbing picture of West Africa which, he said, was "becoming the symbol of worldwide demographic, environmental, and societal stress, in which criminal anarchy emerges as the real 'strategic' danger. Disease, overpopulation, unprovoked crime, scarcity of resources, refugee migrations, the increasing erosion of nation-states and international borders, and the empowerment of private armies, security firms, and international drug cartels are now most tellingly demonstrated through a West African prism."[6] (Conditions have since improved.)

Columnist William Pfaff voiced similar concerns: "The destitution of Africa has been an all but forbidden topic in political discourse. The time has arrived, however, for honest and dispassionate discussion of this immense human tragedy, for which the Western countries bear a grave, if partial, responsibility and which will worsen if not addressed. Much of Africa needs, to put it plainly, what one could call a disinterested neocolonialism."[7]

These are controversial views, and some argue that they show a lack of belief in the survival skills of ordinary people, and may convince the concerned and sympathetic outsiders to give up on Africa. The plight of Africa reflects a central quandary about reporting Africa. Despite the steady decline in news about Africa, the US media's selective, violence-ridden reports have painted a negative and discouraging picture. Yet, if Kaplan and Pfaff are correct, the reality may be bleaker than we believed, and there indeed may be a need for Western nations to intervene. That is not something the Western publics want to hear.

Finally, considering the erratic and sparse coverage of Africa on television and in the news magazines, it is imperative that the handful of prestigious newspapers not dilute their African coverage. Three papers, the *New York Times*, the *Washington Post*, and the *Los Angeles Times*, despite their current financial problems, must continue to produce superior daily reporting out of Africa. Several British papers do an excellent job covering Africa.

Africa remains an enigma. Contradictory news stories often make their appearance. Though usually portrayed as a place of war, disease, and poverty, Africa has been going through a period of one of the greatest population explosions ever recorded. Over 1 billion people now crowd the cities or more accurately the "urban aggregates." Projected populations are for Cairo, 14,800,000; Lagos, 11,400,000; for Kinshasa, 8,600,660; for Johannesburg, 7,350,000; and for Khartoum, 4,500,000; Kenya's population which was 9.3 million in 1965, is expected to reach 65,000,000 by 2050.[8] How, it may be asked, can these poor nations feed and support these teeming masses?

And yet optimistic reports about Africa's future do appear from time to time. McKinsey and Company, a prominent consulting firm, released in 2009 a very upbeat portrait of a continent with growing national economies and an expanding consumer class that offers foreign investors the highest rates of return in the developing world. "A lot of good things are going on in the economies. Since 2000, 316 million Africans have signed up for cell phone service – more than the entire population of America. Africa's billion people spent $816 billion in 2008, more than India's population of 1.2 billion. From 2000 to 2008, African economies grew at twice the rate they did in the 1980s and 1990s.[9] As Pliny the Elder said, "Always something new out of Africa."

## Notes

1. Richard Perez-Pena, "Six New Channels in India to Increase Murdoch's Profile," *New York Times*, August 5, 2008, C3.
2. Sharon LaFraniere, "Cell phones Catapult Rural Africa to 21st Century," *The New York Times*, August 25, 2005, sec. A, 1.

3. Anand Giriddharahas, "Where a Cell phone is Still Cutting Edge," *New York Times*, April 11, 2010, A12.
4. Thomas Friedman, "Low Tech Democracy," *New York Times*, May 1, 2001, sec. A, 27.
5. Beverly Hawk, *Africa's Media Image* (New York: Praeger, 1992), 224.
6. Robert Kaplan, "The Coming Anarchy," *The Atlantic Monthly*, February 1994, 44–76.
7. William Pfaff, "A New Colonialism," *Foreign Affairs*, January/February 1995, 2–6.
8. Shashank Bengali, "Population Boom in Land of Bust," *Wisconsin State Journal*, December 11, 2009, 1.
9. Celia Dugger, "Report Offers Optimistic View of Africa's Economies," *New York Times*, June 4, 2010, A8.

# 10

# Foreign News in Flux

*The cause of the decline and fall of the Roman Empire lay in the fact that there were no newspapers of the day. Because there were no newspapers, there was no way by which the dwellers in the far-flung nation and the empire could find out was going on at the center.*

– H. G. Wells

*The press should be free to go where it wants, when it wants, to see, hear and photograph what it believes is in the public interest.*

– Walter Cronkite

The craft of gathering foreign news by journalists stationed overseas has been undergoing substantial changes in recent years. Because of financial cost cutting and new technologies, less news is reported from abroad and by very different methods. The foreign correspondent – that widely traveled and glamorous specialist of journalism – is becoming a different breed of reporter from the old days of the Cold War. The public today seems less interested in foreign news, and editors and broadcasters are giving them a lot less of it. Yet, on the other hand, as we have seen, the Internet and new media tell a different story: great amounts of news and useful public information are readily available to users of computers.

In the brief two centuries of global news reporting, changes in news are linked to changes in the technology of new gathering. In the nineteenth century, news was collected by reporters who later used telephones, and then the telegraph – hence, the "telegraph editor" long a mainstay on newspapers. For news from abroad, the press relied on journalists' letters

*The World News Prism: Challenges of Digital Communication*, Eighth Edition.
William A. Hachten and James F. Scotton.
© 2012 John Wiley & Sons, Ltd. Published 2012 by John Wiley & Sons, Ltd.

carried by ships – hence the "foreign correspondent" who resided in a foreign capital – a term that has persisted long after news began arriving via international telephones and comsats and now the Internet.

With instantaneous two-way global communication the foreign correspondent and his "foreign bureau" have become anachronisms. News gathering today is more and more a cooperative and collaborative enterprise with more reliance on "other" non-professional media to initially gather news. And as mentioned, global media still get most of their news from print-on-paper journals.

During the decade before 9/11, the news media were somewhat indifferent to foreign news at a time when ethnic conflicts killed millions and globalization touched most American communities. A Harvard study found that during the 1970s, network television devoted 45% of its total coverage to international news. By 1995, foreign news represented only 13.5% of total coverage. Budgets and staff were cut, bureaus closed, and the media emphasized shifts to economic and entertainment/trivia concerns.

Yet serious journalists and editors have long argued that foreign news is important and should be reported thoroughly and well. Many of the best and brightest journalists have spent part of their careers in what must be among the most demanding jobs in journalism. Transnational news gathering is an exacting occupation for the professional newsmen and newswomen who put together the various stories, reports, rumors, and educated guesses that make up the daily international news file. To them, theirs is a difficult, dangerous, and badly misunderstood enterprise. They understand its shortcomings and difficulties far better, they believe, than politically motivated critics or cost-conscious media owners.

In a real sense, the world's ability to learn the news about itself depends on what gets into the news flow in the fifteen or twenty open societies with highly developed media systems. After an important story appears, for example, in New York, London, Paris, Berlin, or Tokyo, it immediately starts flowing through the arteries of the world's news system and will be widely reported elsewhere – but not everywhere, and certainly not every story; the majority of non-Western governments act as gatekeepers, screening news in and out of their nations. These political controls, as well as poverty and illiteracy, deprive the great majority of the world's peoples from learning even the barest outline of major current events. But any major story that "breaks" in the West has at least the possibility of being reported throughout the world.

To the few thousand foreign correspondents, the world's nations are strung out on a continuum from "free" or open at one end to "not free" or closed at the other, and with many variations in between. To illustrate, the Associated Press has little difficulty gathering news in open Sweden, because several newspapers there take AP services and share their own news and photos with the agency. In addition, AP correspondents can use other Swedish media as sources and can develop their own stories or easily gain access to public officials.

Sudan, like other developing nations, offers a different kind of challenge. AP has no clients in Sudan, largely because the Sudan News Agency lacks the hard currency to buy the Comsat-beamed AP world service. The local media are subject to official controls, and AP cannot justify the expense of maintaining a full-time correspondent in Khartoum. Therefore, AP "covers" Sudan by using a local stringer (a part-timer who is paid for what news is used). Periodically, AP may send a staff correspondent to Sudan to do background or round up stories. At other times, AP may try to report on events in Sudan from Nairobi, in neighboring Kenya. Yet as recent events in Sudan have illustrated, the world knew too little about a state that condoned, if not encouraged, genocide against its own people. Despite the efforts of a few hardy reporters who managed to get into Darfur to report the atrocities against helpless civilians, the United Nations has still not taken effective action to halt the genocide.

At the "not free" end of the continuum are a few countries that for years barred all foreign journalists and news agencies. In the Cold War days, when something important happened in Tirana, Albania, for instance, AP and the world usually found out about it belatedly from a government-controlled Albanian radio broadcast monitored abroad, or from travelers or diplomats leaving the country. Albania has since opened, and Western analysts were surprised that Albanian refugees knew about the collapse of communism, which they learned about by listening carefully to English broadcasts on the BBC and the Voice of America (VOA). Much news of the turmoil in Africa is often reported from the safety of neighboring countries.

A foreign correspondent often defines a country as free or not free according to how much difficulty he or she has in reporting events there. This may sound narrow and self-serving, but it has validity: the freedom of access that a foreign reporter enjoys is usually directly related to the amount of independence and access enjoyed by local journalists themselves. If local journalists are harassed or news media controlled by a particular government, so very likely will be the foreign journalists.

With the availability of impressive gadgets used by today's foreign correspondents – satellite telephones, videophones, laptop computers, reliable phone lines (or better yet cell phones), and faxes – the reporter abroad is able to do his or her job better. An important recent gadget is the video telephone so widely used in Afghanistan. Even so, collecting news throughout the world is still an erratic and imperfect process. Some significant events are either not reported or reported long after the fact. Certain areas of the world, such as central Africa, rarely get into the world news flow.

In the dangerous and confusing post-Cold War world, foreign reporters and news organizations went through an identity crisis over what is news. As John Walcott of *Newsweek* said, "The Cold War provided us with a coherent global road map, in terms of what to cover and how to cover it."[1] The press is not used to reacting to a world full of conflicts and violent encounters that, as George Kennan put it, offer no "great and all absorbing focal points for American policy."[2] Now the war on terrorism has provided for some nations a focus for global news comparable to that of the Cold War.

Key challenge is disagreements between journalists and government officials over the very nature of news. To journalists, news is the first, fragmentary, and incomplete report of a significant event or happening that editors think will be of interest or importance to their readers or listeners. To many government officials, news is "positive" information that reflects favorably on their nation (and hence themselves) and serves their country's general interests and goals. Yet those same leaders want to know all that is happening elsewhere that affects their own interests and country. An AP man once said that news is what a government official wants to read about somewhere else, whereas propaganda is what the official wants the world to read about his or her country. Politicians and government leaders in every nation attempt to manage or manipulate the news so that it favors their causes, their programs, their image.

Any major news story is perceived differently by the press in almost every country for these reasons. Media everywhere tend to have a "bias of nationalism" that affects the way a story is reported. What has been called "journalism as politics" permeates foreign news in subtle ways. Moreover, the maxim "all news is local" has validity because editors usually respond more fully to what happens nearby or what affects local interests.

Certainly, before 9/11 the news media, especially television and news magazines, had been paying less attention to foreign news. Always expensive to cover, the consensus in the news business had been that you can expect international news to turn a profit only when it is really domestic news in a foreign setting, such as a US military intervention, when it is "our boys" who are "over there," as in Afghanistan or Iraq. Even among Western nations, there can be profound differences or issues such as free speech and access to news versus the right to privacy. In February 2010, an Italian court ruled that Google had violated Italian privacy law by allowing users to post a video on one of its services. The ruling raised the issue of how much responsibility Google has for offensive material that it passively distributed. But it also called attention to the profound European commitment for privacy which runs head long into the American concept of free expression. This standoff could restrict the flow of information on the Internet to everyone. Because of World War II experiences, the right of privacy is to Europeans a basic human right. Free press advocates usually support the view of Walter Cronkite that the press should be free to go where it wants, to see, hear and photograph what it believes to be in the public interest. That view is basic to the American/British press practices and is being gradually accepted by media around the world. International journalism seems to be groping for uniformity of law to protect journalists and the public interest.

## Television News in Decline: The CBS Case

CBS News, long famed for its international coverage, once maintained twenty-four foreign bureaus. By 2005, it had reporters in only four capitals: London, Moscow, Tel Aviv, and Tokyo. Dan Rather told a group of Harvard students, "Don't kid yourself. The trend line in American journalism is away from, not toward, increased foreign coverage. Foreign coverage requires the most space and the most air time because you are dealing with complicated situations, in which you have to explain a lot. And then there's always somebody around who says people don't give a damn about this stuff anyway. . . . 'If you have to do something foreign, Dan, for heaven's sake, keep it short'."[3]

Tom Fenton, a former CBS reporter, recently wrote that foreign news is down 70 to 80% since the early 1980s, supplemented by "junk news" and "tabloidism." Meanwhile, the all news cable channels – once our great hope – degenerate to celebrity and commentary formulas, offering little credible reporting. One of the most alarming comments in Fenton's book is as follows: "In the three months leading up to September 11, the phrase 'Al Qaeda' was never mentioned on any of the three evening news broadcasts – not once. I, and scores of my fellow American foreign correspondents, had been tracking stories about Al Qaeda and its allies for more than a decade.

But we rarely reported what we knew on network news – because, much of the time, our bosses didn't consider such developments newsworthy."[4] Fenton said CBS relies increasingly on information supplied by video wire services and overseas broadcasters. It is television's equivalent of outsourcing.

In September 2009, CBS News announced that it had formed a partnership with GlobalPost, a foreign news Web site that would provide CBS with reporting from its seventy affiliated correspondents in fifty countries. CBS suggested that the alliance with GlobalPost for which the network will pay a monthly undisclosed fee was really an expansion of CBS News' efforts to cover the rest of the world. Others saw it as indicative of the continued decline of the news organization's proud traditions associated with such greats as Edward R. Murrow, Walter Cronkite, and Eric Sevareid.

Meanwhile a rival, ABC News, has gone through several downsizing stints. In April 2010, the news unit of the Disney Company completed one of the most drastic rounds of budget cuts and firings at a television news operation – roughly one quarter of the staff, over 100 people, were laid off. Then in September 2010, David Westin, the ABC news chief, resigned after fourteen years. ABC News long a solid second to NBC News, found it hard to compete without a cable outlet such as MSNBC, and was unable to increase revenue, share labor, and reduce costs. Television journalists were stunned by these developments and the capability of television news to cover global news seemed seriously diminished.[5]

## Changing Correspondents

"What is commonly referred to as the world flow of information," AP correspondent Mort Rosenblum wrote, "is more a series of trickles and spurts. News is moved across borders by a surprisingly thin network of correspondents. . . . The smaller countries are squeezed into rapid trips during lulls between major stories in the larger countries." Rosenblum quoted a comment from a Latin American academic that "news breaks in South America along the direct line of the international airline route."[6]

In some places it may seem that way, and yet the total flood of daily news reports from abroad is immense. One study estimated that the big four agencies send out about 33 million words a day, with 17 million from AP, 11 million from UPI, 3.4 million from AFP, and 1.5 million from Reuters.

Among the smaller agencies, DPA of Germany was set at 115,000, ANSA of Italy at 300,000, and EFE of Spain at 500,000.

Considering the demand for foreign news and the difficulties of reporting from far-flung places, there are probably too few correspondents stationed overseas. Rising costs and inflation have made maintenance of a staffer overseas quite expensive. Estimates for maintaining a newspaper bureau overseas (that is, at least one reporter) for a year range from $150,000 to $250,000, and the costs keep going up. A television bureau can cost more than $1 million a year. It is not surprising, therefore, that many news media rely on the news agencies for their foreign news. In most countries, that means the Associated Press and Reuters. High costs help explain the drop in overseas television bureaus and the loss of regular staffers in overseas bureaus. The void has been filled to some extent by freelancers or independent part-time journalists. Perhaps more important is the increased news coming from diverse Internet sources not really connected to regular news outlets.

AP and other news agencies are using more and more "locals" – nationals of countries they cover. Western journalism is increasingly relying on foreign nationals to help report the news. Foreign journalists are not only less expensive, but often have a grasp of local languages and knowledge of their own countries that US journalists cannot match. Journalist Scott Schuster attributed the trend to a global acceptance of English as a media language and the global influence of American journalistic methods: "American influence is most profound among broadcasters, and foreign broadcast journalists need only to turn on their television sets to receive lessons on how to do the news American-style," he said. Schuster goes on:

> American methods of news production are being adopted all across Western Europe and in many third world countries. ... During the coming decade journalistic styles in both print and broadcast media are likely to experience continuing international homogenization. The nationality of the reporter will no longer be an issue. Brits will cover Britain. Ghanaians will cover Ghana, and a large number of American journalists will become "foreign correspondents" – covering America for foreign media.[7]

Increasingly, to deal with rising costs and tighter budgets, news media are relying on stringers or freelancers. A study by Stephen Hess of the Brookings Institution of 404 foreign correspondents working for US news media found that 26% are freelancers. Moreover, many of these are underemployed, with

40% saying they do other work as well. All suffer the usual fate of freelancers: low pay, no benefits, and a precarious relationship with their employers.[8] Hess found six types of stringers: "spouses" of other correspondents; "experts," who know languages and the area; "adventurers," like Oriana Fallaci; "flingers," a person on a fling who might start a serious career; "ideologues" or "sympathizers," who are often British; and the "residents," who are often longtime residents and write occasional stories.

A significant change has been the increasing number of women among foreign correspondents, especially today as war reporters. Before 1970, their numbers were small, although there had been a few famous names: Dorothy Thompson, Martha Gellhorn, Marguerite Higgins, and Gloria Emerson. Hess found that, by the 1970s, about 16% of new foreign reporters were women; this doubled during the 1980s to about 33%. This ratio of two men for every woman was also found in Washington media as well as in US journalism generally.

In the past, some women correspondents have earned outstanding reputations, including Caryle Murphy and Robin Wright of the *Washington Post*, syndicated columnist Georgie Ann Geyer, and Elaine Sciolino of the *New York Times*. Christiane Amanpour of CNN became a kind of celebrity because of her aggressive and frankly partisan reporting of such stories as the first Iraq war, civil upheaval in Africa, the civil war in Bosnia, and wars in Afghanistan and Iraq. A significant number of women have been covering the wars for Western media. National Public Radio (NPR) is a major source of reliable news from the world's hot spots and many of its capable reporters are women.

Foreign correspondents today are better educated, know more foreign languages, and have higher-status backgrounds than their predecessors. Current salaries range from about $50,000 to $90,000, with more experienced reporters earning even more.

When not reporting a war, the networks increasingly seem to be relying on news film supplied by the syndicates, Reuters Television, APTV News, and other foreign broadcasters for international coverage. These less costly ways of collecting news have undermined the credibility of some foreign news. A few years ago, if you saw a foreign news story on NBC News, chances are that it was reported by an NBC reporter at the scene, with film shot by an NBC crew. Now, you cannot be sure. The networks are relying more on less expensive, and often less experienced, freelancers and independent contractors whose products are rarely identified on the air, leaving the impression that the story was reported by network staffers. This practice gives rise to a growing concern about quality control. "By the time the tape gets on the air, nobody has the foggiest idea who made it and whether the pictures were staged," contended Tom Wolzien, a former NBC news executive.[9] More loss of authenticity results when US network correspondents, based in London, add voice-overs to stories they did not cover. Bert Quint, former CBS correspondent said, "There's no reason to believe the person [doing the voice-over] because odds are he or she was not within 3,000 miles of where the story occurred."[10]

Not only are foreign correspondents comparatively few, they are unevenly distributed as well. One study found that more than half of all American reporters abroad were stationed in nineteen European countries. During the Persian Gulf crisis, more than 800 Western reporters descended on the region, but few were experts on Middle Eastern affairs. Many of the hundreds covering the wars in Afghanistan and Central Asia have had no previous overseas experience. Such "parachute journalism" does not always provide informed coverage, because so many of these reporters lack previous experience or understanding of the area about which they are reporting.

For readers and listeners, serious questions have been raised about the quantity and quality of foreign news. The debate tends to be circular. AP and other agencies have long maintained that their services gather ample amounts of foreign news, but that their newspaper and broadcast clients do not use very much of it. The media clients in turn argue that their readers and viewers are not very much interested in foreign news. Yet critics say that Americans are uninformed about the world because their news media report so little about it. The widespread shock and fear felt by many Americans after the September 11 terror attacks was in part related to their lack of knowledge about terrorism and the Middle East.

Certainly the generalization that the majority of the public, with access to the world's most pervasive media, are ill informed about world affairs has substance. A panel at Columbia's School of Journalism criticized the audience:

> There is a crisis in international news reporting in the United States – and not one that should simply be blamed on the reporters, the gatekeepers, or the owners. We know there is stagnation, and even shrinkage, in the number of international stories in the media and the number of correspondents in the field for most US media outlets. But the primary reason for this decline is an audience that expresses less and less interest in the international stories that

do appear. What we're increasingly missing, as a culture, is connective tissue to bind us to the rest of the world.[11]

Foreigners traveling in the American heartland are uniformly impressed by the lack of world news in local media and the ignorance shown by most Americans about the outside world. By contrast, the average German, Dane, or Israeli knows more global news because his or her media carry more. Part of the problem is that Americans, like Russians and Chinese, have a continental outlook, living as they do in the midst of a vast land mass that encourages a self-centered, isolationist view of the world. With two friendly neighbors and protected by two oceans, Americans are slow to recognize their interdependence with others. The shock of 9/11 may have modified that mind set, but only temporarily.

The public's interest in foreign news has its ups and downs, depending on the perceived impact of any current crisis on their lives. During the Vietnam War, much concern was focused on happenings in Southeast Asia, but not in Latin America or Africa, where news coverage dropped off. After Vietnam, foreign concerns receded as the nation became enthralled by Watergate and its aftermath. But after the rapid increases and then decreases in the price of foreign oil, the Soviet incursion into Afghanistan, continuing Arab/Israeli conflict, and a rising level of terrorism directed against Americans, the average American's interest (if not knowledge) in foreign news, especially that of the Middle East, clearly increased. Then, during the summer of 1990, after Iraq invaded Kuwait and American forces were moved into Saudi Arabia before war began in January 1991, American and European interest in and anxiety about the Persian Gulf soared.

In late 1994 and early 1995, interest in foreign news plummeted as the US news media became mesmerized with the murder trial of O.J. Simpson and the domestic politics of the Republicans' legislative zeal in Washington, DC, after winning control of Congress in the November 1994 elections.

In 1998, the nation's prosperity and the continuing story about President Clinton's personal problems seemed to push foreign news off the nation's news agenda, at least for a while. The continuing crises in the former Yugoslavia, Iraq, and Israel and the teetering Asian and Russian economies did not go away; they just seemed less urgent and less visible. By mid-1998, nuclear tests by India and Pakistan and the possibility of war in South Asia brought a heightened interest in foreign news. The aerial war over Kosovo and Serbia led by America and NATO held the spotlight while it lasted. But the terror attacks of 9/11 have brought an abrupt, if temporary, change in

Americans' attitude toward the outside world. Many were clearly frightened and saw themselves as vulnerable to the perils faced by Israelis and many Europeans. Recent events such as 9/11, world economic crisis, global warming, and so on, have added to anxieties.

Some critics believed that television had profoundly affected the public's news perceptions. Neil Postman believes television projects a "peeka-boo" world, "where now this event, now that, pops into view for a moment, then vanishes again. It is a world without much sense or coherence. . . .. Americans know of a lot of things but about almost nothing. Someone is considered well informed who simply knows that a plane was hijacked or that there was an earthquake in Mexico City."[12]

Despite ignorance of the world, there is a growing recognition that perhaps the term "foreign news" is a misnomer and that in our inter-dependent world we are potentially affected by any event almost anywhere. Failing overseas economies can threaten the US stock market and pros-perity. American workers who lose jobs in manufacturing due to cheap foreign imports, or farmers unable to sell wheat abroad due to the over-valued dollar, are becoming more knowledgeable about world economic trends. And the Iraq and Afghan wars and other turmoil reminded Westerners of their dependence on Middle Eastern oil and the lack of a conservation policy to deal with that dependence. Since 9/11, many Americans for the first time have believed they could die in a terrorist attack.

The reporting of foreign news has been criticized as being too crisis oriented. An ABC News poll found that among viewers polled, 55% agreed, "Television news only does stories about foreign countries when there's a war or some other violent crisis going on."[13] Media critic Hodding Carter said the networks "concentrate on showing kids throwing rocks at troops or guns going off or planes bombing or rubble falling. These are the repetitive images that block out the complexities." In addition, he cited the "extraordinary lack of continuity and perspective, which is the shadow of all television news."[14] Inevitably, much of what happens in the world will go unnoted. Wherever he or she may be, the average person obviously does not have the time or interest to follow all the news from everywhere. As one editor asked, "Who wants to read about Zaire if there is nothing going on there?" Gerald Long of Reuters explained more fully: "The prevalent school of journalism throughout the world is a 'journalism of exception.' In other words, you don't report that everything is fine in Pakistan. You report that there has been an air crash."[15] This approach contributes to an inevitable imbalance and distortion of reality.

The journalism of exception – reporting civil unrest, the coup d'état, the train wreck, the drought – is at the root of much hostility and antagonism toward Western reporting. Journalists who work abroad say it is difficult to gain access to many parts of the world, particularly Africa, the Middle East, and Asia. Americans who often hold domestic journalists and broadcasters in low esteem, especially on cable television, are mostly uninformed about the dangers of practicing journalists in the Middle East and other trouble spots in the world.

Journalists had particular difficulty in reporting the eight-year conflict between Iran and Iraq and the prolonged civil war involving Serbia, Bosnia, Croatia, and Kosovo. In its early stages, the war in Afghanistan was dangerous and challenging to report. Before 9/11, in India, the foreign cable networks, CNN and the BBC's World Service Television, became a target for Indian politicians looking for scapegoats to blame for secessionist movements, religious strife, and natural disasters. India's own television network, Doordarshan, owned and controlled by the government, is well known for delaying and sanitizing news broadcasts. CNN and the BBC came to India in 1991 while reporting the First Gulf War and later aggressively reported the razing of the Babri Mosque in late 1993 by Hindu fundamentalists, which led to national riots in which 1,800 died. In response, Indian political leaders of both left and right demanded strong action against the networks. However, when things go in favor of the politicians, they praise foreign coverage.[16]

A major point of contention, as mentioned, is that most governments believe the press, including foreign reporters, should serve the host country's national aims, whereas the Western press believes it must decide for itself what news to report. And each foreign reporter will report his or her version of events, as colored by the culture and traditions of his own national media.

## Physical and Psychological Dangers

Foreign correspondents often risk their lives to cover wars, civil unrest, and other forms of violence. Within unstable nations, journalists, both foreign and domestic, are often singled out as targets for arrest, beatings, or assassination. Sometimes they are just in the wrong place at the wrong time.

One difficulty in protecting journalists abroad is that there are now different kinds of journalists. There are now "citizen journalists" who provide news not otherwise available and sometimes their identity cannot be revealed. In 2010, a George Polk award was given for the brief video reports of the violent death of an Iranian woman during election protests in Tehran in 2009. The thirty-seven-second video of the death became a symbol of Iranian opposition and was viewed worldwide. The prestigious Polk Award committee said it wanted to acknowledge the role of ordinary citizens in disseminating words and images in times of turmoil when professional journalists faced restrictions as they in Iran. It was the first Polk Award given anonymously.

Another new category is that of inexperienced reporters from lesser known media who run afoul of autocratic regimes. Two young American women, Laura Ling and Euna Lee, were working on a story about North Korean refugees when they were arrested by North Korean border guards. Later, they were sentenced to twelve years in a labor prison, setting off diplomatic efforts to win their release. They were not working for a well-known news organization but for an obscure television channel, Current television, which lacked the clout to bring pressure on their captors. The Committee to Protect Journalists found that in 2008 at least fifty-six of the jailed journalists worked for online organizations and that forty-five of that total were freelancers.[17]

The admirable Committee to Protect Journalists keeps track of such violence, and reported in 2010 that 830 journalists since 1992 had been killed in the world. Among that eighteen-year total 598 journalists had been murdered; 147 here been killed in crossfire or combat; and eighty-three killed on dangerous assignments.

Numbers killed in the deadliest countries were as follows: (i) Iraq, 142 journalists; (ii) Philippines, 142; (iii) Algeria, 60; (iv) Russia, 52; (v) Colombia, 43; (vi) Somalia, 34; (vii) Pakistan, 31; (viii) India, 27; (ix) Afghanistan, 22; (x) Mexico, 22, (xi) Turkey, 20; (xii) Bosnia, 19; (xiii) Sri Lanka, 18; (xiv) Rwanda, 15; (xv) Tajikistan, 16; (xvi) Sierra Leone, 16; (xvii) Brazil, 16; (xviii) Bangladesh, 12; (xix) Israel/Occupied Palestine, 10; and (xx) Angola, 10.[18]

In twenty-three cases since 1995, journalists were kidnapped, often taken alive by militants or government forces and subsequently killed. The kidnapping and murder of *Wall Street Journal* reporter Daniel Pearl in early 2002 highlighted this terrible phenomenon. In several cases, notably in

Algeria and Turkey, journalists have simply "disappeared" after being taken into government custody.

Among the many killed in Russia some died covering the war with Chechnya, but at least eleven reporters have been murdered in contract-style killings in the four years since President Putin took power. Paul Klebnikov, the American-born editor of *Forbes Russia*, was gunned down outside his office in Moscow in July 2004.

Governments and warring armies are not the only foes of press freedom; sometimes terrorists and thugs attack the press. Louis Boccardi, then president of AP, said, "On the international scene, the world continues to grow more difficult to cover. The physical dangers abound. Dozens of journalists have been killed in the last few years and many more injured in the pursuit of a story, their story, wherever it was."[19]

Finally, it should be said that the Western practice of "journalism of exception" continues to rankle critics of the press everywhere. In America, many feel that the media report far too much negative news. But as Daniel Patrick Moynihan once said, "It is the mark of a democracy that its press is filled with bad news. When one comes to a country where the press is filled with good news, one can be pretty sure that the jails are filled with good men."

The reporting of modern wars – their own wars – have presented special challenges to American and British news media and to reporters who cover them. That problem is discussed in the next chapter.

## Notes

1. Leon Hadar, "Covering the New World Disorder," *Columbia Journalism Review*, July/August 1994, 27.
2. Hadar "Covering the New World Disorder."
3. Stephen Hess, *International News and Foreign Correspondents* (Washington, DC: Brookings Institution, 1996), 61.
4. Tom Fenton, *Bad News* (New York: Regan Books, 2005), 4.
5. Brian Stelter, "Job Cuts at ABC News Leave Workers Stunned and Downcast," *New York Times*, May 1, 2010, B2.
6. Mort Rosenblum, *Who Stole the News?* (New York: John Wiley, 1993), 20.
7. Scott Schuster, "Foreign Competition Hits the News," *Columbia Journalism Review*, May/June 1988, 45.
8. Stephen Hess, "The Cheaper Solution," *American Journalism Review*, April 1994, 27.

9. Hess, *International News and Foreign Correspondents*, 100.
10. Hess, *International News and Foreign Correspondents*.
11. "World News: Truth or Consequences," *Columbia Journalism Review*, January/February 1995, 4.
12. Sally Bedell Smith, "How New Technologies are Starting to Change the Nation's Viewing Habits," *New York Times*, October 9, 1985, sec. A, 10.
13. Sally Bedell Smith, "Why TV News Can't Be a Complete View of the World," *New York Times*, August 8, 1982, entertainment section, 1.
14. Bedell Smith, "Why TV News Can't Be a Complete View of the World."
15. Rosemary Righter, *Whose News: Politics, the Press and the Third World* (New York: Times Books, 1978), 70.
16. Arthur J. Pais, "Anger in India," *Columbia Journalism Review*, May/June 1993, 17.
17. Brian Stelter, "A World at Risk for a New Style of Journalism," *New York Times*, June 15, 2009, B1.
18. Press freedom online Committee to Protect Journalists.
19. Mark Fitzgerald, "A Dangerous Affair," *Editor and Publisher*, November 2, 1985, 18.

# 11

# War Reporting: Fire and Misfire

*The first casualty when war comes is truth.*
— Senator Hiram Johnson, 1917

*We don't want the truth told about things around here.*
— General William Tecumseh Sherman

Four recent wars – the 1991 First Gulf War, the aerial war over Serbia and Kosovo, the winding down of the war in Iraq and the continuing seven-year-plus struggle in Afghanistan – have dramatically altered the ways that armed conflicts are reported to the world. Although long-standing frictions and suspicions persist between the press and military officials, the use of new communication technologies has altered journalism for better or worse. The wars themselves have changed – from short intensive clashes, to asymmetrical struggles against terrorist guerillas – to drawn out counter-insurgency efforts involving nation-building to win the hearts and minds. The West has relearned a basic tenet. Wars are much easier to get into than to get out of.

In the brief Gulf war, television and especially CNN turned much of the world into a global community witnessing a televised real-time war, as the brief conflict evolved from armed confrontation to spectacular aerial bombardment and finally to lightning ground warfare. The war became the biggest global news story in years, and telling it utilized the full resources of the US and European news media as well as much of the international news system. More than 1,600 print and broadcast journalists were on hand to report it.

*The World News Prism: Challenges of Digital Communication*, Eighth Edition.
William A. Hachten and James F. Scotton.
© 2012 John Wiley & Sons, Ltd. Published 2012 by John Wiley & Sons, Ltd.

The 1999 NATO bombing campaign against Serbia, whose ground forces were mauling Kosovo civilians, was a new kind of war: an effort, mainly by US air power, to bomb a nation into submission without deploying ground troops or even incurring casualties. As in the First Gulf War, the press accused the military of withholding news and of "spinning" combat reports for political and strategic reasons. The seventy-eight days of NATO bombing finally forced Yugoslavian dictator Slobodan Milosević to yield and permit 16,000 NATO soldiers to chase the fleeing Serbian forces out of Kosovo and thus bring relief to the battered ethnic Albanians. In that last war of the twentieth century, global news coverage was greatly facilitated by the satellite telephone, twenty-four-hour cable television coverage, and, for the first time, the Internet.

During the opening months of the war against the Taliban in Afghanistan, press and military relationships were still evolving. The Bush administration made it clear that the press would receive less access to combat-related information than in previous conflicts. Yet the news media, here and abroad, poured out a steady torrent of news, speculation, commentary, and pictures about this many-faceted conflict. The world of 2001 was more completely "wired" for 24/7 coverage and journalists from many nations flocked to the region. The Iraq war, launched with great fanfare in spring 2003, at first dominated the world's front pages and television screens as the United States and its coalition forces quickly overwhelmed the army of Saddam Hussein and captured Baghdad. Then, when the blitzkrieg morphed into a tortuous insurgency that after two and a half years (and counting) still had no end in sight, most of the world paid less and less attention. But for reporters still in Iraq, their work became increasingly dangerous and difficult.

The role of the news media in reporting and explaining Iraq has gone through changes. Wars, particularly when they involve Western powers, are always at the top of the news agendas for foreign nations. And as the world becomes more interconnected by global communications, many more people in more places are paying close attention through the news media. But after seven years, as the Iraq war had finally wound down most (but not all) combat troops had departed, most of the journalists had left as well. The public, too, had largely lost interest.

Many journalists traveled to Afghanistan where the United States under a new president Barack Obama, sent 150,000 more troops in order to counter the growing influence of the Taliban. As of late 2010, relations between the military and the press were at a low ebb; Western leaders and the informed publics increasingly dubious that the war was winnable. With the strategic emphasis on counter-insurgency, the news was less and less about combat and more about the politics and diplomacy of dealing with an erratic Afghan president presiding over a corrupt government. And the old mutual suspicions between the press and the military persisted.

## Background of Press Controls

How did the relations between American journalists and the US military become so abrasive? In World War I, some 500 American correspondents covered the conflict for newspapers, magazines, and press associations in France and, unlike British and French reporters, they were free to go to the front lines without military escorts. Still, everything written by such star reporters as Richard Harding Davis, Will Irwin, or Floyd Gibbons was passed through the censorship of the press section of the Military Intelligence Service. Details about specific battles, numbers of casualties, and names of units could be released only after being mentioned in official communiqués.

US military censorship followed the same general pattern in World War II, with the added feature of controlling radio broadcasts. The Office of Censorship was headed by Byron Price, a former AP editor, who handled with distinction the most difficult part of his job: the direction of voluntary press censorship that applied to print media outside the combat zones. In far-flung combat "theaters," reporters were generally free to move about and join military units but were always subject to possible censorship. About 500 full-time American reporters were abroad at any one time, and provided coverage that many considered the best and fullest ever seen. With mobile units and tape recordings, radio coverage greatly increased. Relations between the military and reporters were mutually trusting and supportive. Despite occasional conflicts over withheld information, everyone seemed to be on the same team. During the Korean war, the press-government relations were pretty much the same.

The change began in the 1960s Vietnam War when relations soured and reached their lowest ebb. Reporters and camera crews, working within military guidelines, were given free access without field censorship to roam Vietnam; some called it the best-reported war in history. Yet many in the US military believed critical press reporting contributed to the American defeat by over-stressing negative aspects, including graphic pictures of dead and wounded, highlighting scandals such as the My Lai massacre, and mis-interpreting key events, such as the Tet offensive, which the military pronounced a defeat for North Vietnam, and not a Vietcong victory as the press reported. Such reports, the military argued, aided the anti-war movement at home.

The war reporters felt that the US military had misled and lied to them in Vietnam and that officials consistently painted a much rosier picture of the war than the facts justified. Given the record of deception, the press, it was argued, was correct in being skeptical of the military. A view prevailed within the military that the free rein given to reporters in Vietnam led to reporting that seriously damaged morale and turned American public opinion against its own troops. If news or information is a weapon, then, the generals argued, it should be controlled as part of the war effort.

The brief war in 1982 between Britain and Argentina over the Falkland Islands in the South Atlantic provided a model for the Pentagon on how to manage the press during wartime. Only British reporters were permitted to accompany the task force, and these reporters were carefully selected. The seventeen journalists chosen had to accept censorship at the source and were given a government handbook telling them they would be "expected to help in leading and steadying public opinion in times of national stress or crisis." The Ministry of Defence effectively imposed censorship at the source, and most war information followed a policy of suppression or subtle control of emphasis. After the Falklands War was over, the British press gave a very different picture of the conflict, detailing losses, mishaps, and failures of British forces previously unreported.

For the US, the war news issue surfaced again on October 25, 1983, when US forces invaded the tiny island of Grenada. The Defense Department barred all reporters from covering the initial invasion. After two days of rigorous protests from the press, a pool of twelve reporters was finally flown in with a military escort. By the end of one week, with the fighting winding down, 150 reporters were ferried to the island and allowed to stay overnight. The press, however, was not mollified. Walter Cronkite said the Reagan Administration had seriously erred, arguing, "This is our foreign policy and we have a right to know what is happening and there can be no excuse in denying the people that right."[1] But as in the later Gulf war, opinion polls showed that the public supported the ban on press coverage. As a result of the furor, the Defense Department appointed a commission that recom-mended that a select pool of reporters be allowed to cover the early stages of any surprise military operation and share its information with other press organizations. This seems a fair compromise between the military's need for surprise and the public's need for information. The new guidelines were first tested in December 1989, when US forces invaded Panama. The press arrangements failed miserably. The Pentagon did not get the sixteen-reporter pool into Panama until four hours after fighting began, and reporters were not allowed to file stories until six hours later. Most critics blamed the White House for the mix-up and for insisting that only the military facilitate press coverage. When the First Gulf War loomed, the American generals, Colin Powell and Norman Schwarzkopf, and other Vietnam veterans, were ready to deal with the press.

## The First War with Saddam Hussein

Global television came into its own as CNN and other broadcasters reported a war as it was happening, or as it appeared to be happening – a "real time" war. After hostilities began early on January 17, 1991, reporters described anti-aircraft tracers in the night sky of Baghdad and flashes of bomb explosions on the horizon. On succeeding nights, viewers were provided with live video reports from Tel Aviv and Riyadh of Scud missiles, some apparently intercepted by Patriot missiles, exploding against the night sky, and of television reporters donning gas masks on camera. The press talked of the "CNN effect" – millions anchored hour after hour to their television sets lest they miss the latest dramatic development. Restaurants, movies, hotels, and gaming establishments all suffered business losses: "People are intensely interested in the first real-time war in history and they are just planting themselves in front of their television sets," one expert said. Ratings for CNN soared five to ten times their prewar levels.[2] The First Gulf War was a worldwide media event of astonishing proportions. Global television had never had a larger or more interested audience for such a sustained period of time. Television became the first and principal source of news for most people, as well as a major source of military and political intelligence for both sides. CNN telecasts, including military briefings, were viewed in Baghdad as they were being received in Riyadh or Washington, DC – as well as in other non-Western countries.

The combatants, particularly the governments of Iraq and the United States, tried to control and manipulate the media with subtle and not-so-subtle propaganda and misinformation messages. Western journalists chafed at the restraints on news coverage of the war itself and complained that there was much news they were not permitted to report. Most coalition news came from military briefings and from carefully controlled and escorted "pools" of reporters. Some official news presented at the briefings was actually disinformation intended to mislead the enemy, not to inform the public. For example, viewers were led to believe that Patriot missiles were invariably successful in neutralizing Scud missiles, but such was not the case.

Information was tightly controlled; one observer called it "the illusion of news." For its own self-defined security reasons, the military often held back or distorted the news it did release. In the opening days of the war, much was made of the "smart bombs" that hit their targets with about 90% accuracy. After the war, the US Air Force admitted that smart bombs made up only 7% of all US explosives dropped on Iraq and Kuwait. The Air Force later said that 70% of the 88,500 tons of bombs dropped on Kuwait and Iraq missed their targets.[3]

Peter Jennings of ABC News reminded viewers that much of what was revealed in the opening days of war was speculation, mixed with some hard facts and some rumors in the rushing river of information. But whether they were getting hard news or not, many millions of viewers stayed by their television sets. Public opinion polls showed that the overwhelming majority of Americans supported both the war and the military's efforts to control news; further, some thought there should be more controls on press reporting. A *Los Angeles Times* Mirror poll found that half of the respondents considered themselves obsessed with war news, but nearly 80% felt that the military was "telling as much as it can." About the same proportion thought that military censorship may be a "good idea."

But after the brief war, many in the press felt that the traditional right of US reporters to accompany their combat forces and report news of war had been severely circumscribed. Michael Getler of the *Washington Post* wrote, "The Pentagon and US Army Central Command conducted what is probably the most thorough and consistent wartime control of American reporters in modern times – a set of restrictions that in its totality and mindset seemed to go beyond World War II, Korea, and Vietnam."[4]

President George H. W. Bush and the Pentagon followed a deliberate policy of blocking negative and unflattering news from the US public lest it weaken support for the war. Long after the conflict, the public learned that some Iraqi soldiers had been buried alive in trenches by US plows and earthmovers and that the military had waited months to tell the families of thirty-three dead soldiers that their loved ones had been killed by friendly fire. Not until a year after the war did the public learn that key weapons such as the stealth bomber and the cruise missile had struck only about half of their targets, compared with the 85 to 90% rate claimed by the Pentagon at the time.[5] American casualties were reported, but there were few pictures of dead and wounded. Details of tactical failures and mishaps in the bombing campaign were not released, nor was the information that at least twenty-four female soldiers had been raped or sexually assaulted by American servicemen.

But the shooting war itself was quite a media spectacle, which started just as the evening news programs were beginning at 6:30 Eastern Standard Time (January 16, 1991 in the United States; January 17 in the Middle East). The networks and CNN interrupted their prepared news shows to report that aerial bombing had begun in Baghdad. Then followed one of most memorable nights in television history: the opening phases of a major conflict reported in real time by reporters in Iraq, Saudi Arabia, and Washington.

CNN stole the show that night, as three CNN correspondents, John Holliman, Peter Arnett, and Bernard Shaw, gave vivid eyewitness descriptions of the US air attack from the windows of their Baghdad hotel room. As in old-time radio, reporters relied on words, not video, that first night. Other networks reported the fireworks, but CNN with its previously arranged leased lines stayed on the longest after the lines were cut for the other networks. The next day, General Colin Powell jokingly said that the Pentagon was relying on CNN for military information. The second night gave prime-time viewers another long, absorbing evening, when CNN and NBC reporters in Tel Aviv reported live as Scud missiles landed. Reporters, often wearing gas masks, provided raw and unevaluated information. At one point, NBC reported dramatically that nerve gas had been detected in one Scud attack. Tom Brokaw decried the situation for some minutes, but, after the report proved false, NBC apologized. For the first three days, people everywhere stayed glued to television and radio sets, including shortwave receivers. Networks expanded to near twenty-four-hour coverage for the first thirty-six hours, and even the daytime soap operas were preempted briefly for war coverage. There was not that much to report at that point, and the same facts, theories, and speculations were repeated again and again. Nevertheless, the mesmerized public stayed tuned.

During this early bombing phase of the war, the Pentagon withheld detailed military information, such as the extent of the bombing and destruction within Iraq. Restrictions were placed on interviews with troops and returning pilots. Reporters could cover field combat only in designated pools, with groups of reporters being accompanied by an escort officer. (One reporter likened a press pool to a group of senior citizens on a conducted tour.) All interviews with soldiers were subject to censorship before they could be released.

If the war had gone badly, the press would have had difficulty reporting the negative aspects. With more than 1,600 reporters in the theater, only about 100 could be accommodated by the pools to report on the American force of 500,000. As the ground war neared, the large press corps became increasingly restive and frustrated at this lack of access.

The response of some reporters was to "freelance" – to avoid the pools and go off on their own. Malcolm Browne reported, "Some reporters were hiding out in US Marine or Army field units, given GI uniforms and gear to look inconspicuous, enjoying the affection (and protection) of the units they're trying to cover – concealed by the officers and troops from the handful of press-hating commanders who strive to keep the battlefield free of wandering journalists."[6] Browne noted that nearly all reporters who tried to reach front-line US troops were arrested at one time or another (including reporters for the *New York Times*, the *Washington Post*, the Associated Press, and Cox papers), sometimes held in field jails for up to twelve hours and threatened with revocation of their press credentials. After the ground war began, these freelancers, particularly John Kifner and Chris Hedges of the *New York Times*, produced some outstanding reportage. Forrest Sawyer of "ABC News," who traveled unofficially with Saudi forces, provided some of the earliest and best reports on the freeing of Kuwait City.

## The Triumph of Twenty-Four-Hour Global News

During the American Civil War, in 1861–1865, the demand for news was so great that US newspapers for the first time went to seven-day publication. During the 1963 Kennedy assassination, live television emerged as the preeminent medium for reporting breaking news. This story positioned ABC, CBS, and NBC as major news gatherers, but as still reaching essentially US audiences.

During the forty-two-day First Gulf War, CNN established the importance of a twenty-four-hour news network with true global reach. The concept has certainly changed the international news system, especially during times of international crisis and conflict. The three major US networks were shaken by CNN's success. After CNN's historic scoop on the first night of the war, a number of independent television stations, radio stations, and even several network affiliates relied on CNN in the crisis. Although the three networks had more talented and experienced reporters, they could not compete with CNN either in time on the air or in the vast audiences CNN reached in about 100 countries. The success of CNN encouraged similar services, such as the BBC's World Service Television.

The First Gulf War certainly conditioned viewers everywhere to keep their television sets tuned to CNN (or its later cable imitators) during times of high crisis. Newsrooms from Milwaukee to Cairo to Shanghai routinely keep a television set tuned to CNN or the BBC for the first report of any global crisis. Perhaps the news business today places too much emphasis on immediate and fast-breaking news "as it happens." Video shots of F15s roaring off runways, of "smart bombs" scoring direct hits, of Tomahawk missiles flying through Baghdad, and of tank formations rolling through the desert made memorable viewing. But after the fog of war had cleared, the press and the public found that the war was not quite what they thought it was.

The tragic events in the volatile Middle East also reminded the public that wars and political crises are complex and intricate processes that can still best be reported and explained by the printed word. The best and most complete reporting of the First Gulf War came ultimately from print media, which rounded out the picture and provided the context and perspective necessary for full understanding. During the first several weeks after the cease-fire, it was the print reporters, not television, who dug out and filled in the details of what actually happened during the air campaign and the brief ground war – details that the military on both sides had so effectively screened from public view.

From all indications, the US military as well as the first Bush administration were pleased with the results of their media policy and would do the same thing again. But among American and British journalists, there was a general conclusion that the press had been unduly and even illegally denied access to information about the war.

After the First Gulf War, a report that called military restrictions in the war "real censorship" that confirmed "the worst fears of reporters in a democracy" was delivered to Defense Secretary Dick Cheney. It was signed by seventeen news executives representing the four networks, AP and UPI, and major newspapers and news magazines. The report bitterly complained that the restrictions placed on reporters by the Pentagon were intended to promote a sanitized view of the war. The war was called the first in this century to restrict all official coverage to pools. "By controlling what reporters saw and when they saw it, the military exerted great power to shape and manage the news," the report said. Also criticized were the use of military escorts and "unwarranted delays in transmitting copy."[7] After more than eight months of talks with news executives, in May 1992 the Pentagon issued a set of principles intended to guarantee that journalists had greater access to future military operations than they had in the First Gulf War. However, news media and the government could not agree on whether there should be any official "security review" of news reports before they are published or broadcast. The statement affirmed that "open and independent reporting will be the principal means of coverage of US military operations. The guidelines limited the role of military escorts and said that "press pools are not to serve as the standard means of covering operations."[8]

## Marines in Somalia

The incursion of US Marines into Somalia in December 1992 was intended to provide military protection to the relief organizations trying to feed starving Somalis caught in the cross-fire of warring clans. Under these conditions, the Pentagon decided to place no restraints on the media. Howard Kurtz called what happened the most embarrassing moment ever in media-military relations: "the infamous night in December 1992 when Navy SEALS hitting the beach in Somalia were surrounded by a small army of reporters and photographers who blinded them with television lights, clamored for interviews, and generally acted like obnoxious adolescents. That sorry performance, turning a humanitarian mission to aid starving Africans into a Felliniesque photo opportunity, underscored what the Pentagon had been saying for years: that the press simply could not discipline itself, that reporters would blithely endanger the safety of American troops for the sake of journalistic drama."[9] It was not one of the news media's finer days.

David Hackworth of *Newsweek* wrote, "To lurch from thought control to no control is plain stupid. When the press corps beats the Marine Corps to the beach, everyone loses."[10] The Pentagon wanted full coverage of Somalia, so no controls were placed on the press, and what resulted was a confused circus. There are those, however, who suspected that the Pentagon deliberately orchestrated the fiasco to make the media look bad. Somalia raised the question of whether the media, by its heavy barrage of pictures and stories of starving Somalis, had pushed President Bush during his last days in office to send troops on their humanitarian mission. The answer is unclear, but Bush did react by committing US armed forces to a limited and supposedly feasible assignment of famine relief. When the Somalia assignment expanded in the early Clinton administration to include warlord hunting, it provoked a devastating firefight in the streets of Mogadishu. When eighteen US soldiers were killed and the pictures shown on US television, the American public was unprepared to accept casualties when vital US interests were not at stake. The White House soon announced that the United States was getting out of Somalia.

James Hoge, editor of *Foreign Affairs*, commented, "From its understanding of Vietnam came the military's subsequent emphasis on quick solutions, limited media access and selective release of 'smart' weapons imagery. The public, however, will not remain dazzled when interventions become difficult. As in Vietnam, public attitudes ultimately hinge on questions about the rightness, purpose and costs of policy – not television images."[11]

## NATO's Air War Over Yugoslavia

After NATO bombs started falling on Serbia and Kosovo in 1999, military relations with the press deteriorated abruptly. Critics protested that the lack of detailed after-action reports – routinely provided in earlier conflicts – made it impossible to assess NATO's claims that they were steadily dismantling Milosevic's war-making powers. At both the Pentagon and Brussels NATO headquarters, spokespersons stubbornly refused to provide specific information about bombing sorties. These policies were considered even less forthcoming than in the First Gulf War, which the press had considered overly restrictive. Of course, NATO had its reasons: the need to hold the somewhat reluctant alliance together and the need to retain the support of the American public for military action. But most journalists covering the war were highly critical.

Yet the war was reported and, in some basic ways, differently from others. After being forced to watch seventy-eight days of bombing through the lenses of official video cameras, some 2,700 journalists had a chance to see for themselves when NATO troops rolled into Kosovo in June 1999. Even though military censors blocked specific information, satellite communications enabled reporters from Brussels to Kukes, Albania, and other points to triangulate information more easily than in earlier wars. According to editors, the key device for putting together information into coherent stories was the satellite telephone and, more broadly, satellite communications. The satellite uplink was the key information medium for the air war. "Instantaneous communication has changed everything," said Andrew Rosenthal, foreign editor of the *New York Times*. "The ability of a reporter on the Macedonian border to call a reporter on the Albanian border or to call a reporter in Brussels or Washington instantly made a huge difference. Newspapers were able to put together groups of reporters to do joint efforts in a way that was previously impossible," he said.[12]

For television, the same satellite technology allowed a profusion of images to be transmitted at great speed. Whether the vivid video showed the fate of Kosovar refugees or fleeing Serbian troops, the emotional impact of television was great indeed. Some thought such reportage helped to justify the humanitarian aspects of the hostilities and convinced otherwise dubious viewers to support the NATO effort. The expanded role for the Internet and cable television news meant that there were far more outlets for instantaneous reporting and analysis. CNN, MSNBC, and the Fox Cable Channel also offered frequent and compelling debates about the conflict, even though much of it was discounted by critics as lacking in depth and context. For the first time, the Internet was a player in war reporting, providing a plethora of web sites (that is, blogs) presenting war issues and other information from diverse viewpoints: Serbian, Albanian, Republican, Democratic; and ranging from the in-depth reporting of the BBC to the erratic sensationalism of Belgrade news outlets. As a result, some observers thought that the sum total of these trends amounted to sharper, speedier coverage. David Halberstam wrote: "Despite all the restrictions and just God-awful limitations and dangers, there were enough different people in different places to give you the dimensions you needed."[13]

Even though CNN had more competition this time – BBC World, MSNBC, and Fox – than in the First Gulf War, the Atlanta cable network emerged from the Yugoslav conflict in a much-enhanced *international* role for its news dissemination as a global twenty-four-hour cable news channel. During the First Gulf War, some 10 million households outside the United States had access to CNN. In the Yugoslav war, the number had jumped to 150 million households.

The air war in Yugoslavia demonstrated that the democracies of America and NATO were unwilling to be candid and forthcoming with reliable information to their own peoples while engaged in hostile actions against other states. As in the First Gulf War, the Pentagon gave misleading and exaggerated accounts of the effectiveness of the bombing campaign. Yet despite such deceptions, the events surrounding the air war also showed that today's news organizations can still get much of the news out if they pursue the events with vigor and imagination and make use of their varied tools of communications technology.

## Chasing the Taliban in Afghanistan

The world's press – mainly Americans and Europeans – geared up to cover the war in Afghanistan with essentially the same technologies as well as the limited access to the battlefields that characterized NATO's air war with Yugoslavia two years earlier. But now, global audiences were larger and the news flow, from many more reporters, was much heavier. Unlike earlier wars, individual reporters can now report news from war zones in real time, but often they may have less to tell. Because the military sharply limits access and thus what reporters can know, the war reporter is not in a position to decide what is appropriate and safe to report. Basically, the military today is very uneasy with new media technology. The old battlefield censorship is no longer feasible because reporters carry their means of transmission (that is, satellite phones and videophones) with them. More and more, reporters are kept away from troops and military organizations. As a result, much of what is considered "war coverage" has originated in the Pentagon press briefing room. Today, the global audience is accustomed to getting its news quickly and often. People will check their favorite web sites four or five times a day, or tune in to twenty-four-hour cable stations for the latest developments.

As mentioned earlier, the Afghanistan war may go down in history as our first "videophone war." From the earliest days of the conflict, the closest views of the fighting were provided in live reports by reporters using videophones, which are literally cameras plugged into satellite phones. The videophone has enabled television news crews to venture out to remote and dangerous areas of Afghanistan, untethered to the more cumbersome satellite uplinks that can weigh over a ton. The videophone can fit into two briefcases, one with one or two satellite phones and the other with the videophone. With that and a car battery, they are ready to roll. The videophone is actually a variation on videoconferencing, which businesses have used for years. The videophones, at about $8,000 each, combine videoconferencing equipment with "store and forward" technology that helps compress very high bandwidth feeds so that they can be transmitted by satellite. The satellite phones also cost about $8,000 each. Early in the war, much of what the public saw and heard on television seemed to come from a correspondent reporting live via a videophone from a remote location in Afghanistan.

The networks also used the "traditional" satellite uplinks in places such as Islamabad, Pakistan, to complement the videophones. Videophone reporting has been criticized for being "too sketchy" or almost "undecipherable." Yet the technology will only improve over time, and it does get the television reporter closer to the battlefield.

But what the press has gained in time and convenience, it has lost in access to the military itself. For families of servicemen and women, this was not considered a good precedent. News about casualties caused by "friendly fire" and other battlefield mishaps tend not to be reported if there are no reporters on the ground. The press has been likened to an uncle representing the family. They go to the front line and say, "Well, how is Johnny doing? What's going on here? Who's running this operation? Are there needless frontal assaults?" Walter Cronkite has said that there is another reason people should care about how the military operates: "We must know what they are doing in our name."[14] The journalists' concerns have not yet aroused similar concern from the public. As noted in a recent survey by the Pew Research Center, half of the respondents said the military should have more control over war news than news media have.

During the opening weeks of the Afghan war, almost all significant information was released from the Pentagon, far from the battlefields, and much of it was considered dated and vague. The extremely restrictive policy toward release of information was set by Defense Secretary Rumsfeld, who said that the nature of the war against terrorism made the constraints necessary. Rumsfeld several times stated that defense officials who leaked information might be in violation of federal criminal law. Later, after President Obama ordered a renewed effort in Afghanistan, press/military relations were improved. But there was less reporting of American soldiers living in peril and more about political corruption of President Karzai and the difficult diplomatic relationship with neighboring Pakistan which was accused of harboring and even aiding Taliban terrorist and leaders of the still elusive Al Qaeda. The Afghan war had become the longest in US history; public interest and support had clearly declined. This disillusionment was clearly reflected in Western media.

## The Second War against Saddam's Iraq

The invasion of Iraq and the toppling of Saddam Hussein's regime were quickly accomplished by coalition forces – mainly American and some British – in the spring of 2003. Around the world, millions watched the unfolding of this the most heavily televised war in history. As in the 1991 Iraq war, hundreds of journalists and photographers used new and refined communications gadgets – videophones, cell phones, Internet, and e-mail – to flood the world with words and images.

Combat journalism has changed, as has warfare itself. Technology has markedly changed how wars are waged and for how long. Reporters utilize new tools to gather news and send it out faster than ever. In Iraq, the typical television war correspondent found he needed the following essential carry-along gear that weighed about seventy-six pounds: a digital video camera, five pounds; microphones, cables, and batteries, ten pounds; camera tripod, ten pounds; two satellite phones, twenty pounds each; laptop computer, six pounds; and night scope lens, five pounds.

Reporters in Iraq were comfortable with their technology as never before. Television reporters carried hand-held video cameras and print journalists traded their seventy-pound videophones of 1991 for handy models that can be held against an ear. High-speed Internet lines in the desert meant that journalists could make a connection almost anywhere. One reporter said that today's digital devices enable a reporter to provide a more intimate and multi-faceted view of the war than had ever been seen before. The high quality and diverse nature of the reporting reflected this.

The most important policy innovation of the war was the Pentagon's unexpected decision that journalists be "embedded" with the military units fighting their way across Iraq. For the first time since World War II, and on a scale never seen in military history, some 600 reporters, photographers, and television crew members – about 100 of them from foreign and international news organizations, including the Arab satellite news network, Al Jazeera, had access to troops in combat. Embedding was considered the greatest innovation (and improvement) in press-military relations in many years. The results of the experiment were generally positive. The viewing public had a front-row seat during the invasion, with the "embedders" providing a steady stream of news reports, anecdotes, and human interest stories, along with dramatic and vivid video and photos about the military they accompanied.

One observer, Rem Rieder, commented, "Now that the fighting has stopped, it's clear that the great embedding experience was a home run as far as the news media – and the American public – are concerned. Six hundred journalists had a first-hand view of the combat. That is a far cry from the First Gulf War when reporters were at the mercy of government briefers and that misbegotten press pool."[15] But there were negative aspects to embedding. Some critics saw the reporters as tools of the military – only turning out good news. And it was dangerous duty – several correspondents were killed, including David Bloom of NBC News and Michael Kelly of *The Atlantic Monthly*.

Another important dimension was the role of transnational satellite networks in the Arab world. They became important news sources of war news in Arabic, and were in fact challenging the hegemony of the British and US media. Al Jazeera then reached about 45 million viewers, and broadcast a very different version of the conflict than CNN or BBC World. The Arab networks were accused of sending inaccurate and biased information. But many millions of Arabs were now receiving news and views in Arabic that differed from that sent out by their own closed national media systems.

How good was the televised reporting of the brief shooting war? At their best, reporters managed to humanize the war without becoming cheerleaders for the military. News organizations went to great expense to provide thorough coverage. But critics questioned how clear and complete the coverage was. One journalist said the war was too big a canvas to capture on the small screen of television. Yet at the same time there was so much television coverage that sometimes viewers became confused. The effectiveness of television was limited by the limitations of the medium itself – the mismatch between words and images. Vivid pictures from one fixed position in a battle of no consequence could overwhelm any context provided by a voice-over correspondent.

Embedded reporters could not report visually a key aspect of the ground war – that incessant bombing attacks had attrited Iraqi ground forces before battles began. And sometimes, reporters were too downbeat about the invasion's early setbacks.

## Insurgency and counter insurgency

After the fall of Baghdad, the war changed into another unexpected phase – a deadly and persistent guerrilla war waged against the occupying forces, and at times the Iraqi public itself. Attacks against US and coalition forces, usually as roadside bombings of cars and trucks or seemingly random suicide bomb attacks in crowded urban areas, took a steady toll of soldiers and civilians during the following two and a half years. The more serious media stayed on and maintained full coverage of the confused and discouraging events in Iraq. By 2005, many journalists had left Iraq – from a total of 2,000 at one time down to 200.

For the reporters, life became much more dangerous. One reporter said it was like being under house arrest and not able to do your job. Just leaving their hotel meant facing the chance of being kidnapped or shot. Increasingly, reporters relied more and more on Iraqi stringers or "fixers" to go out and gather information. Some reporters began to share their bylines with Iraqi colleagues. Every day was a gamble; ten Iraqi fixers were killed; Reuters lost three cameramen; and in all thirty-five Iraqi journalists had been killed. Being pinned down this way, many reporters felt they were getting only part of the story. They said the war looked different on the other side and they were not able to report it.

One of the best, Dexter Filkins of the *New York Times*, said the "business of reporting in Iraq has become a terribly truncated affair, an enterprise clipped and limited by the violence all around. . . .. Even in areas of the capital thought to be relatively safe, very few reporters are still brazen enough to get out of a car, walk around and stop people at random. It can be done, but you better move fast."[16] Ironically, it appeared that being embedded with troops at the front was the safest place to be. But not always: Filkins spent two weeks with a US Marine company during the siege of Fallujah. In some of the deadliest urban warfare since World War II, 25% of the Marines Filkins was with were killed during sixteen hours of continuous conflict. About this experience in Iraq, Filkins said the "list of hits and near misses was long enough to chill the hardiest war correspondent: we have been shot at, kidnapped, blindfolded, held at gunpoint, detained, threatened, beaten, and chased."[17]

An American freelancer, Steven C. Vincent, was abducted and shot dead in the port city of Basra in August 2005. It was believed that Vincent was targeted for writing about the rise of conservative Shiite Islam and the corruption of the Iraqi police in Basra. Vincent was one of nineteen correspondents killed in attacks in which they were the apparent targets. Soon after, on September 29, 2005, an Iraqi journalist and photographer working for the *New York Times* (as did Vincent) in Basra was found dead after being abducted from his home by a group of armed men. Like Vincent, Fakher Haider had been reporting about the rising violence among Basra's rival Shiite militias, which had apparently infiltrated the police.

Reporting the drawn-out insurgency in Iraq certainly contrasts sharply from riding along with combat troops as they quickly and decisively overwhelmed the army of Saddam Hussein in 2003. As public interest waned, more and more media organizations pulled out their reporters and relied more on local Iraqi reporters to cover the news. NBC News, with the largest US evening news audience, appeared to rely heavily on one veteran reporter who reported all the major stories in Iraq even he was no longer stationed full time in Baghdad but just flew in and out frequently. There was a large turnover of reporters including many women who shuttled back and forth. There are few journalistic celebrities as in Korea and Vietnam such as Homer Bigart, Marguerite Higgins, and David Halberstam all highly regarded and well known. The best regarded reporter today was Dexter Filkins who wrote Pulitzer Prize stories about the Marines' battle at Falluja as well as superior interpretive reporting from Afghanistan. There seemed to be fewer scoops and more sharing of news The US public often learned about Afghanistan from the BBC and Independent Television News from the United Kingdom on US public television. Nevertheless on the Internet a good deal of war news appeared but somehow seemed less distinctive and authoritative than similar reports on the front pages of the *New York Times* and *Washington Post*.

But the public and the media, while losing hope for a successful ending and withdrawal of troops from the Near East. has not, like Korea and Vietnam, lost its support for troops overseas. The press assiduously reports all casualties and reminds the public to heed the needs of the returning soldiers.

## First Amendment Concerns

From Grenada to Panama to Kosovo and, recently, to Afghanistan and Iraq, the press has been barred from fully covering wars or military incursions that it has historically and traditionally reported. This is important because the US Supreme Court has ruled that the press, in order to inform the public, has a First Amendment right to those places that "historically" and "traditionally" it has had the right to cover, such as trials and town meetings. The Supreme Court has also ruled that the press has a First Amendment right to be present at all "public" events. Certainly, an invasion lasting more than several hours or a full-scale war is a public event.

Perhaps the press's Constitutional rationale for war coverage was best expressed by Justice Hugo Black in the Pentagon Papers case:

> The Government's power to censor the press was abolished so that the press would remain forever free to censure the Government. The press was protected so that it could bare the secrets of government and inform the people. Only a free and unrestrained press can effectively expose deception in government. And paramount among the responsibilities of a free press is the duty to prevent any part of the government from deceiving the people and sending them off to distant lands to die of foreign fevers and foreign shot and shell.[18]

The press has no "right" to report sensitive military information that could aid an enemy, nor would it want to do so; but, we believe, it does have a right to be there, to keep a watchful eye on the military, just as it does on the proceedings of a criminal trial. When wars go badly, as they often can – with incompetent leadership, confused tactics, and unnecessary "friendly fire" casualties – it is essential that the press, as independent representatives of the public and of the forces themselves, be there to report, then or later, what occurred. The peoples of Iraq and Afghanistan had no independent press reporting back to them about the military disasters and political incompetence that led to the battlefield deaths of thousands of their young men – a basic difference between a democracy and a dictatorship.

This view is not shared by Professor Jane Kirtley, who has argued that no First Amendment right of access to military operations exists. She wrote, "The message from the court is clear: with no constitutional right to accompany troops the press should be grateful for whatever access the military decides to allow."[19]

Thus, apparently, the Supreme Court of the United States is unlikely to come to the defense of the US press in this matter. Perhaps the best hope of the press is to protest and complain until a significant portion of the public supports their own right to know. In the First Gulf War, it was apparent that the American news media and their owners did not complain loudly and vehemently enough about the pool and censorship restrictions before the bombs started dropping. The more open policy of embedding troops with combat units in the second Gulf war may have been a result of press pressures for more openness. Also, of course, it was very good public relations by the Pentagon to do so.

Few Americans were willing to second-guess the military policy of harsh controls over war news. A sitting president is not likely to modify such restrictions of free expression in wartime until forced to by political pressures. Yet it is imperative for the press to keep pushing for greater access to news relating to our military.

Ironically, the greatly expanded capability of global television and the Internet to report instantly on any new information in a modern war provides perhaps the major rationale for governments to control and censor war news. And when American or British journalists are denied access to war news, the rest of the world is denied access as well.

## Notes

1. "Media Access to Grenada Stirs Controversy," *AP Log*, October 31, 1991, 1.
2. "Tourism Shaken by CNN Effect," *New York Times*, January 28, 1992, sec. A, 8.
3. Tom Wicker, "An Unknown Casualty," *New York Times*, March 20, 1991, sec. A, 15.
4. Michael Getler, "The Gulf War 'Good News' Policy is a Dangerous Precedent," *The Washington Post National Weekly Edition*, March 25–31, 1991, 24.
5. Howard Kurtz, *Media Circus* (New York: Times Books, 1993), 215.
6. Malcolm Browne, "The Military vs. The Press," *New York Times Magazine*, March 3, 1991, 45.
7. Jason DeParle, "17 News Executives Criticize US for 'Censorship' of Gulf Coverage," *New York Times*, July 3, 1991, sec. A, 4.
8. Robert Pear, "Military Revises Rules to Assure Reporters Access to Battle Areas," *New York Times*, May 2, 1992, sec. A, 8.
9. Kurtz, *Media Circus*, 214.
10. David Hackworth, "Learning How to Cover a War," *Newsweek*, December 21, 1992, 32.
11. James F. Hoge, Jr., "Media Pervasiveness," *Foreign Affairs*, July/August 1994, 139–40.
12. Felicity Barringer, "A New War Drew on New Methods to Cover It," *New York Times*, June 21, 1999, sec. C, 1.
13. Barringer, "A New War Drew on New Methods to Cover It."
14. Kim Campbell, "Today's War Reporting: It's Digital But Dangerous," *Christian Science Monitor*, December 4, 2001, online edition.

15. Rem Rieder, "In the Zone," *American Journalism Review*, May/June 2003, 6.
16. Dexter Filkins, "Get Me Rewrite. Now. Bullets are Falling," *New York Times*, October 10, 2004, sec. P, 1.
17. Filkins, "Get Me Rewrite. Now. Bullets are Falling."
18. *New York Times v. United States*, 403 US 713, 717 (1971).
19. Jane Kirtley, "Accompanying the Troops," *American Journalism Review*, April/May 2005, 60.

# 12

# Public Diplomacy and Propaganda

*When it came to radio waves the iron curtain was helpless. Nothing could stop the news from coming through – neither sputniks nor mine-fields, high walls, nor barbed wire. The frontiers could be closed, words could not.*

– Lech Wałęsa

*In wartime, truth is so precious that she should always be guarded by a bodyguard of lies.*

– Winston Churchill

*The Internet has become a choke point in the struggle for a free press.*
– Joel Simon

Public diplomacy and propaganda have much in common with the armed forces: in peacetime, they are somewhat ignored and diminished, but during time of war, these activities are mobilized by governments to join the fray and to win the "hearts and minds" of both followers and adversaries. In modern times, government-sponsored shortwave radio, which reaches many millions almost anywhere on the globe, has been a preferred medium in political warfare – in World War II, the Cold War (including the Korean and Vietnam wars), and other international crises – and now, since 9/11, along with international television it has come to the fore in the war on terrorism. For Western governments, the tools, strategies, and messages of political warfare had been neglected, but were quickly being sharpened for the conflict in Afghanistan and Iraq with the additional tools of satellite television and the Internet.

*The World News Prism: Challenges of Digital Communication*, Eighth Edition.
William A. Hachten and James F. Scotton.
© 2012 John Wiley & Sons, Ltd. Published 2012 by John Wiley & Sons, Ltd.

Commentators have seen the current struggle in large part as an effort to convince world public opinion of the rightness of the anti-terrorism cause. The conflict in Afghanistan was quickly seen in part as a propaganda war between the West and the radical Islamists, as personified by the elusive Osama bin Laden. Western efforts to penetrate the opinions and attitudes of Arabs, as well as Muslims in general, were fitful and ineffective due in part to the widespread unpopularity at what was seen as President George W. Bush's war against Iraq and the failure to project an effective information (that is, propaganda) campaign via global radio and regional satellite television programming in Arabic. In mid-2005 the US public diplomacy effort had a new leader, Karen Hughes, a top Bush aide, but the campaign to reach and persuade the Middle East of the rightness of US goals was still sputtering.

Under the Barack Obama administration, America's efforts to influence world opinion have come into sharper focus. Secretary of State Hillary Clinton has declared Internet freedom to be a plank of American foreign policy.[1] An attack on one nation's computer network "can be an attack on all." She warned that the United States would defend itself from cyber attacks. Internet Freedom was in effect placed alongside freedom of expression and the press as policy values essential to democratic states. Further, the current state department, while still communicating by traditional diplomatic methods, has been also using the Internet and various social media, especially Twitter, Flickr, Facebook, YouTube, and so on, to communicate directly to non-Americans around the world. This policy initiative had the effect of drawing a line in the sand between the open nations of the West and the authoritarian-leaning states like China, Saudi Arabia, Iran, Vietnam, and Malaysia – all of whom are trying to control or repress the Internet and its progeny.

Although the looming frictions on the Internet are a global phenomenon, the focal point for the clash of ideas and propaganda is still found in the Middle East cauldron, especially Iran, Iraq, Afghanistan, Pakistan, and the perennial standoff in Palestine and Israel. Also, of course, the widespread political unrest and instability all across the Arab world has exaberbated the diplomatic challenges for the Western nations.

## Our "Truth" vs. Your "Propaganda"

Since the end of the Cold War in 1989 and before September 2001, global broadcasting over shortwave radio had not, however, receded in volume but had less impact than global television. On any given evening, an Arab in a café in Algiers, a Peruvian llama herder in a shelter in the Andes, or an African in a Ghanaian village can share a common communication experience. By merely flicking on a shortwave radio receiver and twisting the dials, each will hear the same polyglot cacophony of sounds detailing the news, unfolding diverse feature programs, and playing all sorts of music. The variety of languages spoken is immense, but each listener can, with little difficulty, find a program he or she understands. Nowhere is the prism of international communication more apparent. In shortwave radio broadcasting, one person's "truth" or news is another person's "propaganda," and vice versa. And again, one person's music is another's "noise." Transnational radio (now supplemented by global television, the Internet, and AM radio) is also a major conveyor of what is sometimes called public diplomacy.

For more than forty years, public diplomacy (a government's overt efforts to influence other governments and their publics) and shortwave radio were dominated by the great East-West struggle called the Cold War, which in effect ended in 1990 with the reunification of Germany and the withdrawal of Soviet troops from Central Europe. But public diplomacy and propaganda wars continued on other polemical battlefields: in the Persian Gulf after Iraq invaded Kuwait; in the tragic and protracted struggle among Serbs, Croats, and Bosnian Muslims in the former Yugoslavia; in the Israeli/Palestinian struggle; and in clashes over human rights in China.

With the globalization of the economy, international frictions were for a time more concerned with economic competition and business contentions between nations, rather than with political and ideological differences. Concerns about incipient war in, say, the Korean peninsula, in Kashmir, or in the Middle East were partially replaced by worries about the flagging economies in Indonesia, Japan, or Argentina, and how these trends might undermine more stable economies of the West. For a time, political espionage was replaced by economic espionage and concerns about the global pirating of videos, movies, CDs, and computer software. For example, 90% of the software used on China's computers is reported to have been pirated. The privacy issue has been pushed aside by national security concerns raised by international terrorism.

Much of the torrent of messages constantly washing over the globe is not neutral or "disinterested" information (that is, news) but "purposive" communication – words, sounds, and images intended to influence people's perceptions and opinions. A great deal of what refracts through the prism of international radio is purposive and is often called "propaganda"; that is, the systematic use of words or symbols to influence the attitudes or behaviors of others. *Propaganda* is a loaded term, a pejorative epithet subjectively defined as a "persuasive statement I don't like." No one – journalist, broadcaster, writer, or educator – wants to be called a propagandist. Transnational communicators put on their ideological blinkers when they insist, "We deal in information or truth. They deal in propaganda."

International political communication (IPC), a cumbersome term though it is, is a useful and neutral expression encompassing such terms as public diplomacy, overseas information programs, cultural exchanges, and even propaganda activities and political warfare. A useful definition for IPC is as follows: the political effects that newspapers, broadcasting, film, exchanges of persons, cultural exchanges, and other means of international communication can achieve.

However, a distinction should be made between official and private communications and between international communications designed to have a political effect and those that are not. Here, then, are four broad categories of IPC:

1　Official communications intended to influence foreign audiences (that is, public diplomacy), such as those of the Voice of America, Deutsche Welle, Radio France Internationale, and the BBC's World Service. Most international shortwave broadcasting falls into this category, and almost every nation with the capability will sponsor some broadcasting efforts across its borders.
2　Official communications not intended to influence foreign audiences, a small category indeed. One example has been the US Armed Forces Radio and Television Network. At its peak, AFN operated some 200 radio and thirty television transmitters serving American forces overseas and had large eavesdropping audiences. This is much less of an IPC factor today.
3　Private or commercial communications intended to influence foreign audiences politically, including various organizations and groups working to promote international understanding – for example, peace groups advocating a freeze on nuclear weapons. Terrorist organizations belong here because they are technically non-governmental. Every terrorist act is an effort to influence opinion.
4　Private communications without a political purpose. Among these would be Western news agencies, advertising agencies, and distributors of motion pictures, television programs, videos, and so forth. Activities of relief organizations, important in poor countries, belong in this

classification as well. The vast flood of American mass culture (much of it movies, music videos, pop recordings, and television programs, most of it produced within a five-square-mile area of Hollywood), has both negative and positive effects, but not intentional effects on international political communication.

Without doubt, the overseas impact of private US communications is far greater than that of US public diplomacy, but the actual influence is difficult to assess. As we have seen, Western pop culture has certainly contributed to political change in Eastern Europe in recent years. Unintended effects sometimes can be more profound than those caused intentionally.

The international news media of all nations play a significant role in international political communication. The privately owned media organizations of the West serve their own commercial purposes by distributing and selling news and entertainment around the globe without intentional political aims. Yet at the same time, the news media transmit a good deal of purposive official information – that is, propaganda – because all governments work hard at getting their versions of news and events into the world's news media. Much of the news from official sources in national capitals is intended to serve foreign-policy goals. News and propaganda are not mutually exclusive categories. The media serve the purposes of public diplomacy when they carry a story of President Obama's views of Osama bin Laden or of Afghanistan, yet what a US President or British Prime Minister says is always "news." A continuing problem for professional journalists is that of separating legitimate news from self-serving official "interpretations" of the news, whatever the source. Nevertheless, the two are often identical.

News media of authoritarian nations, less independent of official controls, often serve as unquestioning conduits of political communication from their own governments. Editors in Beijing or Tehran usually face no professional dilemmas over whether to carry stories supporting their governments' foreign policies. Less-developed nations are mostly on the receiving end of public diplomacy, because most lack the communication capability to compete effectively on a global basis.

## International Radio Broadcasting

In this day of direct-broadcast satellites, global television, and the Internet, the powerful and pervasive medium of international radio broadcasting, long capable of carrying messages around the world almost instantaneously is still important in the poor nations of the South. According to audience surveys, listening on shortwave radio continues to increase. A BBC study found that 143 million people tune in weekly and according to sales figures, there are about 600 million shortwave radios around the globe – half in Asia and Africa. That is indeed mass communication, beamed mainly at the most populous and poorest nations.

In the 1930s, politicians such as Nazi Germany's Josef Goebbels talked of international radio as a "limitless medium" and saw it as a powerful instrument of international diplomacy, persuasion, and even coercion. For more than half a century, transnational radio has been just that – a key instrument of international political communication as well as many other things. The medium enjoyed a rapid and diverse expansion and by the late 1930s was being used by national governments, religious organizations, commercial advertisers, domestic broadcasters, and educators to carry their messages across national borders.

As the twentieth century was closing, the total number of national broadcasters rose to more than 150, and the number of hours broadcast almost doubled that of the 1960s.[2] Shortwave radio messages are sent from transmitters directly throughout the world to receiving sets, but international radio's growth and diversity continue today with the utilization by national broadcasters of local AM and FM with signals sent down by satellites. The BBC does this with 800 stations around the world, 200 of them in the United States. But most in affluent nations do not listen much to international radio and so are unaware of how pervasive it is: 1,600 shortwave stations, the voices of 160 countries. These stations offer a choice of some sixty or more language services, broadcasting for a total of 100 hours a day or more. The formats are equally diverse: newscasts, talks, interviews, editorial comments, press reviews, documentaries, and a good deal of music. News on the hour, every hour about domestic and foreign events is a common feature, but other informational programs try to reflect the broader cultural, social, and economic aspects of particular nations through drama, music, sports events, and religious services. Today, international broadcasters often have web sites as well to transmit their messages over the Internet.

Here, we are concerned with the largest international broadcasting operators. Currently, in order of numbers of weekly listeners they are Britain, the United States, Germany, and France. The BBC World Service broadcasts in forty-three languages to 149 million listeners weekly. The

Voice of America broadcasts fifty-three languages to about 86 million weekly. Deutsche Welle goes out in thirty-five languages and uses 1,700 journalists. Radio France Internationale uses eighteen languages to reach about 30 million weekly.[3] The most widely used languages, in descending order of usage, are English, Russian, Mandarin Chinese, Arabic, Spanish, French, Japanese, Indonesian, Portuguese, German, Italian, Persian (Farsi), Swahili, Hindi, Hausa, and Korean.

A significant portion of international political rivalries and frictions are refracted through the prism of international broadcasting: the nationalistic and ethnic animosities in the post-Cold War world; the Arab versus Israeli tensions as well as those between moderate and radical Arab regimes; the North-South disputes between rich and poor nations; plus dozens of smaller regional controversies and disagreements between neighboring nations. More recently, increasing concerns about terrorism have dominated. Any major global crisis will be widely reported, analyzed, and commented upon on shortwave radio.

As the Cold War was winding down, Radio Moscow and its related Soviet broadcasters were on the air 2,257 hours weekly during 1988.[4] The United States countered with sixteen hours daily of Russian language VOA broadcasts into the Soviet Union, while US-backed Radio Free Europe broadcast into Eastern Europe, and Radio Liberty broadcast in non-Russian languages to various parts of the Soviet Union. In 1988, the United States was broadcasting globally 2,360 hours weekly; China, 1,517 hours weekly; the United Kingdom, 756 hours; and India, 444 hours.[5] By June 1994, after the demise of the Cold War, the United States had dropped to 2,000 hours weekly and Russia to 1,400 hours; China was steady at 1,600 hours, the United Kingdom was up to about 1,800 hours, and India was steady at 500 hours.

Amid the cacophony of sometimes strident and pejorative voices clashing over the international airwaves, it is important to remember that international radio also is a substantial news source for many millions, but nowhere is the truism that one person's news is another person's propaganda more apparent. Listeners can twist the dials to find a version of world events that suits their own needs and world views; this is especially true for people living under autocracies that lack popular support. News on international radio may often be acrimonious and self-serving, but without question it provides a diversity of news and views for untold millions. The importance of shortwave news is demonstrated, for example, when a political crisis or attempted coup occurs in an African nation. At such times, local broadcasters usually go off the air, and local residents habitually tune to the BBC or the VOA to learn about what is really happening in their own country.

With so much of what fills the night air (when reception is best) perceived by many as propaganda, the credibility of an international station's news and commentaries is crucial for its reputation among foreign listeners. The international broadcaster that has long enjoyed the best reputation for believability and objectivity is the World Service of the BBC. As a public corporation, the domestic BBC radio is financed by license fees paid by each British householder under the age of seventy-five with a television set. The BBC World Service is not funded by license fees; instead, it receives about $160 million annually in parliamentary grants-in-aid. The government, in consultation with the service, has the final decision over which languages are broadcast, but editorial control of the programs rests entirely with the BBC. The World Service broadcasts in English and forty-four other languages and, according to its research, reaches 143 million regular listeners in a week. Of those, 122 million listen directly, whereas about 27 million, with some overlap, listen to rebroadcasts on local stations. Of the total audience, 35 million listen in English. The World Service receives about half a million letters a year; the total in 1996 was 671,002. Languages used in most letters were English, with 119,897, followed by Hindi, 107,602; Burmese, 103,602; Tamil, 86,102; and Arabic, 38,303.

During Britain's brief war with Argentina over the Falkland Islands, Prime Minister Margaret Thatcher bitterly criticized the BBC for not sufficiently supporting the British war effort. Some saw this as evidence of the BBC's independence – the independence that draws so many listeners to the BBC during times of crisis.

Shortly after the BBC World Service announced the start of the Gulf War in January 1991, it expanded its Arabic-language radio broadcasts to fourteen hours a day, five hours longer than before the crisis.[6] Today, an estimated 10 million Arabs from North Africa to the Persian Gulf listen in, a far larger number than listen to either the Voice of America or Radio Moscow. Currently, the BBC plans an ambitious news and information expansion for the Arab world. In 2008, the BBC started an ambitious news and information for the Middle East – a new Arabic language television channel, The channel, BBC Arabic TV, started broadcasting twelve hours daily to the Middle East, Persian Gulf region and North Africa and later around the clock programming operating with a $50 million annual budget. Arab critics wondered whether the BBC could succeed in a region where

Britain is sometimes viewed with animosity. But the BBC World Services have beamed radio services to the region in Arabic since the 1930s and have long established BBC's credibility.[7]

Another powerful voice in the region is the BBC's Persian-language television service on the air since 2009 and reaching an audience of 6 to 8 million Iranians – a powerful fraction of Iranian viewers in a population of 70 million. The Iranian government has singled out several foreign newscasts as biased; CNN's English broadcasts, Voice of America, and BBC. But the BBC's Persian service was considered the main threat. As always with the BBC broadcasters strive for political independence and impartiality. The Persian channel also goes to Persian speakers in Afghanistan and Tajikistan and has an annual budget of $25 million.

## US Activities in Public Diplomacy

In the past, US activities in public diplomacy shared many similarities with those of the United Kingdom, but with some important differences. The United States Information Agency (USIA) was one of the key organizations, working closely with but separately from the State Department. The Voice of America began broadcasting in 1942 and was largely under the aegis of the USIA. During the Cold War, the VOA's efforts were supplemented by Radio Free Europe, which broadcast 555 hours weekly in European languages to Eastern Europe, and by Radio Liberty, which broadcast 462 hours weekly in Russian and fourteen other languages (but not English) to the Soviet Union.

The USIA, usually operating with a budget of about $900 million, employed about 12,000 people between Washington and some 275 US Information Service (USIS) posts in 110 countries. Typically, a USIS post worked under a US ambassador and included a public library. USIS personnel cooperated with local media by providing news and related material, holding exhibitions, running language courses, giving seminars of various kinds, and arranging visits and cultural exchanges of both Americans and local people. (However, on October 1, 1999, the USIA was abolished and the State Department absorbed most of its activities.)

The USIA and the VOA have long had an identity crisis. Are they objective news and cultural organizations reflecting the diversity of American life and culture, or are they arms of the State Department, vigorously advocating US foreign policy objectives? (This dispute has risen again during the war against terrorism.) Past managerial participation by such well-known journalists as Edward R. Murrow, Carl Rowan, and John Chancellor suggested the former. At other times, as during the Vietnam War and the Reagan administration, the latter role has been stressed. Under Reagan, the VOA was accused of repeatedly compromising its news integrity by broadcasting misleading and biased reports.[8]

Another policy issue debated within public diplomacy circles is audience targeting, revolving around the question of who we are trying to influence. If it is the ruling elites of the world's nations, then the person-to-person efforts of diplomatic posts and various cultural and educational exchanges seem called for. If the target is the mass public, then expanded and more aggressive radio broadcasting seems appropriate.

After 1981, the agency undertook the development of a government television network called Worldnet, with the potential of linking sixty overseas television systems to the USIA headquarters in Washington. In addition to producing cultural and public affairs programs for local overseas networks, Worldnet employed satellite links for two-way televised news conferences between foreign journalists and American public figures. Part of the programming in its first years included a two-hour program of news and features to Europe, five days a week. During the First Gulf War crisis, President George H. W. Bush used Worldnet to address foreign publics.

Another Reagan project was Radio Marti, a VOA-linked facility patterned after Radio Free Europe to broadcast news and commentary specifically to Cuba. Named for a Cuban independence hero, the radio station went on the air in May 1985, broadcasting news, entertainment, and sports in Spanish for fourteen hours daily from studios in Washington and a 50,000-watt AM transmitter in the Florida Keys. A Television Marti service was later added and has since been more controversial. Opponents had argued that since Cubans regularly listen to non-jammed US radio and television stations from Miami, the new service was unnecessary.

## Public Diplomacy after the Cold War

The dramatic and unexpected ending of the Cold War during 1989–1990 and the accompanying demise of communist regimes in Eastern Europe profoundly altered public diplomacy, because East-West rivalries had so long dominated the propaganda wars. Most agreed that the West had "won" the Cold War. However, there was not the same certitude about many aspects of the victory. Foreign radio broadcasting by the VOA,

Radio Free Europe, and Radio Liberty, as well as the BBC and the other Western broadcasters, had proved far more effective than most Western experts had supposed. In 1990, journalist Morton Kondracke commented, "If ever there was an American foreign policy success story, it's in international broadcasting. By the testimony of everyone from Václav Havel (of Czechoslovakia) to Lech Walesa (of Poland) to ordinary people in the streets of Bucharest and Beijing, democracy would not be what (and where) it is today without the two US foreign broadcast networks, the Voice of America and Radio Free Europe (RFE)/Radio Liberty (RL)."[9]

Michael Nelson, in his book *War of the Black Heavens: The Battles of Western Broadcasting in the Cold War*,[10] argues that the Western radio programs presented a compelling message of the good life that undermined communist regimes and connected listeners with the cultures of Europe and North America. Nelson believes that radio, not diplomacy or the global economy, raised the Iron Curtain.

Despite their Cold War successes, US planners talked of consolidating the US radio services as well as cutting back on their budgets because they no longer seemed needed. But due to the uncertainty of economic reforms and political instability in Russia, unrest in the former Soviet Republics, and unresolved crises in the Balkans, the survival of both Radio Liberty and Radio Free Europe seemed necessary. President Václav Havel of the Czech Republic and the new democratically elected leaders of Poland and Hungary all pleaded that the stations be saved, because they considered those broadcasts irreplaceable. The administration and Congress agreed to continue funding them. So, with pared-down budgets, RFE and RL moved to Prague in 1995 from Munich, where they had been since the CIA established them in 1951.

The success of RFE and RL during the Cold War led to proposals in Congress for a similar broadcaster to beam news and persuasive communications into China, ruled by a communist government and beset with human rights problems. The VOA and the BBC had played a key role during the Tiananmen Square events in 1989, by providing the only Mandarin-language news reports not controlled by China's government that were received throughout the Chinese hinterland, where most Chinese live.

Congress agreed in early 1994 to establish a new radio service, Radio Free Asia, to beam news and other programming to mainland China, Burma, Cambodia, Laos, North Korea, and Vietnam – all essentially authoritarian nations with serious human-rights problems. The station was modeled after RFE and RL, with grants to the new station set at $30 million a year. Radio

Free Asia got off to a shaky start in September 1996. Neighboring countries loudly opposed it and it was resented by other international broadcasters. Most Chinese who listen to radio broadcasts are devoted to the BBC, the VOA, and Radio France Internationale, all of which had bolstered their Asian broadcasting in the two previous years.

By early 2001, Tibet and China's western deserts were the scene of a radio battle for the hearts and minds of restive minorities in the region. The VOA was transmitting in two Tibetan dialects, and Radio Free Asia had eight hours daily of Tibetan broadcasting. Other foreign broadcasters represented Muslim separatists and Saudi religious programming. Beijing was fighting back by expanding programming in local languages and extending Chinese radio into remote corners of Tibet and the Muslim region of Xinjiang. Further, the Chinese were building facilities to jam foreign broadcasts. The jamming was called China's new Great Wall and part of the effort to rein in the restive western province, with its threat of Muslim fundamentalism and terrorism.

On April 30, 1993, President Clinton signed the International Broadcasting Act, establishing the International Broadcasting Bureau, which for the first time combined all US government international broadcasting services under a Broadcasting Board of Governors. The board oversees the operation of the VOA, Worldnet television service, and Radio and TV Marti to Cuba, as well as Radio Free Europe/Radio Liberty and Radio Free Asia. These services transmit nearly 2,000 hours a week in sixty languages. No one knows how much money is wasted due to duplication. No one knows how many people are listening. The VOA says surveys show 65 million, but that figure could be 86 million. RFE/RL may have 20 million "listeners," defined as persons who tune in one or more times a week.[11]

US global broadcasting employs about 3,500 people. Besides the shortwave audience, millions more listen to VOA programs placed on local AM and FM stations around the world. The VOA's original programming, all of it produced in studios in Washington, DC, totals almost 700 hours a week. Most programs concern news and news-related topics. Music programs, from jazz to rock, classical to country, are popular.

Radio Free Europe/Radio Liberty broadcasts from Prague, including its Czech and Polish affiliates, more than 500 hours weekly in twenty-three languages. Its programs target Central Europe, Russia, and the various republics of the former USSR, several of them near Afghanistan.

In 1994, the VOA began distributing, via the Internet, its newswire and selected newscasts and program audio files in nineteen languages, along with VOA frequency and satellite information. The VOA launched a web page on the Internet in May 1996. (The BBC World Service offers similar information on the Internet.) Using a network of fourteen relay stations worldwide, the VOA transmits its programs to its global audience via satellite, shortwave, and medium wave. The connection is instantaneous, so listeners may never realize that the signal passes through several different channels before it reaches their receivers.

Since 9/11, there has been concern that since the abolition of the United States Information Agency in 1999, the nation's ability to conduct public diplomacy has been diminished. On a per capita basis, France and many other countries, including Spain, spend more money on public diplomacy than does the United States. Yet public diplomacy is needed by a nation at war.

After the Soviets withdrew from Afghanistan in 1989, the United States began losing interest in Pakistan. After budget cuts, five American cultural centers there were either closed or greatly reduced in scope. Pakistan was only one of many countries where the United States cut its public diplomacy programs in the early and mid-1990s. Across the Arab world, where anti-Western propaganda is a staple, the Voice of America broadcasts are barely audible and reach less than 2% of the population in the twenty-two countries targeted. The budget in 2001, which allotted $370 billion for the military, gave $22 billion for all non-military spending abroad, including foreign aid grants, VOA and radio projects, and budgets of the State Department, which has absorbed the USIA functions. Funding for foreign exchanges such as the Fulbright grants, measured in constant dollars, fell by nearly a third from 1993 to 2000. But now policy makers in Washington are listening again to advocates of increased cultural exchange and public diplomacy.[12]

In 1994, when public diplomacy was being dismantled, historian Walter Laqueur warned:

> No specialized expertise is needed to realize that, far from being on the verge of a new order, the world has entered a period of great disorder. This refers to all kinds of regional conflicts as well as to the proliferation of the means of mass destruction, all of which makes nuclear war in the not-too-distant future a distinct possibility. . . . Cultural diplomacy, in the widest sense, has increased in importance, whereas traditional diplomacy and military power (especially of the high technology variety) are of limited use in coping with most of these dangers.[13]

The "long thin war" against terrorism has no end in sight. Without question, public diplomacy and propaganda have important roles to play; and very likely Congress will substantially strengthen various facets of our public efforts – the VOA and more targeted broadcasting, cultural exchanges, and more person-to-person contacts with foreign nationals overseas.

A key question for policy makers at war is whether the Voice of America should be a propaganda tool, pushing hard for American policy objectives or whether VOA should be a reliable source of accurate, unbiased news. A former VOA director, Sanford Ungar, commented recently that before 9/11, the VOA had evolved into a highly effective and credible player in the worldwide flow of information across borders. In many hot spots around the world, its correspondents are among the best and most courageous. Its two-source rule prevents it from making mistakes common to some other international news services. It reflects the daily experience of American democracy, warts and all. . ... Now more than ever, the Voice of America has important work to do. It must be able to interview anyone anywhere at any time, without fear of rebuke or reprisal, in order to provide honest and full coverage of momentous events. The State Department should keep its hands – and editing pencils – off the news.[14]

## New Broadcasting Board of Governors

In June 2010, a new Broadcasting Board of Governors was confirmed by the US Senate. The bipartisan board whose new chairman is Walter Isaacson, a prominent journalist and biographer, will supervise the Voice of America, Radio Free Europe/Radio Liberty, Radio Free Asia, the Arabic language service Radio Sawa and Al Hurra TV and finally, Radio and TV Marti.

America's strongest competition has long been the BBC which produces radio services in thirty-two languages and, as mentioned, television programs in Arabic and Persian and has a weekly global audience of 180 million people which is about 10 million more than the combined audiences of the US international stations. The BBC keeps its global audience listening in on an annual budget of $420 million. America spends almost twice as much – $750 million annually to reach a smaller audience. Reasons for the disparity were duplication for some foreign broadcasts and the lack of centralized control. There were hopes that the new Broadcasting Board of Governors (BBG) will rationalize itself and make the US efforts more cost effective. In any case the BBG indicates that

US foreign policy is still committed to international radio in order to pursue foreign policy goals.

## The Propaganda War in the Middle East

As the Pentagon geared up for war in late 2010, the White House began to mobilize its resources for political warfare. Although the 9/11 attacks had evoked sympathetic responses from the Western nations, in much of the Arab world terrorism was applauded and hailed throughout the Arab and Muslim nations. Subsequent television statements by Osama bin Laden made it clear that a war of words had begun, and the United States and its allies were at best playing catchup or even losing.

After the United States invaded Iraq, against the vocal opposition of most of the United Nations and even such traditional NATO allies as France and Germany, much of world public opinion was overwhelmingly against the war. American popularity was at an all-time low throughout this period. America's long-time support for Israel had been an important contributor to anti-American feelings.

For Americans, there was a broad chasm between the way Americans saw themselves and the way they were seen by other peoples. Traditional cultures have long been troubled by the invasion of their cultures by powerful outside interests which have featured social mobility and cosmopolitan thinking that has undermined the traditional ways of clans, religious elders, and dictators. And, of course, just the presence of over 150,000 Western soldiers in Iraq created animosity in neighboring Arab nations and subsequent problems for US public diplomacy.

These factors represented a great and perhaps insurmountable challenge to the Voice of America and subsequent satellite television efforts. The first efforts to reach Islamic audiences were ineffective. The State Department brought in Charlotte Beers, a former advertising executive, to use her marketing skills to make American values as much a brand as Ivory Soap. She soon quit and was replaced by Margaret Tutwiler, the next undersecretary of state for public diplomacy. She lasted a year.

A major effort was Al Hurra ("the free one" in Arabic), a satellite news station that began broadcasting in northern Virginia, with a $62 million first-year budget, to provide an alternative to pan-Arab news stations such as Al Jazeera and Al Arabia. The purpose, according to President Bush, was to cut through the barriers of hateful propaganda and provide reliable news across the region. But Al Hurra earned little praise from its target audience. Many Arab commentators were quick to condemn the new station. The consensus was that the station was an abysmal failure and it was beset with poor ratings.

The next US entry in the propaganda war was Radio Sawa, an Arabic-language pop music and news station, which was touted as a success in reaching out to the Arab world. But a State Department report on the station charged that Radio Sawa was so interested in building its audience for music that it failed to measure whether it was influencing minds. It too had not been a critical success in the war of ideas.

In early 2005, Karen Hughes, a close adviser to President Bush, was appointed to launch a bold new approach to US public diplomacy. But apparently there was no hurry, as Hughes did not assume her post for six months. At the same time, a government report criticized the administration for failing to develop a strategy to improve the image of the United States at a time when data showed that anti-Americanism was spreading and deepening around the world.

At her confirmation hearing, Hughes said she wanted to enlist the private sector, including the music, film, and travel industries, in a reinvigorated effort to help the Muslim world understand America. She said that the long-term way to prevail in this struggle is through the power of our ideas. Another aspect of Hughes's assignment is to publicize the President's campaign for democracy in the Middle East.

## New Battle Lines

As the year 2011 began, the Internet has become the battle ground of international political communication. Although China's efforts to control its Internet and its progeny – Google, Facebook, Twitter, and so on – have been the most publicized, across Southeast Asia Malaysia, Thailand and Vietnam have turned to coercion and intimidation to rein in online criticism. There nations have been arresting bloggers and individuals posting contentious views online. In Saudi Arabia where 29% of Saudis use the net considerable filtering of political and pornographic web sites takes place. In Iran where 32% are online, the government operates one of the most extensive filtering systems and has developed its own technology to do so. Opposition web sites were blocked during the contentious 2009 Iran presidential elections. Internet-freedom advocates worry that more governments beyond Southeast Asia and the Middle East will follow suit and tighten Internet controls.[15]

To exploit the Internet potential to open closed societies, the Obama administration announced in March 2010 that it will permit technology companies to expand online services such as instant messaging, chat and photo sharing to Iran, Cuba, and Sudan. The more people who have access to the range of Internet technology, the harder it is for any autocratic government to crack down on speech and free expression, one official said.

Secretary of State Clinton in her stress on Internet freedom said that "viral videos and blog posts are becoming the Samizdats of our day" referring to censored publications passed around clandestinely in Soviet-era Russia. Other targets of closed societies are Cuba and Sudan plus North Korea and Syria.

The Obama administration in 2009 established a new unit in the State Department to counter militant propaganda in Afghanistan and Pakistan, engaging in a war of words that always goes with a war. Proposals have been considered to give the team up to $150 million for local FM radio stations to counter illegal militant broadcasting and for an expanded cell phone services. The project would also step up the training of local journalists and help produce audio and video programming as well as pamphlets, posters, and CDs denigrating the Taliban and their message. US officials concede it has been losing the information war that accompanied the insurgency in Afghanistan and Pakistan.

Meanwhile the US criticism of Internet censorship has annoyed the Chinese leaders who accused Secretary Clinton of jeopardizing relations between the two countries. The day after her speech, a spokesman for China's foreign ministry called on the United States to stop using the "so-called Internet freedom question to level baseless accusations" He also insisted the Chinese Internet is open. China has the most Internet users of any nation – 384 million officially, but also the most sophisticated system of Internet censorship nick-named the Great Wall.

Editorially the *New York Times* supported Mrs. Clinton's speech writing that she picked the right battle by calling for censorship's end and naming governments that suppress the free flow of information, including China, Iran, Egypt, Saudi Arabia, Vietnam, Tunisia, and Uzbekistan.[16] The speech "had pointed echoes of the Cold War, including a warning that "a new information curtain is descending across much of the world."

Foreign governments and international organizations will continue to influence the flow of news and we can expect that the news media and the expanding millions of "netizens" and their digital gadgets will influence those nations as well.

## Notes

1. Mark Landler, "Clinton Making Case for Internet Freedom," *New York Times*, January 20, 2010, 6.
2. "Candor Becoming a Staple of Shortwave," *New York Times*, March 13, 1989, 18.
3. Daya Kishan Thussu, *International Communication* (London: Arnold, 2000), 161.
4. "Candor Becoming a Staple of Shortwave."
5. "Candor Becoming a Staple of Shortwave."
6. Deborah Stead, "BBC is Expanding its Arabic Radio Broadcasts," *New York Times*, February 18, 1991, 27.
7. Eric Pfanner, "BBC to begin New TV Service for Middle East," *New York Times*, March 4, 2008, pA15.
8. Carolyn Weaver, "When the Voice of America Ignores its Charter," *Columbia Journalism Review*, November/December 1988, 36–43.
9. Morton Kondracke, "Fine Tuning," *New Republic*, May 28, 1990, 8.
10. Michael Nelson, War of *the Black Heavens: The Battles of Western Broadcasting in the Cold War* (Syracuse: Syracuse University Press, 1997).
11. Mark Hopkins, "A Babel of Broadcasts," *Columbia Journalism Review*, July/August 1999, 44.
12. Stephen Kinzer, "Why They Don't Know Us," *New York Times*, November 11, 2001, sec. A, 5.
13. Walter Laqueur, "Save Public Diplomacy," *Foreign Affairs*, September/October 1994, 19.
14. Sanford J. Ungar, "Afghanistan's Fans of American Radio," *New York Times*, October 5, 2001, sec. A, 23.
15. James Hookway, "Web Censoring Across Southeast Asia" *Wall Street Journal*, September 14, 2009, A10.
16. "A Good Fight" (editorial) *New York Times*, January 23, 2010, A16.

# 13

# Forecast: Changeable with Cloudy Periods

*Western values and assumptions have been internalized to a remarkable degree in almost every major culture . . . . What the West has done to the rest of the world has been done indelibly. Nothing can be the same again. History has been changed by the West which has made the world One World. What seems to be clear is that the story of Western Civilization is now the story of mankind.*

– J. M. Roberts

Modern mass communications, from newspapers and television sets to communication satellites and computer technology, are among the many devices and cultural artifacts of Western society that have so inexorably spread throughout the world since 1945. Words on paper, electronic impulses, and images on tape, film, and recordings have penetrated the minds and cultures of non-Western peoples with tremendous impact. Along with pop and classical music, Hollywood movies, television programs, and youthful life styles have come ideas and ideology: equality, human rights, democracy, freedom of expression, individual autonomy, and free enterprise. John Locke, Thomas Jefferson, John Stuart Mill, Abraham Lincoln, and Adam Smith were Westerners, as was Karl Marx.

International communication, travel, industrialization, commerce, and trade have all participated in this Westernizing process, an aspect of globalization, which perhaps should be termed the *modernization* of the world because so many non-Western societies now contribute to the

*The World News Prism: Challenges of Digital Communication*, Eighth Edition.
William A. Hachten and James F. Scotton.
© 2012 John Wiley & Sons, Ltd. Published 2012 by John Wiley & Sons, Ltd.

process. The practices of Western mass communication have been so widely dispersed and accepted by people everywhere that the adjective *Western* perhaps should be reserved for historians, as Professor Roberts has suggested.[1] The September 11 events, and 2011 upheavals in the Arab nations – as well as the tsunamis, hurricanes, and other natural disasters – showed the crucial role that professional journalism, free of government controls, plays at a time of crisis by supplying reliable and verifiable news to the world. In many nations, the familiar anchors of network television have not only reported the news but have also reassured, steadied, and consoled millions of viewers. When national security is endangered or great natural calamities threaten, people everywhere are reminded how important it is to know and understand the greater world.

## Checklist of Global News Impacts

To summarize some main points of this book, we list ways that the new global journalism has influenced and, yes, even changed our world, for high-speed, international news communication is something new and different – in matters of degree if not in kind. Some of these effects have been global or geopolitical, others have directly influenced the media themselves, and some effects have been felt mostly by individuals.

- *Glorious digital disruption.* For over ten years, disarray among the traditional global news media has been accompanied by a greatly increased digital flow of news and information mainly through the Internet that also threatens the survival of the major ink-on-paper journals and magazines as well as broadcast television and radio news. Great media companies are taking severe revenue losses in circulation and advertising. The future of global media is murky and has been compared to fifteenth-century Europe when Gutenberg's moveable type revolutionized the communication culture and religion in ways no one could have predicted.
- *The triumph of Western journalism.* Since the fall of the communist "second" world, the Western concept of journalism and mass communication (really the US-/UK model) has become the dominant model throughout the world and is widely emulated. In journalism, many non-Western nations have adopted not only the equipment and gadgets of the Western press and broadcasting but also its practices,

norms, ethical standards, and ideology. Throughout the developing and former communist nations, print and broadcast journalists today increasingly seek editorial autonomy and freedom from government interference. These journalists understand and aspire to the professional values of fairness, objectivity, and responsibility as well as the "checking effect" – the role of the press as a watchdog of government and authority. They want to report the news as they see it – not some government's version of events. But, of course, many autocratic nations still have controlled media.

- *Globalization of media.* The internationalization of mass communication has grown hand in hand with the globalization of the world's economy. In fact, the expanding international business media play a key role in "servicing" the world economy by supplying rapid, reliable economic and financial news. Globalization has its other traits and independent news media provide forums for dissent and complaints. The media spread has been a dynamic process and has provided more diversity and variety to the global mix, particularly in China and its neighbors.

- *Mass culture accepted.* For better or worse, Western mass media also have conditioned much of the world to use media for entertainment and leisure. (Political indoctrination by media has been rejected by many people.) But with the war on terrorism, political persuasion – that is, propaganda – has increased on global media. Ever-growing audiences accept and enjoy the movies, television, pop music, and even the ever-present commercials. Today, the most traditional of parents find it almost impossible to prevent the influence on their children of that most powerful engine of mass education the West has yet produced, commercial advertising. Parents and others over thirty years old almost everywhere must be offended and repelled by the noisy, brassy music videos, but there is no doubting their appeal to teenagers literally everywhere. Yet in lands under the sway of religious fundamentalism, opposition to Western mass culture remains strong, and yet even modern and traditional cultures tend to meld and combine.

- *Global audiences growing.* Each year, literally millions more people are being drawn into the global audience, mainly through competing satellite and cable services, computers, and shortwave radio. With satellite dishes and antennas sprouting everywhere, the lands of Asia, particularly China and India, are flocking to join the global village.

Recent terrorism events and tsunamis saw a tremendous surge of interest for global television news. Some Asian nations welcome global television, but others see it as a threat to their cultural identity and political stability. Across the former third world, governments have had only limited success in blocking satellite services. Governments are finding it nearly impossible to prevent people from getting news and entertainment from the skies. Satellite dishes, which are growing smaller, cheaper, and more powerful, are easily put together from imported kits.

- *Vast audiences for global events.* Great events – the terror attack on the World Trade Center and Pentagon, or the quadrennial Olympic Games – can attract significant parts of the global audience. About 3.5 billion people watched some of the 1996 Olympics in Atlanta. The biggest share of that audience was in China, because more than 900 million Chinese had access to television sets, and three channels broadcast events there all day long. And during the 2010 World Cup in South Africa a vast global audience watched the games on television.

- *History speeded up.* Nations and people today react faster to important events because information moves so quickly and widely. A bomb explodes in an airliner and security measures tighten up in airports everywhere. War breaks out in the Middle East and the price of gas at the pump goes up everywhere. Actions that would have been taken later are now taken sooner, thus accelerating the pace of change.

- *"The whole world is watching."* The reality that many millions can watch on television as tanks rumble across borders, troops storm ashore in a distant land, or police fire on peaceful protesters gives much greater import and consequences to news reports. A camcorder's report of Los Angeles police beating a man named Rodney King set off repercussions lasting for years. Video taken by camcorders in the hands of European tourists and broadcast on television showed the horror of the Asian tsunami. A discarded "home videocassette" showing Osama bin Laden rejoicing over the New York City terror attacks provided what many considered the "smoking gun" that proved his complicity in the attacks. Americans are often surprised to understand that the world often learns full details about shootings, massacres, and all about a famed golfer's marital troubles. It is news that Americans consider to be local but can be gossip or sensation to global publics.

- *Diplomacy changed.* Foreign relations and the ways that nations react to each other are clearly influenced by public (and world) opinion formed by global communication. Television viewers concerned by watching starving children in Somalia can exert pressures on their government to intervene with military force in a place they later regret going to. Media discussions and debate between diplomats and leaders can clarify policy and influence nations or alliances to act. Nonstop coverage by CNN and the BBC provides the opportunity to monitor news events constantly and disseminate timely diplomatic information. But some politicians are more concerned than elated by global, real-time broadcasting, fearing a loss of control and the absence of quiet time to make deliberate choices, reach private agreements, and mold the public's understanding of events.

- *Autocrats' loss of control.* Authoritarian regimes can no longer maintain a monopoly over news and censor what their people know. They cannot stop news from coming into their nation or getting out. Shortwave radio, fax, the Internet, cell phones and videophones, and communication satellites have changed all that and blunted the power of state censorship. Throughout the Middle East, the growing impact of the Internet and Al Jazeera has meant that millions of people have access to new and information not sanctioned by their governments. This is a step toward open government. During times of crisis, dictators can no longer seal their borders and control information. The news will get out. And the "social media" – Twitter, Facebook, and so on – are making the censors' tasks even more difficult.

- *"Revolution" by personalized media.* Internet blogging, desktop publishing, camcorders, and cell phones have turned individuals into communicators who can reach out to their own audiences. Even photocopiers and audiocassettes have been shown to facilitate political upheavals or revolution. So-called "citizen journalists" have become an important adjunct to professional journalism but it is too early to say how significant and lasting. Few now doubt that the Internet and social media played a crucial role in the political upheavals that shook up the Arab world from Morocco to Yemen.

- *Surrogate media for fettered people.* Independent media from outside now provide news and information for people who are captives of their own governments. By publicizing human-rights violations, torture, and political imprisonment, independent media help those victims to survive. It has been argued that a famine never occurs in a nation with a free press because the press, by reporting incipient food shortages, will bring pressures on its government to act before people begin dying. Western reporting of the harsh and brutal life of Afghans living under the Taliban augmented the argument for US intervention. The Committee to Protect Journalists (CPJ) and Amnesty International have proved helpful in aiding imprisoned journalists.

- *Reporting pariah states.* The foreign press's persistent reporting about pariah states, such as South Africa under apartheid or the Philippines under Marcos, can apparently help to facilitate political change by forming world public opinion, which in turn can lead to actions by governments. Persistent American and European press reporting of the civil war in Bosnia and growing evidence of genocide by Bosnian Serbs undoubtedly pushed the Clinton administration and NATO to intervene and impose a cease-fire.

- *The "copycat" effect.* With global news so pervasive and widely available, sometimes imitative acts occur that have unexpected consequences. A terrorist's car bombing in one country, widely shown on television, is replicated 3,000 miles away. Somali clansmen defy US soldiers in Mogadishu, and a few days later, Haitian thugs are encouraged to stage a near-riot as US troops try to land at Port au Prince, causing the US forces to withdraw. Like a newly published book, an important news story can have a life of its own – extending its influence far beyond expectations.

- *Profit-driven media.* The international communication system has grown and expanded so rapidly because there was money to be made by globalization of the world economy. The profit motive is, of course, a powerful force for technological change. The INTELSAT system, a crucial early component in expanding the reach of global news, expanded so rapidly and effectively because there were real profits from a more efficient and cost-effective way to make international telephone calls. A partial exception is the "public media" as exemplified by the BBC in the UK and the NPR and Public Television in the US which are supported by public contributions. These are major contributors to world news flow. Business journalism has flourished because a globalized economy requires reliable and unbiased information to function effectively.

Whatever their faults, the "media barons" – Rupert Murdoch and Ted Turner, among others – are entrepreneurs who will take risks and are willing to innovate. When Turner proposed a twenty-four-hour global news channel, many thought he was crazy.

Now a kind word for the much-criticized media conglomerates. Commenting on the global activities of News Corporation, Time

Warner, the Walt Disney Company, Bertelsmann AG, Sony, and CNN, John Keane commented, "These global media linkages have helped to achieve something much more persuasively than the maps of Geradus Mercator ever did: to deepen the visceral feelings among millions of people (somewhere between 5 and 25% of the world's population) that our world is 'one world' and that this worldly interdependence requires humans to share some responsibility for its fate."[2]

- *Globalization of advertising and public relations.* The two persuasive arms of Western mass communications, advertising and public relations, have become globalized as well. Here again, the Anglo-American model, speaking English, is the world standard. Though often criticized, advertising and public relations are necessary and inevitable components of market economies and open societies. Moreover, advertising and public relations often make news and are, in fact, an aspect of news. Peoples with diverse and impenetrable languages are increasingly conversing in English or its hydra-headed variations dubbed Globish.

## The Downside of Global Media Effects

Rapid change causes dislocations and inequities, and global communication certainly has its negative impacts as well.

- *The fragility of democracy and open societies.* The worldwide surge of the late 1980s toward democracy and market economies – from Eastern Europe to Tropical Africa and South Asia – provided the promise and possibility of press freedom and independent media in nations long under one-party or military rule. Recently, more than half, or 99 out of 191, countries held competitive elections with varying but promising guarantees of political and individual rights. Yet most efforts to move from authoritarianism to democracy have failed more often than not after most revolutions, according to Seymour Martin Lipset. He wrote that cultural factors appear more important than economic ones. Some of the factors that have promoted democracy in the past are capitalism, economic growth, a moderate opposition, British influences, and Protestantism.[3] As a result of ethnic and nationalistic clashes, the democratic outlook for some nations in Eastern Europe, the Middle East, and Africa today is not promising. The "failed states" of the Arab world, which have been unable to modernize economically or to acquire democratic rule, have been a major breeding ground for terrorists.

The failure to relieve economic misery in the newly democratic governments in Africa has led to disillusionment with democracy, and this may lead to new military or civilian dictators. L. Gray Cowan said, "In most of the African countries where they have had elected democratic governments, the fundamental problem is that they are left with precisely the same economic and social problems they had before."[4]

The rise of democracy and a free press has been associated with market economies, but market economies do not guarantee democratic societies. Currently, the capitalist nations of Indonesia, Thailand, and Malaysia have modern media systems and rising standards of living, but are not yet fully democratic and are facing financial difficulties as well.

Even the robust and successful Western nations have proved vulnerable to sneak terrorist attacks. The chief characteristics of globalization – open borders, lenient immigration policies, individual freedoms including privacy protection, and ample free trade – has made the United States and Europe particularly vulnerable to terrorist attacks. Terrorism has been rightly called the dark side of globalization. And when thousands of civilians are killed or endangered, national security becomes a dominant imperative and government controls are tightened.

- *Poor nations lag in the information age.* Optimism about the trends in global communication is based mainly on what is happening in the prosperous societies of the United States, Europe, and Japan, and in the modernized sectors of China and India. Among the poorer nations of the Southern Hemisphere, especially in Africa, development and growth of media and their audiences have been painfully slow in large part because the stubborn problems of poverty, overpopulation, poor health, illiteracy, and economic underdevelopment still defy solution. African countries and some other nations are not acquiring the technology and infrastructure needed to travel on the information superhighway. In absolute terms, the poorer nations are falling further behind and becoming further marginalized. In addition, the onrush of rapid technological change is further widening the gap between rich and poor nations. The lack of skilled workers, an industrial base (including investment capital), and a literate and educated middle class precludes the poor nations from participating fully in the information revolution, particularly the Internet. When most of a country's population still lives as illiterate peasants on subsistence agriculture, as in much of Africa, Asia, and parts of Latin America, terms such as "transnational data flows," "free flow of information," or "logging on" have little practical meaning. Further, deep political and cultural differences still contribute to hatred, envy, and animosities among many millions toward affluent Westerners. The communication revolution has been coming about through education, communications, technology, and dynamic free-market economies – regrettably all in short supply in too many developing countries.

- *Trends toward media monopoly.* The financial activities of the big players in international communication – Murdoch, NBC, Time Warner, Disney/ABC, the BBC, Sony, formerly Viacom/CBS, and Bertelsmann – seem to be moving in one direction: toward consolidation and monopoly of the main structures of international communication. (But some media giants, like Vivendi, do fail.) Bigger conglomerates and fewer competitors mean greater profits but less variety and diversity. Problems of regulating these transnational entities are already proving formidable, especially in light of recent megamergers among US media giants. (The US government today has been backing off from anti-trust regulation of media giants.) Primarily involved with profitable entertainment enterprises, these conglomerates show slight concern with quality news dissemination. Critics fear that consolidation means a loss of diverse opinions and less competition among competing news media.

- *Declining standards.* Some critics ask, where in this commercial scramble for profits and power is the concern for serious journalism and quality entertainment? Europeans, for example, lament the decline of public service broadcasting and of quality drama and entertainment. Serious international news is often pushed aside for stories that are more sensational and celebrity oriented. Entertainment values are degrading news values.

- *Shortcomings of audiences.* In the affluent West, the majority of people attending to mass media have only a superficial interest and knowledge of world affairs. They may know that Russia is having economic problems, but they do not understand the reasons. Most Americans were deeply shocked by the 9/11 attacks, in part because the news media, as well as the government, had paid scant attention earlier to the possibilities of surprise terror attacks on America. In less affluent nations, most people lack the education and standard of living to pay attention to world events. In many cases, their own inadequate media are incapable of providing significant foreign news.

# Indications of Improvement

The expanding capacity to communicate information rapidly around a world that has become ever more interdependent has begun to erase some differences and perhaps improve understanding among diverse societies. The better educated and more affluent people of most nations – the media users – know more about the outside world and have access to more information than ever before. The educated elites of the developing nations, though small in number, travel more and are more conversant with world affairs than were their predecessors under colonialism. However, the euphoric reaction of some in the Islamic world to the 9/11 attacks was a sobering reminder to Westerners of the widespread hatred and anti-Americanism and anti-Westernism found abroad. Americans, who like to be liked, were shocked that so many do not like them.

The international news system, despite its inadequacies, moves a great deal of information, data, and pictures much faster than ever before, and there is every indication that this flow will expand in the years ahead. Walter Goodman, a frequent critic of television, had some good things to say about the little box: "Television, that product of the West, is by its nature on the West's side when it comes to freedom of information. Censors may hedge it in and manipulate it, but they cannot contain it; the content flows across boundaries and over the globe. When communism fell, television, which every East bloc country boss thought was his to run for purposes of celebrating himself and suppressing his critics, was among the forces that gave it a shove. . ... Television's natural impulse is to reveal, not conceal."[5] The same can be said about the Internet and its proliferating progeny. History seems to be on the side of openness and the free exchange of information.

These are some of the reasons why the West's version of world news and events, largely gathered and disseminated by American and Western European journalists, often antagonizes and annoys non-Western governments and peoples, despite their reliance on these sources of information.

To assist governments in dealing with their formidable problems of poverty, massive debt, environmental degradation, disease, and sometimes famine, some leaders would harness mass communications – a clear invocation of the developmental concept of the press. But under the Western concept, the press must be free of government to maintain liberty, to make democracy possible, and to provide reliable and objective news.

Liberty is not the same as social justice or economic equality. History shows that when press freedom is sacrificed for some "greater good," political liberty and human rights usually disappear.

To the Western journalist, the press must be independent of authority, not an instrument of government, so that it can report the news and expose the abuses of governments at home and abroad. Now more than ever, because of their global reach, governments (and corporations) need watching. But whether democratic or authoritarian, only governments – not multinational corporations or media conglomerates – have the power to start wars, nuclear or conventional; to conscript soldiers and send them off to dubious wars; to punish dissidents; to establish gulags; to "ethnically cleanse" people with a different religion – or to deal with terrorists. Media in both North and South must contend with governments that try to control, manipulate, and suppress what the news media wish to report – and often succeed. Democratic government and private ownership give the press a better chance of resisting government control and serving the public interest, but they are no guarantee of independence. (But also it should be remembered that when national security is threatened, as after 9/11, people quickly turn to government for help to counter subversive terrorism.)

Modern history is replete with regimes marred by incompetence, venality, corruption, and brutality. Some journalists believe that the world's free press has done far too little, rather than too much, critical reporting about economic failures and political abuses, especially among developing nations. This basic impasse over the proper purpose of international news communication and the relations between the press and government will continue. But the greater the threat from abroad, the greater will be the interest and need for foreign news.

## What Can Be Done

Improvements in international news communication must come from several quarters. Western journalists and mass communicators can do much to improve their own effectiveness. And governments and journalists of the communications-poor developing nations can do more to involve themselves in transnational news, both as senders and receivers. Much can be accomplished as well by nations and journalists working together through international organizations to arrive at some consensus on policy questions and proposals for improved news communication. But it should be remembered that most journalism is essentially local and parochial – it serves the interests and needs of its own audiences. Therefore, the front pages of the leading papers in Japan, Turkey, Norway, and Nigeria will always feature quite different stories. And yet, high-quality foreign news is still essential and does bring diverse peoples closer together.

A central argument in journalism today is about journalistic authority – who has it and what is it worth. One view is that the democratizing power of the Internet has rendered traditional forms of journalism obsolete and implies that the public should not pay for the news. This is a new world in which readers want to have to ability to make their own judgments and express their own priorities and learn from their peers as much as from traditional sources of authority. Reliance on professional journalists is seen as elitist and stifling.[6]

Opposing their view is a conviction that a significant number of serious readers feel the need for someone with training, experience, and standards – reporters and editors – to help them learn and understand the news. This view doe not preclude the use of "citizen journalists" who add to the news flow. But the authority of professional journalists is both an aid for readers too busy to sort out the news for themselves as well as a civic good for a democracy to have trustworthy information upon which to make its decisions.[7]

But as discussed earlier in this book, a central concern for the news business today is to find ways to pay for news gathering in today's digital environment. A new business model to improve the profitability of news media is essential for its survival. Proposals and suggestions for revised business models are frequent and useful. The *New York Times*, the flagship of global news coverage, has announced that it is going to charge fees for access for certain news stories in 2011. Online users of the *New York Times* will have free access to a certain number of stories a month and then will have to pay once they have exceeded a cap. Think of it as an article cap similar to a salary cap in sports. The *New York Times* says the model will provide a second revenue stream to support the advertising model and also fund its journalism. Print subscribers to the *New York Times* will have full access without an article cap. The most prominent newspaper to date with a similar plan is the *Financial Times* of London which allows readers ten articles a month for free and charges $4.25 for unlimited access. Other publications are considering similar plans. Mobile devices offer hope as well for print media. The fact that consumers pay fees for their various iPhones, iPads, and other mobile devices offer a way for journalism to back away from its earlier mistake of offering its digital news free of charge.

## Western Initiatives

Western media, with their greater resources, should gather and report more news of the non-Western world and do it with more understanding of the problems and concerns of those nations. The coups, the economic disasters, the civil wars, the famines, and other disasters must be reported, of course, but the press also should provide more sustained, comprehensive coverage of social and cultural aspects in a historical perspective. The public requires more general knowledge of the greater world so that if, say, Iran or Pakistan suddenly dominates the news, readers can react more knowledgeably.

Even in non-crisis times, television news needs to expand its foreign coverage and, furthermore, do more than provide blanket coverage of a single running story, such as a notorious celebrity trial, while virtually ignoring other important stories elsewhere.

CNN's around-the-clock coverage of the first Iraq War revealed the inadequacies of networks' formats. Commercial networks should revive the hour-long news documentary, which has almost disappeared from television screens, and not leave it entirely to public television. News media in general need to show more responsibility and sense of public service – and to cover foreign news even when no crisis looms.

More Western media should invest more money and human resources in covering foreign news and not leave the immense task to the few media groups that do maintain correspondents abroad. And newspapers and broadcasters without their own reporters abroad should do a better job of using the considerable amount of foreign news available from news services and syndicates.

Foreign-news editors could make much more use, as well, of academic sources. Hundreds of area specialists who have current and reliable information about every corner of the world are to be found throughout universities.

Programs to train journalists from abroad should be continued and expanded. Western news organizations have helped to establish national news agencies and trained personnel to run them. For years, a steady stream of journalists and broadcasters has come to Europe and America for training and internships, but training journalists in their home countries or regions still has merit and perhaps priority.

Western media organizations might also consider selectively establishing newspapers in non-Western countries. Although fraught with political risks, some previous ventures have markedly raised the level of journalism in those countries. Two of the best newspapers in black Africa, the *Daily Times* of Nigeria and the *Daily Nation* of Kenya (now both African owned) were started by foreign publishers as commercial ventures. India has a number of vigorous newspapers today because British interests started newspapers there during colonial rule. Since independence, these papers have been managed completely by Indians and have served that nation well.

Closer Western ties can be established between journalists of different nationalities through professional groups such as the Journalists Without Borders and the Inter-American Press Association. This can lead to better understanding and cooperation. Journalists of various nations working together in professional organizations can assist developing nations in such practical matters as subsidies for expensive newsprint, which is almost entirely produced in northern nations, obtaining media equipment such as used presses and broadcast electronics from Western media, and helping to obtain cheaper preferential rates for news transmissions via Comsats and cable.

## Non-Western Initiatives

The dynamic changes of economic and communication development in recent years have rendered as obsolete such terms as "developing nations" or "third world" China, India, Taiwan, South Korea, among others, today have much in common with the so-called West. And in the Middle East, an information revolution based on digital media and international broadcasting, as shown by the influence of Al Jazeera and the lowly cell phone, has blossomed. There is no turning back but still a long way to go.

To balance the flow of information better, the news media in developing nations must be improved and expanded, but this will not be easy, because any nation's mass media grow and expand along with general economic and social development and the modernization of individuals. Educated and informed individuals are required for media jobs as well as for media audiences. Although training and technical assistance from outside can be helpful, the impetus for media improvement must come from within.

A few Western news agencies and other media ideally should not dominate global news gathering as they do now, but they themselves are incapable of correcting the inequities of the system – nor should it be expected they can. Newspapers and broadcasters in Africa or South Asia should not have to rely upon a news agency based in London or New York City to find out what is happening in their own region. A much greater diversity of news sources is needed for the world's media to draw upon. For that reason alone, the persistent efforts in Asia, Africa, and Latin America to establish regional news agencies and broadcasting exchange agreements should be encouraged, despite the difficulties involved. Happily, some regions are producing more and more of their own movies, television programs, and popular music. The rise of the Al Jazeera satellite television news service in Qatar, broadcast in Arabic all over the Middle East, was an important addition to news diversity in a region of government-controlled news.

How soon and how effectively developing nations can improve their news media may well depend on how their governments respond to the following policy questions.

1   Will non-Western nations cooperate effectively in developing regional and continental telecommunications and news exchange?

In Africa, for example, long-distance telecommunications can have a revolutionary potential for the sub-Saharan region by providing a truly continental system of telecommunications where none has previously existed. An integrated system of regional satellites, Internet connections, cable systems, ground stations, improved AM and FM broadcasting, and microwave relays can have important implications for intra-African exchanges of news, educational broadcasting, telephone service, television programming, and high-speed data transfers. Recently there have been hopeful signs out of Africa that these kinds of communications improvements are being made.

2   Will non-Western governments show more concern both for their own peoples' right to know and for an unimpeded flow of information throughout the world?

Too much of the world news controversy has involved the claims of professional journalists versus the claims of governments over regulation of news and information. In today's world, any person, whether born in Pakistan, Norway, Peru, or Tanzania, has the right, at least in theory, to acquire information that affects his or her own welfare and future. And the government under which that person lives should respect that right – a hopeless ideal, some will say, since so many of the world's poor peoples live under authoritarianism and are far removed from information sources. Nevertheless, that is the direction in which the world has been moving.

To participate in global news flow requires that information, news, technical data, and cultural fare be permitted to move unimpeded across borders. It also requires that journalists be protected by law from government intrusion into their activities.

3 Will non-Western nations encourage more diversity and freedom in news and information?

Regional and alternative news agencies can be helpful and should be actively fostered. A key question is whether the governments will provide their own journalists and broadcasters with greater autonomy and independence. Journalism flourishes best in an atmosphere of freedom from authority and corporate interference, but few journalists in non-Western nations enjoy such latitude. Too many, unfortunately, either work for autocratic governments or are at the mercy of arbitrary political interference. Too few governments in the world today permit their own journalists the freedom to probe serious internal problems, much less allow them to criticize even mildly the performance of those in authority. In general, these nations will continue to lag behind the information societies of the West until they evolve into constitutional, democratic societies with market economies. That will take time, and some nations obviously will not opt for that path to development. But to date, few one-party nations have shown the flexibility and dynamism to join the information societies.

In conclusion, what has happened to international news communication in the past quarter-century is, of course, only one aspect of the broad trend of the revolution in information processing and diffusion that has been transforming the modern world and its economy.

For the foreseeable future, the current system of international communication will probably retain its present basic structure, with the flow of information and news steadily expanding and audiences steadily increasing. Modifications will come mainly from the adoption of more technological and economic innovations in the media themselves. In recent decades, communication technology and economic forces have proved powerful forces for change. The future of global journalism is tied to the future of political democracies where a free press can flourish. More open societies mean greater flow and exchange of news across borders, whereas autocracies try to block or distort the flow of news.

But more than that, a reliable flow of global news and other essential information is an absolute necessity for our interdependent world, and the "closed" nations that try to block out that flow will find themselves unable to compete and prosper. Global politics and wars influence and shape international communication, and in this uncertain and danger-fraught era, the world's news media will play a central role in helping people everywhere better understand the world beyond their borders. As the media remind us, the world faces unprecedented challenges – global warning, water and food shortages, widespread poverty, and growing populations – which international organizations and nation states seem unable to cope with. An enhanced and improved system of global news media appears essential for the world to survive.

## Notes

1. John M. Roberts, *The Triumph of the West* (Boston: Little, Brown, 1985), 290–295.
2. John Keane, "Journalism and Democracy Across Borders" in *The Press*, G. Overholzer and K. H. Jamieson, eds. (New York: Oxford University Press, 2005), 94.
3. "New Democracies Face Long Odds for Survival," *Stanford Alumni Review*, September 1993, 5.
4. Howard French, "African Democracies Fear Aid Will Dry Up," *New York Times*, March 19, 1995, sec. A, 1.
5. Walter Goodman, "Even If Used as a Weapon, Television is True to its Nature," *New York Times*, January 20, 1998, sec. B, 3.
6. Bill Keller, "Editor in Chief," *New York Times Book Review*, April 25, 2010, 1.
7. Keller, "Editor in Chief."

# Selected Bibliography

Abdulla, Rasha. *The Internet and the Arab World*. New York: Peter Lang, 2007.

Alleyne, Mark D. *News Revolution: Political and Economic Decisions About Global Information*. New York: St. Martin's Press, 1997.

Anokwa, Kwadro, Carolyn Lin, and Michael Salwen (eds). *International Communication: Concepts and Cases*. Belmont, CA: Wadsworth, 2003.

Auletta, Ken. *Googled: The End of the World as We Know It*. New York: Penguin, 2009.

Avolon, Ami. *The Press in The Middle East*. New York: Oxford University Press, 1995.

Baoguo, Cui (ed.). *Report on Development of China's Media Industry*. Beijing: Social Sciences Academic Press, 2007.

Boyd, Douglas A. *Broadcasting in The Arab World*, 2nd edn. Ames: Iowa State University Press, 1993.

Chadwick, Andrew. *Internet Politics: States, Citizens, and New Communication Technologies*. New York: Oxford, 2006.

Chang, T. K. *China's Window on the Window on the World: TV News, Social Knowledge, and International Spectacle*. Cressfield, NJ: Hampton Press, 2009.

Chang, Won Ho. *Mass Media in China: The History and the Future*. Ames: Iowa State University Press, 1989.

Couldry, Nick and James Curran (eds.). *Contesting Media Power*. New York: Rowman & Littlefield, 2003.

Christians, Clifford, *et al. Normative Theories of the Media in Democratic Societies*. Urbana, IL: Illinois Press, 2006.

Curtin, Michael. *Playing to the World's Largest Audience: The Globalization of Chinese Film and TV*. Berkeley, CA: University of California Press, 2007.

Dizard, Wilson P. *Old Media, New Media*. New York: Longman, 1994.

---

*The World News Prism: Challenges of Digital Communication*, Eighth Edition.
William A. Hachten and James F. Scotton.
© 2012 John Wiley & Sons, Ltd. Published 2012 by John Wiley & Sons, Ltd.

Dizard, Wilson P. *Meganet: How the Global Communications Network Will Connect Everyone on Earth*. Boulder, CO: Westview, 1997.

Demers, David. *Global Media: Menace or Messiah?* Cressfield, NJ: Hampton Press, 1999.

Downie, Leonard and Robert Kaiser, *The News About the News*. New York, Vintage, 2003.

Fenton, Natalie. *New Media, Old News: Journalism and Democracy in the Digital Age*. London: Sage, 2009.

Fenton, Tom. *Bad News: The Decline of Reporting, The Business of News and the Danger to Us All*. New York: HarperCollins, 2005.

Flournoy, Don and Robert K. Stewart. *Making News in the Global Market*. Luton, UK: University of Luton, 1997.

Friedman, Thomas L. *The Lexus and the Olive Tree: Understanding Globalization*. New York: Anchor Books, 2000.

Friedman, Thomas L. *The World is Flat: A Brief History of the 21st Century*. New York: Farrar, Straus & Giroux, 2005.

Friedman, Thomas L. Hot, Flat and Crowded. New York: Farrar, Straus and Giroux, 2008.

Geyer, Georgie Anne. *Buying the Night Flight*. Washington, DC: Brassey's, 1996.

Gwertzman, Bernard, and Michael T. Kaufman (eds.). *The Collapse of Communism*. New York: St. Martin's Press, 1990.

Ha, Louisa and Richard Ganahl. *Webcasting World Wide*. Mahwah, NJ: Lawrence Erlbaum, 2007.

Hachten, William A. *Growth of Media in the Third World: African Failures, Asian Successes*. Ames: Iowa State University Press, 1991.

Hachten, William A. *The Troubles of Journalism: A Critical Look at What's Right and Wrong with the Press*, 3rd edn. Mahwah, NJ: Lawrence Erlbaum, 2005.

Hallin, Daniel C. and Paolo Mancini. *Comparing Media Systems: Three Modes of Media and Politics*. New York: Cambridge University Press, 2004.

Hawk, Beverly G. *Africa's Media Image*. New York: Praeger, 1992.

Heisey, D. Ray and Wenxiang Gong (eds.). *Communication and Culture: China and the World Entering the 21st Century*. Amsterdam: Editions Rodopi, 1994.

Herman, Edward S. and Robert W. McChesney. *The Global Media: The New Missionaries of Corporate Capitalism*. London: Cassell, 1997.

Hess, Stephen. *International News and Foreign Correspondents*. Washington, DC: Brookings Institution, 1996.

Hoyt, Mike, John Palettella, *et al. Reporting Iraq*. New York: Mellville Howe, 2010.

Jones, Alex. S. *Losing the News*. New York: Oxford, 2009.

Kaplan, Robert D. *The Ends of the Earth*. New York: Vintage, 1996.

Kovach, Bill and Tom Rosenstiel. *The Elements of Journalism*. New York: Three Rivers, 2007.

Lynch, Mark. *Voices of the New Arab Public*. New York: Columbia University Press, 2006.

McChesney, Robert and John Nichols. *The Life and Death of American Journalism: The Media Revolution That will Begin World Again*. Philadelphia: First Nation Books, 2010.

McCrum, Robert. *Globish: How English Became the World's Language*. New York: Norton, 2010.

McKensie, *Comparing Media Around the World*. New York: Pearson, 2006.

McPhail, Thomas L. *Global Communication: Theories, Stakeholders, and Trends*. Boston: Blackwell, 2006.

McQuail, Denis. *Mass Communication Theory*, 3rd edn. Newbury Park, CA: Sage, 1994.

Merrill, John C. *Global Journalism: Survey of International Communication*, 3rd edn. New York: Longman, 1995.

Mickiewicz, Ellen. *Changing Channels: Television and the Struggle for Power in Russia*. New York: Oxford University Press, 1997.

Miles, Hugh. *Al-Jazeera: The Inside Story of the Arab News Channel That is Challenging the West*. New York: Grove Press, 2005.

Mueller, Barbara. *International Advertising: Communicating Across Cultures*. Belmont, CA: Wadsworth, 1996.

Nacos, Brigitte L. *Mass-Mediated Terrorism: Central Role of the Media in Terrorism and Counter Terrorism*. New York: Rowman & Littlefield, 2002.

Naisbitt, John and Patricia Aburdene. *Megatrends 2000*. New York: Avon, 1990.

Nelson, Michael. *War of the Black Heavens: The Battle of Western Broadcasting in the Cold War*. Syracuse, NY: Syracuse University Press, 1997.

Overholzer, Geneva and Kathleen Hall Jamieson (eds.). *The Press*. New York: Oxford University Press, 2005.

Pan, Philip. *Out of Mao's Shadow*. New York: Simon and Schuster, 2008.

Parks, Lisa and Shanti Kumar (eds.). *Planet TV: A Global Television Reader*. New York: New York University Press, 2003.

Paterson, Chris and Annabelle Sreberny (eds.). *International News in the 21st Century*. Eastleigh, UK: John Libbey/Luton Press, 2004.

Rugh, William. *Arab Mass Media*. New York: Praeger, 2004.

Pavlik, John V. *Journalism and New Media*. New York: Columbia University Press, 2000.

Scotton, James and William Hachten. *New Media for a New China*. London: Wiley-Blackwell, 2010.

Seib, Philip. *Headline Diplomacy: How News Coverage Affects Foreign Policy*. Westport, CT: Praeger, 1997.

Semati, Mehdi (ed.). *New Frontiers in International Communication Theory*. Lanham, MD: Rowan and Littlefield, 2004.

Shenk, David. *Data Smog: Surviving the Information Glut*. New York: Harper Edge/ HarperCollins, 1997.

Silvia, Tony. *Global News: Perspectives on the Information Age*. Ames: Iowa State University Press, 2001.

Stevenson, Robert L. *Global Communication in the Twenty-first Century*. New York: Longman, 1994.

Strobel, Warren. *Late-Breaking Foreign Policy: The News Media's Influence on Peace Operations*. Washington, DC: US Institute of Peace Press, 1997.

Thussu, Daya Kishan. *International Communication: Continuity and Change*. London: University of North London, 2000.

Tumber, Howard and Jerry Palmer. *Media at War: The Iraq Crisis*. Newbury Park, CA: Sage, 2004.

Van Ginneken, Jaap. *Understanding Global News*. Thousand Oaks, CA: Sage, 1998.

Walker, Andrew. *A Skyful of Freedom: Sixty Years of the BBC World Service*. London: Broadside, 1992.

Weaver, David H. (ed.). *The Global Journalist*. Cressfield, NJ: Hampton Press, 1998. (Boulder, CO: Paradigm Press, 2005.)

# Index

*The World News Prism: Challenges of Digital Communication*, Eighth Edition.
William A. Hachten and James F. Scotton.
© 2012 John Wiley & Sons, Ltd. Published 2012 by John Wiley & Sons, Ltd.